THE FIVE STRATEGIES OF THE VIRTUES PROJECT™

These strategies help us to live more reverent, purposeful lives, raise morally conscious children, create a culture of character in our schools, and enhance integrity in the workplace. They are being used worldwide to build safe and caring communities.

Strategy 1: Speak the Language of Virtues

Strategy 2: Recognize Teachable Moments

Strategy 3: Set Clear Boundaries

Strategy 4: Honor the Spirit

Strategy 5: Offer Spiritual Companioning™

"Great spiritual nuggets for a healthy spiritual pathway."
—Gerald G. Jampolsky, M.D., author of *Love Is Letting Go of Fear*

Linda Kavelin Popov is the author of *The Family Virtues Guide,* and is one of the founders and directors of The Virtues Project International. She travels around the world in support of the project's initiatives, speaking to communities, businesses, and governmental organizations. The United Nations Secretariat has honored The Virtues Project as a model for global reform for people of all cultures. She lives in the Gulf Islands near Victoria, British Columbia.

Other books by Linda Kavelin Popov

The Family Virtues Guide
Sacred Moments
The Virtues Project Educator's Guide

A PACE
OF
GRACE

*The Virtues
of a Sustainable Life*

LINDA KAVELIN POPOV

A PLUME BOOK

To my beloved Dan, who walks beside me with true grace.

PLUME
Published by the Penguin Group
Penguin Group (USA) Inc., 375 Hudson Street, New York, New York 10014, U.S.A.
Penguin Books Ltd, 80 Strand, London WC2R 0RL, England
Penguin Books Australia Ltd, 250 Camberwell Road, Camberwell, Victoria 3124, Australia
Penguin Books Canada Ltd, 10 Alcorn Avenue, Toronto, Ontario, Canada M4V 3B2
Penguin Books India (P) Ltd, 11 Community Centre, Panchsheel Park, New Delhi – 110 017, India
Penguin Books (NZ), cnr Airborne and Rosedale Roads, Albany, Auckland 1310, New Zealand
Penguin Books (South Africa) (Pty) Ltd,
24 Sturdee Avenue, Rosebank, Johannesburg 2196, South Africa

Penguin Books Ltd, Registered Offices: 80 Strand, London WC2R 0RL, England

First published by Plume, a member of Penguin Group (USA) Inc.

First Printing, July 2004
10   9   8   7   6   5   4   3   2   1

℗ REGISTERED TRADEMARK—MARCA REGISTRADA

LIBRARY OF CONGRESS CATALOGING-IN-PUBLICATION DATA
Popov, Linda Kavelin.
A pace of grace : the virtues of a sustainable life / Linda Kavelin Popov.
p.   cm.
Includes bibliographical references.
ISBN 0-452-28543-7 (trade pbk.)
1. Conduct of life.   2. Virtues.   I. Title.
BJ1581.2.P67 2004
179'.9—dc22   2003070768
Printed in the United States of America
Set in Minion
Designed by Erin Benach
Illustrations by Pat Walker

Acknowledgments

I am deeply grateful to Horace Holley and Dr. Helen Schuchman, who served as my inspiring muses; my longtime agent and cherished friend, Theresa Park of Sanford J. Greenburger, for her discernment about the nature of this book and her tireless encouragement to "go deeper"; Gary Brozek, my articulate, persevering editor at Plume, for honoring the true spirit of the book and helping me to separate the wheat from the chaff; to Penguin for keeping it in the family; to Kate Marsh for her excellent research assistance; to my husband, Dan, whose constant support and cheerleading helped me to persevere; to Jean Forrest for encouraging me to complete the book as she completed her earthly journey; and to the individuals from the global Virtues Project community, patients, families, and staff from Hospice Victoria, and my friends and loved ones, whose stories illuminate *A Pace of Grace.*

Contents

Introduction

Affirmation of life is the spiritual act by which man ceases to live unreflectively and begins to devote himself to his life with reverence in order to raise it to its true value.
—Albert Schweitzer

Until life caught up with me, I was a dedicated member of the Stress Generation. I didn't mean to be. It just happened. A few weeks before September 11, 2001, I struck up a conversation with an East Indian cabdriver in Vancouver as he drove me from the airport to a downtown hotel where I would be speaking at a conference the next day. We chatted about how he felt, living so far from most of his family. He told me he longed to have them here but that his relatives had no wish to come to North America. When I asked about it, he said, "When I go home to India, it is pure peace, no worries. People still have bills, they still pay the bills, but they are not busy—overdone—as people are here." Overdone. I blushed in recognition. What an apt description of the typical stress-filled North American lifestyle, I thought, and the perfect word to describe what had led to my own collapse several years before in 1997.

After a lifetime in the healing professions, I lapsed. I had no idea how far I had been swept into the swift current of stress until a life-threatening health crisis literally knocked me off my feet. Like so many others in this era of excess, the demands of my life had outgrown my capacity to sustain it. I had drifted from a gentle path of reflection, reverence, and service to a fast-paced life of constant international travel and an attempt to manage a growing global project, which had become an all-consuming passion. I felt like the goddess Kali, all of her arms busy juggling, but without her steady knowing gaze of serenity and grace.

It all began with a simple desire to be of service, yet there I was careening toward a vortex of exhaustion. I know full well I'm not alone. Too many of us are constantly overdoing because we have overextended our lives, our financial resources, and our personal energy supply. Most days, we don't even stop to breathe. And now, watching the nightly news has become a health hazard. The turmoil in the world seems worse than ever, the economy is uncertain and unpredictable.

You see things and you say, "Why?"
But I dream things that never were;
and I say, "Why not?"
—George Bernard Shaw

The deepening world conflict set in motion after the terrorist attacks on New York and Washington on September 11 has cast an unsettling shadow of anxiety and insecurity over an already overwhelming way of life. We are engulfed in an epidemic of stress in a culture of chaos.

I have always been privileged to pursue the work of my dreams—fulfilling a passionate prayer I uttered while circumambulating our backyard garden at age five: "God, please let me help people when I grow up." I worked for decades in community mental health, consulted government leaders in the halls of Washington, companioned the dying at a hospice, conducted healing retreats with indigenous and inner-city communities, yet even the best of intentions didn't protect me from burnout.

In 1990, my husband, Dan Popov, my brother John Kavelin, and I founded The Virtues Project. It began one April morning in 1988, over brunch at the stately, ivy-covered Empress Hotel overlooking the inner harbor in Victoria, British Columbia. John was enjoying the final day of his week of respite from his frantic career as a show producer for Walt Disney Imagineering in Los Angeles. He began to talk about wanting to be of more direct service to the world. The three of us experienced a crystalline, life-changing moment as we feasted on scones and salmon. We were discussing the state of the world—the rising tide of violence, the school shootings, the growing hole in the moral ozone—and one of us (I don't recall who) said, "Someone should do something about it." Suddenly we looked up from our plates, gazed deep into each other's eyes, and in that moment the dream of serving together was born.

John moved up to Victoria, and we began working together. It occurred to us that violence was a symptom, and meaninglessness was the disease, therefore the cure would have something to do with the meaning of life. So we set off to find it. For years, Dan had studied the world's sacred texts. He pointed us toward the six thousand years of spiritual guidance contained in the Jewish, Hindu, Christian, Buddhist, and Moslem texts. He researched those and more. We were startled by the luminous simplicity of the answer that emerged.

Running through the great spiritual teachings of all cultures, like a silver thread of unity, are the virtues, described as the qualities of the Creator and the attributes of the human soul. Love, justice, kindness, courage, joy, and peace are the essence of who we are.

The virtues are God's grace to us, a gift in our lives. What we do with them is our gift to God. They are both our spiritual legacy and our destiny. Many sacred traditions also describe the virtues as a very high order of angels, pure expressions of the Divine nature, higher than the archangels.

We found that virtues are at the heart of the value system of every culture on earth and are expressed in the oral traditions of the First Nations. They are a universal vocabulary of character, a context that enables people to integrate spirituality into everyday life, whatever their belief system. Several years after we initiated The Virtues Project, a First Nations shaman in northern Canada told me, "Linda, The Virtues Project is the bridge between the cultures." On our second trip to the Solomon Islands, Dan and I were invited to meet with the prime minister. We were surprised to recognize him as a participant in a virtues workshop two years before. He told us that he had attained his position after receiving the Virtues Card of service in that workshop. "It set the course for my life," he told us.

In 1990, in a converted garage beside the home we shared on a five-acre property, we self-published *The Virtues Guide*, a kind of handbook to help parents to morally and spiritually mentor their children. The book offered simple ways to awaken the virtues within ourselves and our children, describing fifty-two of the three-hundred-plus virtues we discovered in the world's sacred texts. To say we *published* a book sounds a bit too lofty, given the fact that we were photocopying it onto three-hole paper and Saran wrapping it for shipment. Within two months of completing the guide, we received orders from more than twenty countries, where news of the book had spread by word of mouth alone. In 1997, to our amazement, the book caught the attention of all the major publishing houses in New York and was put up for auction. Penguin republished it as *The Family Virtues Guide* (this time with binding!), and Oprah Winfrey invited me to present it on an episode of her show in 1998, "Doing the Right Thing." It has become an international best seller.

The Virtues Project has evolved into a grassroots movement in more than sixty-five countries. In 1994, the International Year of the Family, the United Nations Secretariat recognized it as a model global program for families of all cultures. Suffice it to say the project took over our lives; seven years after we started it, my life was completely out of control. I found myself sinking under the weight of an unsustainable lifestyle, and finally I crashed.

I was one of the children who fell ill at the end of the polio epidemic of the 1950s, just before the discovery of the polio vaccines by Salk and Sabin. The symptoms that struck me down in 1953, when I contracted bulbar polio at age eleven, returned. Among baby boomers an epidemic of post-polio syndrome has affected many of those who had polio during the 1940s and '50s.

Post-Polio Sequelae is not the only hazard of the Stress Generation. Countless individuals find themselves succumbing to energy-related diseases such as chronic fatigue syndrome and fibromyalgia as well. Like many people with post-polio syndrome, chronic fatigue, and other energy-related diseases, I had overspent my life's energy. I was an overachiever—passionate about my work and compulsively working long hours, overfilling my schedule, constantly multitasking, and traveling too much. I was hooked on the adrenaline flowing from the stress and the excitement—which are physiologically just a hair's breadth apart.

I experienced a profound shock when the fatigue of post-polio took over my life. As the weeks went on and the fatigue failed to lift, I imagined how a high-spirited racehorse might feel after years of running freely in an expanse of pasture as far as the eye could see. I suddenly felt as though I was confined to a small fenced enclosure, which gradually kept contracting. I wondered when the boundaries of my energy would stop closing in. The world had been my pasture, with annual speaking trips to Australia, New Zealand, Fiji, and Europe, with invitations from Asia, Russia, and South America in the offing. Now I could no longer drive, had difficulty walking some days, and often could only concentrate and hold my head up for a couple of hours a day.

One winter morning, several months after my initial diagnosis, I awoke at 5:00 A.M., my normal and preferred time to start the day. Prior to the onset of post-polio, this had been a time of light, clear energy for me. It was the beginning of my two-hour sacred time, when I would pray, meditate, journal, exercise, and plan my day. One of the greatest losses I had experienced since the severe onset of post-polio was that my capacity for concentration had withered. I no longer had the ability to meditate and receive clear answers in prayer, a counsel I had relied on for years. Visual meditation had been a daily delight and sanctuary for me, and my primary source of spiritual guidance. When post-polio hit, my meditation screen went dark. I was desolate in the bleak absence of Divine help when I needed it most. Although I dutifully continued to pray and journal a bit each day, I felt no response, as if calling a telephone number that had been disconnected.

Darkness greeted me on that winter morning when I opened my eyes. As I gradually became conscious, an oppressive fatigue restricted my breath. I felt as though an enormous cat was lying on my chest. When I attempted to get out of bed, my legs went out from under me, and I plunged into a dark inner place of hopelessness and fear.

I struggled out to my prayer corner in the living room by holding on to furniture and leaning on walls. I literally fell to my knees, sobbing, and cried out, "Help me, God! I don't know what to do. I don't know how to live like this." I anticipated silence, expected no response. Suddenly, the familiar voice of Spirit spoke: "I will give you ten rules for health. Write them down and follow them." The commanding power and clarity of this inner voice startled me, but I immediately pulled myself up to my prayer chair, grabbed my journal, and began to write. It felt like taking very rapid dictation.

When it was over, I read through the Ten Rules. They were simple, practical, and surprising—demanding a radical change in my lifelong habits of overdoing at the cost of self-neglect. The first rule was Purity and Cleanliness. It contained detailed instructions about purifying my diet—what foods to eat, the required amounts of water to drink, and the necessity of immersing my body in water each day. The meditation ended with the tenth rule: Plan a sustainable life. That morning, this phrase utterly mystified me. I had absolutely no idea what the word "sustainable" meant. I had a vague understanding of the words "sustain," meaning to support life, "sustenance," which means food, and "sustainable," something that endures over time. Although the phrase baffled me, I did have an alarming sense that if I failed to follow the Ten Rules, I would probably not survive.

During the next year, following these Ten Rules for Health literally saved my life. While they contain specific practices given to me for my personal condition, I believe the principles within them can serve as a catalyst for anyone who wishes to emerge from the fog of energy depletion or joyless hyperactivity. To be wise, consult your own physician and health practitioners about the Ten Rules, to make certain they are right for you. They are meant to serve as a reference and a tool for you as you read *A Pace of Grace*, supporting you to become a loving steward of your own energy and providing a step-by-step approach to a more graceful way of life.

The Ten Rules, a list of which follows, consist of simple but radical lifestyle changes. In following these rules, my energy has returned tenfold. I am now living sustainably for the first time in my life and have been strengthened in subtle ways that have taken my life and relationships to a deeper level of joy and mindfulness.

One year after following the Ten Rules as faithfully as I could, my health was dramatically improved. I had a follow-up appointment with the post-polio specialist. He looked at me and said, "You've certainly come a long way. How did you do it?" I showed him my Ten Rules for Health. "This is the best energy-restoration program I've ever seen. Where did you get it?" I smiled and told him about my prayer experience. He asked me if he could share the Ten Rules with his other patients.

Others asked me to share the energy-conservation practices in the Ten Rules, and they were published on the Internet on a post-polio network and on The Virtues Project Web site. I decided to develop a new workshop called "A Pace of Grace" in a few cities in Canada and the United States. People with chronic fatigue, fibromyalgia, and burnout, as well as individuals with what I call the "E-Type" personality—"Everything to Everybody"—flocked to the workshops to learn how to live a sustainable life. One day it struck me that a book would make these simple tools accessible to even more people.

Too many of us have suffered a severe loss in our quality of life amidst the stress of terrorism, war, and economic instability that keep us on edge, wondering when something else will happen to shatter our world. My friend Alice, a New York stockbroker, said that even a year after September 11, "Every time I hear a plane overhead, I feel a shock running through my body." Charlie Smith, a longtime executive of a mental health association in the Midwest, confesses that he is constantly feeling depleted by using up his personal energy supply too often and for too long without pausing. "I always have too much on my plate. But that's my life. I don't see an end in sight."

One of my favorite cartoons, by Jerry Van Amerongen, shows a woman in a tiny office crammed with books and papers. Tipped out of her chair, legs dangling in the air, she lies buried under one of the piles of files that has just toppled off an overloaded shelf above her. The caption is something like, "Gloria finds herself organizationally challenged." Like Gloria, we strain to keep up with the growing detritus around us—the sheer mass of details in this complex world we have created. We are overstimulated and dominated by electronic connections through cell phones and e-mail.

Too many of us have fallen into a lifestyle that feels crazed and out of control. We find ourselves overwhelmed by pressures to go faster and do more. Even retirement no longer provides sanctuary from stress and hurry. It is too easy to fill our calendars with countless obligations and activities. Somehow, overdoing has become a way of life, and we have created the most time-stressed era in history. A friend recently said to me, "The hard drive in my brain is full. I'm just totally exhausted. I can't take on any more—not one more thing." Many of us feel the same way.

Yet there is hope. More and more people are heeding a wake-up call in the midst of these troubled times. We are reevaluating how we spend the currency of our lives in light of the values we care about. We no longer take for granted the simple pleasures of life—a laugh with a friend, fishing at sunset, snuggling into a deep, welcoming couch with a good book and blanket on a rainy Saturday, performing an act of kindness for a stranger. Yet we don't make much room for these small blessings. The workaholic lifestyle we have created too easily sweeps us back into a pace of life that fails to sustain our grace.

Now is the time to ask ourselves how we can take back a sense of control over our lives in order to live in a spiritually and emotionally sustainable way. We need to discern how we can preserve our ideals and create islands of peace in our lives and relationships. How can we be the calm in the wind?

In the years that I have been practicing the Ten Rules for Health, I have moved into a deep current of inner joy. I feel as if the aging process has reversed, and photos from the last decade of my life confirm it. At the very heart of these revitalizing lifestyle choices is what I call a pace of grace. By choosing to live our lives each day at a pace that balances and sustains us physically and spiritually, we can receive a greater measure of the grace that is intended for us. Every day is full of rich possibilities—moments of grace that allow us to enjoy our lives and create joy for others—if we are mindful enough to be present to the grace each day holds. It is possible—and I believe essential—to live more gracefully in the midst of a world that is out of control.

Whether you are an at-home parent or a nine-to-five commuter, in retirement or starting a family, there has never been a better time to explore your true priorities, to find your pace of grace, to shape the lifestyle that reflects your deepest desires, to love what you do and do what you love—to bring new life and energy to your work and your relationships.

A Pace of Grace gives you a simple four-part program that supports you to purify your life, pace yourself, practice spirituality, and plan a sustainable life. Through these simple practices, you will be able to redesign your life to integrate a deeper level of grace. Each chapter ends with an Exercise of Grace for sustainable, more balanced living. You will discover a wide variety of ways to cultivate a pace of grace, from creating a daily routine of reverence to being active peace builders in all your relationships, and enhancing your inner sense of order by reshaping the order and beauty around you. It offers steps for sustaining soul-satisfying relationships and creating genuine community, as well as examining ways to play and experience joy.

The energy-restoration practices of the Ten Rules are woven throughout the book along with the virtues of a sustainable life and occasional prayers to give you opportunities to pause and reflect. We structure the practice of the virtues around five spiritual life-skill strategies that have come to light in the years my family and I have stewarded The Virtues Project. The Five Strategies of The Virtues Project form the frame of reference and a "frame of reverence" for living by the virtues of our character. They provide a focus and a litmus test for success in creating a gracious, grace-filled life.

Living by our virtues is the key to leading our lives, rather than following old habits of mindless living that leave no space for a spiritually centered, well-balanced life. The virtues allow us to live each day lovingly, purposefully, reverently, joyfully, truthfully, moderately, and gracefully. I truly believe that the cultivation of our virtues can guide us to the highest expression of ourselves, individually and collectively.

This book is an offering of gratitude for what I have learned on my own healing journey. The health crisis in my life has been a great gift, as all tests are if we are ready to receive the lessons they contain. Moderation—until recently an unfamiliar virtue—is my new best friend. My new pace of grace allows me to live more peacefully, fully, and deeply. I accomplish more in less time. I savor every moment of every day. My mantra has become "I love my easy, grace-filled life." Once again, I am writing, speaking, and traveling internationally but at a far more mindful pace, with lots of space for rest and play. I continually seek to do what I do best and delegate the rest.

My intent in sharing these simple virtues-based practices is to restore hope to others whose "hard drive" is full, or who are feeling stressed, whether by health issues, financial challenges, or simply the need to reclaim a sense of peace and balance in the midst of uncertainty. My hope is that *A Pace of Grace* will be a helpful companion in discovering your own path to a more sustainable rhythm of life, day by day and moment by moment.

I have one caveat. You can't enact the virtues and practices of sustainability described in this book through teeth-gritting determination. Rather, they invite a gentle shift in your spirit. I know that many of you are much like I was. "I'm going to work so hard at not working hard, so that I'll be the most grace-filled person on the planet." I know people who go to the gym religiously to reduce stress. Not that there's anything wrong with that, but you can't always sweat and strain your way to serenity. Luxuriate in these practices, try them on, bask in them with the knowledge that they can refill you and enrich you. I invite you to do the exercises at the end of each chapter as you read along. Take your time. Keep a pace of grace. Fill your own cup and you will have an overflowing sufficiency to give to everyone you love and anything you do. If you choose to cultivate the virtues of a sustainable life, I promise you they will enrich the quality of your life forever.

Linda Kavelin Popov, October 2003

Ten Rules for Health

1. **Purity and Cleanliness** Outside, bathe daily. Inside, eat pure, water-based foods. Eight glasses of water a day. Dark greens, legumes, rice, root vegetables. A little meat. Cut oils by two-thirds.

2. **Breathe (Pranha)** Learn Yoga. Walk or exercise every day for ten minutes, then fifteen, then twenty. No more. Breathe fresh air every day. You haven't breathed deeply in years.

3. **Proper Vitamins** Increase B, C, and E. Speak to a homeopath and listen to what she says.

4. **Proactive Rest** Take two rests each day. Do it as a routine. Stop *before* you get tired.

5. **Pace Yourself** You have four hours a day for work, sometimes six. Choose carefully. Keep your correspondence current. Enjoy! Enjoy!

6. **Pray Every Hour** Let your movements be a prayer, your work, your daily food.

7. **Pursue Peaceful Activity** Cut television down. It depresses you. Read what comes to you. Listen to music, clear and clean in small ways, watch the fire, write letters to your friends.

8. **Play!** Spend time in ways that give you joy and make you laugh.

9. **Prioritize** Put your first passion first. It is your most productive activity.

10. **Plan a Sustainable Life.**

Note: I received these Ten Rules as an answer to prayer during the onset of Post-Polio Sequelae. I offer them as principles that you may find helpful in your own life, and I encourage you to adapt them to your individual needs, as you and your physician see fit.

To download a free decorative poster of the Ten Rules for Health, go to www.paceofgrace.net.

The Five Strategies of The Virtues Project

These strategies help us to live more reverent, purposeful lives, to raise morally conscious children, create a culture of character in our schools, and enhance integrity in the workplace. People use them worldwide to build safe and caring communities.

STRATEGY 1: SPEAK THE LANGUAGE OF VIRTUES

Language is the vehicle of our thoughts. The Language of Virtues awakens spirituality. It shapes character. The way we speak and the words we use have great power to discourage or to inspire. When the language of our thoughts and words is infused with virtues, it transforms our relationships. It helps us to replace shaming and blaming with personal responsibility and respect. It brings out the best in others and ourselves. It helps us to become the kind of people we want to be.

STRATEGY 2: RECOGNIZE TEACHABLE MOMENTS

Recognizing the gifts in our tests and challenges and discerning the life lessons in the events of each day help us to cultivate character in our children, others, and ourselves. When we have the humility and confidence to accept accountability and learn from our mistakes, every stumbling block becomes a stepping-stone.

STRATEGY 3: SET CLEAR BOUNDARIES

Virtues-based boundaries, which focus on respect, restorative justice, and reparation, create a climate of peace and safety. Personal boundaries help us to build healthy relationships and protect our time, our energy, and our health.

STRATEGY 4: HONOR THE SPIRIT

First, this means respecting the dignity of each person. This strategy also encourages us to make time for reflection, develop routines of reverence, experience natural beauty, and participate in the arts. Celebration and ceremony for special life events and sharing our stories are also ways to help us connect with the meaning of our lives.

STRATEGY 5: OFFER SPIRITUAL COMPANIONING

By being deeply present, and listening with compassion and detachment, we connect spirit to spirit. This counseling tool uses "cup-emptying" questions to get to the heart of the matter. When receiving companioning, we are empowered to define our Teachable Moments and reflect on the virtues we need to call on. It supports us to make moral choices and creates intimacy in relationships. It is a powerful tool for healing grief, anger, and trauma.

The Virtues Project inspires the practice of virtues in everyday life by helping people of all cultures to discover the transformative power of these universal gifts of character. The virtues are spiritual life skills that help us to live our best lives.

⚶ Virtues: The Gifts Within ⚶

Acceptance	Flexibility	Patience
Accountability	Forbearance	Peacefulness
Appreciation	Forgiveness	Perceptiveness
Assertiveness	Fortitude	Perseverance
Awe	Friendliness	Prayerfulness
Beauty	Generosity	Purity
Caring	Gentleness	Purposefulness
Charity	Grace	Reliability
Cheerfulness	Gratitude	Resilience
Cleanliness	Helpfulness	Respect
Commitment	Honesty	Responsibility
Compassion	Honor	Reverence
Confidence	Hope	Righteousness
Consideration	Humanity	Sacrifice
Contentment	Humility	Self-Discipline
Cooperation	Idealism	Serenity
Courage	Independence	Service
Courtesy	Initiative	Sincerity
Creativity	Integrity	Steadfastness
Decisiveness	Joyfulness	Strength
Detachment	Justice	Tact
Devotion	Kindness	Temperance
Dignity	Love	Thankfulness
Diligence	Loyalty	Tolerance
Discernment	Mercy	Trust
Endurance	Mindfulness	Trustworthiness
Enthusiasm	Moderation	Truthfulness
Excellence	Modesty	Understanding
Fairness	Nobility	Unity
Faith	Obedience	Uprightness
Faithfulness	Openness	Wisdom
Fidelity	Orderliness	Zeal

See www.paceofgrace.net for a definition of each virtue.

PART ONE

PURIFY YOUR LIFE

*Help us to be the always hopeful
gardeners of the spirit
who know that without darkness
nothing comes to birth
as without light
nothing flowers.*
—May Sarton

⇒ ONE ⇐
How Are You?

We get caught up in all the problems and hassles, and forget the joy of it all.
—Richard Carlson, author of *Don't Sweat the Small Stuff*

At fifty-three, I climbed my first mountain. I have the hero picture to prove it. The mountain was a craggy, terrifying peak near the Llewellyn Glacier in northern British Columbia, looming above a rushing river. When I made it to the top, I said to the guide, "Well, I live here now. You'll have to send food. There's no way I will ever make it back down."

I did manage to go down the "easy" way, clinging to trees and brush, rather than rappelling down on a rope backward. I was cut and bruised but unbowed and totally exhilarated, having won the challenge to my fear of heights. My accomplishments gave me a new zest for life, and an appetite for exercise. I began to do some weight training, and I hiked and climbed every chance I got. I spent hours pulling out the wild broom that had overtaken much of our five-acre property. I began to build a prayer garden outside the east-facing window in front of my prayer corner—digging, shoveling, moving dirt. I felt incredibly virtuous. I was buffing up for the first time in years. Little did I know that excessively pushing my body to new heights was the worst thing I could have done. A few months later, I hit a wall.

I will never forget what my doctor said to me after pronouncing his postpolio syndrome diagnosis. "Linda, this will take you to a deeper level of transformation. You need to be grounded, to stop spending so much time with the angels. You have to stop flying around the world. You must stop this pace. If you don't, you will be very, very ill."

I was forced to recognize the truth of what he said but found it inconceivable that I would have to give up the life I loved. How could I relinquish it, and why, I wondered, would God want me to give up this work of service, which was the very purpose of my life? I was frightened. I had no idea how, when, or if my physical deterioration would stop. I asked my husband, Dan—the soul of patience—to give me two solid weeks to tell him every complaint I had, every

nuance of change I noticed. After two weeks, I needed an extension! The symptoms were rapidly proliferating. I noticed new areas of muscle weakness every
few days. One evening we went out for dinner, and when we were ready to leave
I found I was unable to get up out of my chair. My muscles simply would not
obey my brain. I wept silently as Dan turned a bit pale and then lifted me out of
the chair.

The FOG Syndrome: Fatigue, Overwhelm, and Guilt

I have since come to realize that post-polio and other energy diseases are not the
only destroyers of quality of life. An epidemic of fatigue, overwhelm, and guilt
connected with an unsupportable lifestyle affects millions of us. We have never
been more challenged to develop ways to live sustainably.

According to some studies, 70 percent of Americans are concerned about
burnout or consider themselves already in a state of burnout. Seventy-five percent of teens feel they have little or no leisure time. A recent U.S. poll showed that
an overwhelming majority of Americans consider the true mark of a successful
life to be not a raise, not a promotion—but abundant family time.

Our overfilling of time has become epidemic and spread far beyond urban
and suburban environs. This was brought home to me several years ago while
visiting with the elders in a remote First Nations village in northern Canada. I
was invited there by my friend Robert, a member of the Tahltan First Nation. We
drove for hours through wilderness forest in his battered blue truck, ending in
dirt road switchbacks winding down to a deep river canyon, with nothing in
sight but the wild beauty of this sacred area, a legacy of the Tahltan people for
more than 10,000 years. Finally Robert and I arrived at the tiny village where we
were to pay our respects to the elders and seek their permission to camp on the
land. I entered a small house where a circle of elders was waiting. After a few
minutes of tea and conversation, one of the elders looked at her watch and said,
"Oh, I have to go. I'm so busy these days. My next committee meeting is in five
minutes." I had to laugh.

We suffer on a daily basis from a sense of being overwhelmed and anxious
about "not getting it all done." Faced by impossible demands on our time, we feel
constantly pressured and inadequate to complete the tasks we set for ourselves in
our daily work. FOG immerses young parents as they balance job responsibilities with the relentless tasks of caring for a baby or toddler and the sleeplessness

that often accompanies the early years of their child's life. We soldier on, pretending we are okay while feeling secretly guilty that we aren't managing our lives as well as everyone else seems to be doing.

A large percentage of mothers choose to continue to work outside the home, reluctant to lose their places in their professions, and many feel financially compelled to earn money to support their families. FOG often descends, bringing with it low-level chronic depression mixed with anxiety. Many women feel overwhelmed and guilty, overcome by a sense that there is never enough time or energy in the day to give quality time to their children while simultaneously meeting the demands of their work outside the home. When we are always juggling multiple roles, our relationships with our mates suffer as well. We feel as though we are living parallel lives, with so little time for loving, meaningful connection. Too often our interactions consist of small "business meetings" about who will do car pool, pick up the dry cleaning, or attend a school conference with a child's teacher. Separation from our extended family, which used to provide a nurturing support system, has isolated us and put an incredible strain on all our resources.

Love takes time. Friendship takes time. Spiritual practice takes time. Yet our culture fails to support the mindful use of time to meet our contemplative needs. How often has someone casually asked you, "Are you keeping busy?," as if that is the ideal and natural way to be?

The need for Grace Time

One of our greatest unmet needs is time for solitude. Taking refuge in the bathtub just isn't enough. Many fathers feel frustrated by a lack of "cave time"—time to unwind, free of the relentless demands of work or home.

A friend once confessed to me his guilt over a habit he had developed of stopping and parking the car on the way home rather than getting there as quickly as his wife wanted him to, just so that he could put his head back against the seat and breathe a while. His children were taught to give him a grand welcome when he arrived, jumping on him, hugging, and doing a "show and tell" about their day. "I love them, but it is just too much after a long day of constantly dealing with people."

When we are running on empty, we simply don't have enough energy or time in the day to experience the abundance or grace or joy of life. At the end of the day, we are left wondering what we have really accomplished, and more often than not we have a sense that we have failed someone, something, somehow. We feel overwhelmed when the commitments we make to family, friends, and especially work are more than we can actually handle. I once wrote in my journal: "With my current schedule, which I continue to overfill, I have no time for free-floating thought, so instead I have free-floating anxiety." It was shortly after that that I became seriously ill.

The trap of self-importance in identifying totally with my work for "a worthy cause" and the seduction of running on adrenaline had kept me from mindfulness and stolen away my life energy. We need what I call "Grace Time," a term that is more descriptive and positive than "down time"—to revive, to recover our energy, to daydream, and to putter. Without it, we endanger our energy supply and court disaster in our health.

The paralysis of fatigue

Failure to pause for a moment of grace, if chronic and constant, leads inevitably to fatigue, no matter how healthy you consider yourself. One of the most troubling symptoms of post-polio, chronic fatigue, or fibromyalgia is the paralyzing fatigue. It closely resembles depression. Fatigue makes us too tired to think, to dream, to remember. It keeps us from what is most important—a joyful life lived mindfully, deliberately, and purposefully. Because fatigue is invisible, people around us may not recognize its death grip. "Oh, you're looking fine," they say in a reassuring tone, which just adds to the problem. Now we feel both invalidated and exhausted! In "A Pace of Grace" workshops, I find this one of the greatest complaints of people who suffer from fatigue. "I wish it were visible," one participant said. "If I had my arm in a cast, I would get more understanding. Sometimes I feel people judging me as if I'm a malingering hypochondriac."

Without habits of rest and rejuvenation to sustain us, even in the most vigorous person fatigue becomes cumulative and leads to disorientation and memory loss. Memory overload and disorientation associated with the fatigue of living beyond our energetic means is now creeping into the lives of individuals in their twenties and thirties.

Overwhelmed and never enough

The overwhelming lifestyle we have created continually feeds the belief that we are not enough. For many of us, this is an old wound in our self-esteem, having experienced that "not enough" sense as children, when our parents failed to praise or appreciate and instead criticized and found us wanting. I remember a time when I was about thirteen and hadn't yet given up on my mother someday loving me as she loved my brothers, the twin apples of her eye, born when I was about two. One night, I swallowed my pride and did the dishes without being asked. Shy, and awkwardly hopeful of her praise, I casually tossed the dish towel down, saying, "There." "Why can't you do it cheerfully like your brothers? Why do you have to be so sullen?" she said, missing the affirming moment by a mile. Needless to say, that was my last spontaneous act of service in our house, and I settled into a chronic sense of grief about not being enough for my mother, no matter what I did.

The go, go, go routine of our overwhelming, unsustainable lifestyle both feeds and alleviates the guilt of "not-enoughness." The more we take on, the deeper we dig ourselves into a hole of overwhelm, and at the same time the pace we keep cuts us off from our feelings. We are left with a vague disquiet that steals away our grace.

Guilt, the gift that keeps on giving . . .

Unfortunately, we have become habituated to guilt. We all experience guilt to a certain degree, although not all guilt is alike. For example, a friend of mine in New York works as an editor of children's books. She finds that on a daily basis she has far more to do than she can actually accomplish. Her guilt is the natural result of having too much to do and not enough time to ever have a sense of closure. In the age of e-mail and cell phones, it sometimes feels as though we are trying to empty the ocean with a teaspoon. Just when we feel we're getting through the day's influx, a new wave comes in. Guilt is both the effect and the cause of the sense that we are never enough. We feel as though we can never do enough, or be enough.

Guilt also occurs because we know deep down we are neglecting the most important things—our relationships, our bodies, and our souls. We strive to survive and wonder, "When will I have time for myself and more time for my family?"

THE CALL OF CREATIVITY

As a woman moves beyond her reproductive years, she is ready for her productive years. She is ready to birth her own wisdom and creativity. Many women are finding that their postmenopausal years bring fresh energy, creativity, and a re-laxed joy. They feel more at home in their own skin. Men in their forties and fifties, having worked hard for years, begin to wonder if all this hard work is really what life is all about, and ask themselves, "Is this all there is?" If they are able to withstand the pull of the culture to regress and recapture their lost youth, they too experience an expansive sense of freedom and life-giving creativity.

Our fifties can be a time of spiritual transition, often bringing a life-giving crisis of meaning—the years in which our wisdom ripens. At this age, people ex-perience a spiritual restlessness, an awareness of how quickly life is going by and a knowledge that most of us are well past the midpoint of our time on earth. An inner craving arises to find our true calling, to give birth to a new, perhaps more meaningful dream while living more simply and mindfully.

Forty-five million baby boomers in North America are now in their fifties and sixties, and many of them suffer from the FOG of Fatigue, Overwhelm, and Guilt. At this time in life, our bodies and our spirits are often sending mixed sig-nals. We find that while our bodies are slowing down, we feel a call to give more to life and to get more from life. Our spiritual energies are increasing, and our bodies are telling us it is time for a more contemplative lifestyle. We begin to question the things with which we have identified ourselves. We have paid our dues, raised our children, put in our time at work. We want financial freedom, the freedom to travel, and even more the freedom to be our authentic selves.

I met Margaret, a vivacious woman with a shock of bright silver hair and jewelry to match, at an awards banquet where I was the dinner speaker. She was retired from years as a psychiatric social worker (my first career), and was enjoy-ing an extremely successful second career as a consultant for Victorian Epicure, a networking sales organization offering healthy spices and cookware through home presentations. Her vision for this time in her life had been to do work that would give her "fun, freedom and finances." Margaret was positively radiant as she went up to the podium to receive an award as a top achiever. She had just re-turned from a cruise to which she was able to treat her entire family. The beauty of this second career is that she is pursuing a true passion to give young at-home moms a way to earn a living and pursue their first priority of parenting at the same time. Best of all, she does it at her own pace. She can work, or not, when-ever she chooses. She balances work and play as she sees fit.

We often find that a deep desire emerges in elderhood to give something

back, to make our contribution, and
to leave a legacy in some creative way.
One of the most time-honored roles
of the elder is that of the wise mentor.
Yet too often we find ourselves working harder than ever, either in our jobs
or in frantic volunteerism. At work
and at home we are overwhelmed by
busyness that keeps us from our true
calling.

> *We are spiritual beings
> having a human experience,
> not human beings having a
> spiritual experience.*
> —Pierre Teilhard de Chardin,
> Catholic theologian

LISTEN TO YOUR SPIRIT

Scientists claim that we use only 10 percent of our intelligence. I believe we
use only 1 percent of our spiritual capacity—our virtues of creativity, courage,
reverence, discernment, wonder, joy, and the other powers of our souls. In the
midst of the FOG of Fatigue, Overwhelm, and Guilt, there are quiet signals being transmitted from within. We may experience a dim awareness that we are not
living as we are meant to live. No matter how hard we work, a profound and often subtle calling of our souls causes a faint but persistent sense of loss. We need
to listen to it.

Gifts have come to us out of the economic downturn, the falling of giants,
revelations of corporate greed and insider trading, and the lapses of integrity by
world-renowned executives. These events help us to be aware as never before of
what really matters in this world, and to recognize that we have allowed this graceless, grasping, hyperactive lifestyle to overtake our lives. It is time to weed out
what chokes off life and beauty. It is time to cultivate our inner gardens, to dig
into discernment—to go, as my doctor said, to a deeper level of transformation.

Like any life crisis or loss, my illness concealed a gift—a seed pearl of awareness, a truth I had neglected all my life. My life was worth saving—my life—
regardless of what I could or could not do for others. I was brought face-to-face
with a truth that rarely comes until the end of one's life. We are more than the
roles we play and the images we have of ourselves. I am not my job, my role as
mother or wife or daughter or author or speaker. I am not my body. We are in-
trinsically worthy and deserving of care, particularly self-care.

The virtues, the very purpose of our lives, are first about being and then reflected in our actions. Our culture tells us that what we do is all that matters. All the sacred traditions reveal that our life is inherently meaningful because we are the expression of Divine love, justice, kindness, and truthfulness in the world. The world distracts us from this simple truth, and everything we do to feed the illusion that life is all about what and how much we do devalues us and costs us our health and well-being.

TAKING THE FIRST STEP

The first step of transformation is to awaken one of your most powerful virtues—truthfulness. Take an honest look at your life. Is your life overdone? Are you feeling sustained? How are you, really? You may need to stop the world and get off for a while by taking a retreat to find some solitude. Or you may choose to take some quiet solitude each day to dig in your inner garden. Take a look at the size of your plot. What is populating your life? What have you taken on? What if you decide right now that you will do something about the impossible pace of life? Does your way of life reflect the values you really care about—friendship, learning, beauty, creativity, intimacy, or service? Does your life bring you joy?

RECOGNIZE YOUR
TEACHABLE MOMENT

One of the Five Strategies of The Virtues Project is Recognize Teachable Moments, which means to call on your virtue of truthfulness to discern the lesson of the moment and the gifts in your tests. Reflect on the meaning of what is happening in your life and determine the guiding virtues you need to do the right thing and to live more consciously. In order to heal what blocks you from a sustainable life, the Teachable Moment requires you to be truthful about the habits that block you from living by your true values. First, as the Twelve Steps program of Alcoholics Anonymous teaches, you must admit how your life has become unsustainable. Then you can put into practice the virtues that will help you achieve a life of integration and balance, a pace of grace. Know that this is your soul work. There is nothing more important. This is what you came here for.

⊷⊨ *The Virtue of Truthfulness* ⊫⊶

Then have done with falsehood and speak the truth to each other, for we belong to one another as the parts of one body. —Ephesians 4:25

Truthfulness is being honest in our words and actions. Telling the truth means we don't lie, even to defend ourselves. We don't listen to gossip or prejudice. We see the truth for ourselves. Being true to ourselves means being who and what we are without trying to be more than we are to impress others. We live by our own true natures. Look into your heart and speak what is true for you.

Signs of Success

I am practicing Truthfulness when I . . .

- Speak only the truth
- Investigate the truth for myself
- Don't let others tell me what to think
- Discern the difference between fact and fantasy
- Admit my mistakes
- Don't exaggerate or deceive to impress others

Affirmation

I am truthful. I speak the truth. I see the truth with my own eyes. I know that I am enough. I am content to be my true self.

Put Guilt in Its Place

The first step in facing the truth in a Teachable Moment is to eliminate judgment and needless guilt. Healthy guilt serves *only* as a signal for change. We aren't meant to bathe in it or wear "Eau de Guilt" like daily cologne. With the help of truthfulness, take a long, loving look at what is real and unreal in your life. What needs to change? What is the wheat and what is the chaff? I once commented to an editor for whom I have great respect, "You seem so peaceful and mindful. What is your secret?" He said, "Well, every so often I have my own Boston Tea Party. I throw everything overboard, cast my life upon the waters. Then, I watch what sinks and what comes floating back."

You may find, as I did, that as you emerge from denial and recognize the stress you have allowed to dominate your life, grief comes welling up. Emotions held at bay through the distractions of overdoing will naturally rise to the surface. You may recognize that you have made self-destructive choices, driven yourself too hard, given too much and received too little, perhaps chosen relationships that have drained you of your life energy. Let the grief come, and then let it go. Let it flow. Take time to let yourself mourn for lost health, lost time, lost joy. Take an honest look at your own sources of Fatigue, Overwhelm, and Guilt. In telling the truth, be open to the lessons with courage and curiosity. Ask yourself, as a beloved and trusted friend would, "How are you?"

If your compassion does not include yourself, it is incomplete.
—Jack Kornfield,
American Buddhist,
author of *A Path with Heart*

⊶➦ EXERCISE GRACE ☞⊷
What Stresses You and What Blesses You?

Take some quiet time each day this week to reflect on what is going on in your life and to assess the state of your energy. If you can, take a weekend retreat. Think about which elements in your life stress you and which elements bless you. In a personal journal, write the following questions as well as your thoughts and feelings about each. Reflect and revisit the list each day for the next week. Make a list or draw a diagram of your responses around each question, putting the question in the center of a page and writing your responses around it. Take the time to reflect deeply on each question. Once you have done this reflective work, you may want to share your responses with a friend or a small sharing circle.

WHAT STRESSES ME?

When do I feel most stressed?

What fatigues me?

What conditions, activities, people, and relationships in my life drain me?

What is my greatest fear?

What am I worried about?

What overwhelms me?

What do I feel guilty about? What triggers guilt for me?

What do I want to change about the way I spend my time and energy?

What do I want less of in my life?

WHAT BLESSES ME?

What makes me smile?

What gives me joy?

When do I feel the most peaceful?

What activities do I find most satisfying?

When do I feel most alive?

What relationships and activities restore me and give me sustenance?

Who do I enjoy?

Who do I want to spend more time with?

What do I want more of in my life?

The remaining chapters will lead you deeper into the virtues and practices of a sustainable life. I invite you to continue doing the exercises at the end of each chapter as you read along. Take your time. Keep your pace of grace.

SUMMARY OF CHAPTER 1: HOW ARE YOU?

- Take an honest look at how you are affected by the FOG Syndrome: Fatigue, Overwhelm, and Guilt.
- Take Grace Time—daily time for solitude, recovering your energy, daydreaming, and puttering.
- Keep a pace of grace by making gentle transitions from work to home.
- Resist the tyranny of guilt. Use guilt only as a signal for change.
- Respond to the call of your creativity.
- Listen to your spirit—focus on being more than doing.
- Take the first step of transformation—admit the truth about what keeps you from a sustainable pace of grace.
- Recognize your Teachable Moments with compassion for yourself and faith that you can change.
- Take time to reflect on what stresses you and what blesses you.

Facing the truth frees us to create change, to flush out the habits that block the flow of grace in our lives. Our overdone life is like a dried-out field awaiting irrigation while the water pools behind a logjam of unhealthy habits. Looking honestly at the level of stress in our lives is the first step. Now we can wade in and do something about it.

⊷⊶ *TWO* ⊶⊷

‌Purify Your Body

He leadeth me beside the still waters. He restoreth my soul.
—Psalms 23:2–3

On the morning I received the Ten Rules for Health, I leaned back in my prayer chair, my journal still open on my lap, watching the dawn sky lighten from deep gray to rose and coral. All I could hear was the soft ticking of a clock and my own breath. A few birds began to warble their dawn songs. The shock of having fallen out of bed, unable to bear my own weight, gave way to a gentle sense of being held. I was not alone. There was a way out of this desert place.

I looked down at my journal and slowly read each of the Ten Rules. Something resonated in my heart, a small leap of awareness, as I noticed that the first word on the page was the virtue of Purity. The first rule was about water—the primordial element, the source of life. The exact words I heard were:

Rule 1: Purity and Cleanliness

Outside, bathe daily. Inside, eat pure, water-based foods. Eight glasses of water a day. Dark greens, legumes, rice, root vegetables. A little meat. Cut oils by two-thirds.

This said to me, you are parched, dear one. Irrigate your body. You are malnourished. Nurture yourself with life-giving foods of the earth—fruits, vegetables, and grains. These simple practices of purifying and cleansing my body both inside and out seemed manageable. It dawned on me that I had the power to revive myself. I felt baptized by hope.

The sacred traditions of many cultures consider purification a catalyst for redemption and the symbol of grace. Hindus purify themselves by entering the sacred river Ganges. First Nations healers often cleanse themselves in a lake or river, even in winter, before they pray. Jesus was being baptized in the Jordan River in Judea when the dove came to him, revealing that he was the son of God.

I realized, reading this first rule, that water is the essential source of health. I was shocked to realize that this basic element needed to sustain life was lacking in my life. I found immediate relief by taking the simple step of drinking more water and mindfully immersing myself in water. However, as I continued to unravel the detailed instructions in the first two rules, I found that they required a radical shift in my way of life and a rather daunting leap across a chasm of self-neglect, which had widened during the years I was so enmeshed in my work. I had to develop new habits of drinking, eating, and even breathing.

I was surprised, and to be candid, somewhat humiliated to find that I had a great deal of resistance to investing so much energy and thought into self-care. Wasn't this selfish? Even my belief that the Ten Rules were given to me as spiritual guidance didn't give me sufficient justification to follow these practices without guilt!

Supposedly, I knew a lot about self-care. I was a self-care maven! For thirty years, it had been practically a theme song in my psychotherapy practice, my consultations to managers, and presentations at conferences. I had even given "Healing for the Healers" retreats, for heaven's sake. But when I found myself so ill and incapacitated, an old fear of being self-centered loomed like a mountain in the middle of my path to recovery. As I discovered the radical nature of the self-care required by the Ten Rules for Health, it felt more like a lifestyle of self-indulgence. Before we can purify our bodies with water we have to rid our minds of the notion that we aren't worthy of feeling good.

PURGING OUR GUILT

At a women's seminar I had given years before, a young mother of three expressed shock at the notion of taking time for daily personal reflection. I had just finished saying that everyone needs a routine of reflection, a daily time set aside to rejuvenate and restore. (This was one practice I have always protected as part of my own self-care.) She raised her hand and said, "But isn't that selfish?" "What troubles you about being selfish?" I asked. She spluttered, "It, just, would be . . . *selfish*! What about the rest of the family? I can't afford to take time for myself." I remember thinking, "Honey, you can't afford *not* to take time for yourself. If you don't, how soon will you begin resenting all this 'sacrifice' for your family?" I proceeded to give her several practical reasons for the fact that "You can only give fully to others when your own cup is full."

Don't you find the word "self-ish" an interesting one? It is not merely a word describing what pertains to the self. It is heavily loaded with negative connotations. "Boyish" simply means youthful and boylike. "Foolish" means acting like a fool. "Selfish" implies that to focus on the self is somehow sinful and inappropriate. "Unselfish" or "selfless" implies one who has the virtues of consideration, generosity, and a willingness to meet the needs of others while sacrificing one's own needs in the process.

One of the gifts I received from my illness was that it brought me face-to-face with my own demons of self-neglect and abuse in the name of service. I realized I had grown up with the subtle message that I am here only to serve others and that the greatest sin is selfishness. I believe this message is particularly part of the raising of girls. Many of us, in our growing-up years, watched our mothers catering to the males in the family. The messages our parents sent us during our childhoods were "Children are to be seen and not heard," "Don't cry or I'll give you something to cry about," "Keep a stiff upper lip," "Don't be so selfish," "Think about the starving children in Armenia." I never did get why my eating my peas was going to help those children across the world.

I am an assertive woman and am not afraid to ask for what I need, so I was shocked to realize that I felt so undeserving. I had stranded myself in a desert of neglect, convinced I was just too busy for self-care. I had not paid attention to my own body. I had not asked *myself* for what I needed.

During my initial experience of post-polio I could hardly move, so I had lots of time to reflect. Gradually, I discerned a subtle egoism in the "unselfishness" of the busy martyr role, the insidious pull to sacrifice my health out of an inflated sense of self-importance. This elusive understanding dawned as, more and more, I experienced the freedom of detaching from the undone tasks, of listening to my body first. After attempting to work a couple of hours, I would move toward the couch muttering, "No one's going to die if they don't get an e-mail from me today."

The commitment to be "selfish" enough to take care of my body was an essential step in purifying myself from my own logjam of self-neglect. A few months after receiving the Ten Rules, I received a lifeline that lifted me to a new level of understanding about the spiritual meaning of self-care and inducted me into a more deeply nurturing relationship with my body.

Listen to Your Body

I took the ferry to Vancouver for my first appointment with Dr. Cecil Hershler, a post-polio physician and sports medicine specialist. When I opened the door to his office suite, I noticed a delicate whiff of jasmine incense. His receptionist, wearing a pastel summer dress, greeted me pleasantly from behind the desk. When I met Dr. Hershler, he shook my hand warmly and sat back as if he had all the time in the world. After drawing out the story of my symptoms and listening intently, he gave me three profoundly simple prescriptions:

Listen to your body.

Have compassion for your body.

Take care of your body.

I was touched by the tenderness in these words. It brought to mind something my friend Barbara said when our mentors' circle gathered that summer (see more on mentorship in chapter 14). She said to me, "Linda, you never had good mothering. It's time for you to be a good mother to yourself." This was very helpful in moving me from my habitual task focus of "getting it all done" to concentrating on the task of the hour, which was healing myself.

Respect the Mind-Body Connection

As a psychotherapist, I was very aware that spiritual well-being is deeply and inextricably related to physical health. The body, mind, and spirit are a continuum of energy. When we are physically healthy, we have more emotional equilibrium, mental clarity, and spiritual awareness. We can attend to things beyond our physical comfort. We are more open to the experience of grace, the simple gifts life offers. By the same token, when we are happy, we are more likely to feel better physically. If you have ever experienced depression, you know how hard it is to get your smile muscles to work, much less get up and exercise or prepare a healthy meal. It all goes together.

Medical doctors are not always able to tell what is the cause and what is the effect of disease, since the physical, mental, and emotional facets of our lives are so interconnected. As a therapist, I always looked at the whole picture of a patient's life before diagnosing their problems. Mary, widowed at sixty-four, came to see me because she was obsessively worried and fearful and unable to leave her house. Whenever she tried, she would have a heart-pounding panic attack. It took suicidal desperation for her to call me for an appointment and then make the trip to my office. Mary was in such a state of anxiety that many therapists would have hospitalized her. It was my practice to do everything possible to seek a less radical solution, by making a holistic assessment and treatment plan. As her story unfolded and we unraveled the mystery of her affliction together, two elements emerged that surprised me. When I asked her to describe her day, including her sleeping and eating habits, she innocently revealed that she hadn't been eating properly since her husband had passed away four months before. She was subsisting on multiple cups of coffee and two bowls of dry high-sugar cereal day in and day out. She was dehydrated, literally malnourished, and protein deprived. Secondly, she had not dealt with her grief at all.

Whenever we suppress feelings, they leak out in other ways that affect the mind-body system. An unhealed emotional wound continues to bleed. When I guided her to say good-bye to her husband and to tell him what he meant to her, there in my office, she wept her first tears of loss. At a later session, she vented some anger at her husband and was able to break through to her virtue of forgiveness. Within a week she began to purify her blocked emotions and started eating a balanced diet of eggs, fish, chicken, fruit, grains, and vegetables, and drank at least four glasses of water a day. She looked radiant, and her symptoms completely disappeared. "This is a miracle," she said. I cringe to think that she might have been hospitalized and heavily medicated to further suppress her symptoms, likely receiving a label of depression or agoraphobia, which would follow her the rest of her life. By undertaking simple purification steps for her body and her emotions, she set in motion her own natural innate healing powers.

Sustain Yourself with Water

When I started to practice the first rule in earnest, I found it a challenge just to recognize when I was hungry or thirsty or had to go to the bathroom. I had developed the habit of working so intently, concentrating so fully on what I was doing, that it became easy to neglect even these simple bodily needs.

Before I received the Ten Rules for Health, I was simply too busy to drink much water. Nor did I like to drink, for some reason. I confess that I didn't appreciate having to interrupt my busy day to run to the bathroom, and I assumed that if I drank more I would go more. This is a myth! If we continually

⤙ The Virtue of Purity ⤚

*O pious one, you must purify the character! For any human being, the
purification of his own character is [done] thus: he purifies his character
with good thoughts, good words, good deeds.*
—Zoroastrian teachings, Vendidad 10:10

Purity means having a clean body, a clear mind, and a peaceful spirit. It is being
ourselves, our true selves. Purity is putting only healthful things in our bodies
and our minds. It is keeping our living spaces clean and orderly. We can purify
our character by freeing ourselves from harmful thoughts and actions. When
unwanted thoughts come, replace them with peaceful, positive thoughts. Use
clean language. Act only in ways that feel right within our spirit. When our intent is pure, our actions will be too. Purity is cleaning up our mistakes by making amends when we have done something we regret. We can always restore our
purity by choosing to change. It is never too late to make a fresh start. Living a
pure life is staying true to our ideals, living as we truly choose to live.

Signs of Success

I am practicing Purity when I . . .

- Keep myself and my space fresh and clean
- Put only healthful things in my body
- Protect my mind and spirit from unhealthy influences
- Use clean language
- Clean up my mistakes
- Stay true to my ideals

Affirmation

*I am committed to living a pure life, free of unwanted influences. I keep my
mind and body clean. I am willing and able to clean up my mistakes. My actions reflect my true values.*

hydrate the cells of our bodies, they absorb the water. If we drink only once in a while, it is like watering a parched plant—the water runs off instead of penetrating the soil. Have you ever noticed what happens when you water a dry, neglected houseplant? The water runs right through it and pools beneath the pot. However, once a plant is properly and regularly watered, it gently absorbs the moisture into its roots and leaves. We are the same way.

One of the ways to take care of our bodies is to learn to recognize when we are thirsty. Research reveals that 75 percent of Americans are chronically dehydrated, and for 37 percent of them the thirst mechanism is so weak that it is often mistaken for hunger. When we drink more, we eat less. If you feel thirsty, some research says that at that point you are already dehydrated.

I had a pattern of careless and often addictive eating, of going for days with little water, answering the craving for sustenance with high-carbohydrate, salty, sugary, high-fat "fixes." Once I began to drink fresh clean water, the craving for these things lessened. I have an occasional dessert, and most evenings I have one small piece of good chocolate, but addictive bingeing is a thing of the past. Eating addictively just kept me eating addictively. I have found the purifying effect of water a powerful, natural remedy in helping to heal food cravings.

A simple way to remember to drink is to keep a bottle of water with you at all times. Make sure you empty it before adding new water, and wash it at the end of each day. This keeps it clean and free of bacteria. Obtain a source of water that is as pure as possible, either arranging a delivery service for filtered spring water or using a good filter at your tap.

Without sufficient water, your skin becomes dry and dehydrated. As you increase your water intake, your skin will take on a new radiance. You are continually flushing away impurities that, without water, your skin typically releases as blemishes. Hydrating your cells is one of the greatest and least expensive beauty secrets. I have learned to tell whether I am drinking sufficient water by looking in the mirror. If the skin on my face begins to look pinched or fine wrinkles appear, I know I am getting dehydrated. I increase my water supply the next day and my reflection shows me the effect immediately.

Dehydration is also linked to fatigue. According to some researchers, lack of water is the number-one trigger of daytime fatigue. Immersing yourself inside and out in water purifies and nourishes every cell in your body. Drinking more increases your energy. Continually rehydrating your cells offers a constant energy supply. Without water, you will find you crave salt and sugar because of the urge to instantly boost your depleted energy. Fast foods and soft drinks are a debilitating, false source of energy, a poor substitute for the water of life.

The notion of listening to my body reminded me of an experience I had had years ago at a summer retreat center in Maine where I was giving a weeklong course. I developed a bad headache that aspirin couldn't touch. It was so severe by the third day that I had to cancel my presentations for that day. At lunch, a woman from my class asked me how I was. I told her I was still suffering from this terrible headache the like of which I had never had before. She made a recommendation that sounded bizarre to me in those days before meditation became part of my daily spiritual practice. She said, "Linda, why don't you meditate? Your body knows what is happening and will give you the answer. Just find a quiet spot and ask for the source of the headache." Skeptical yet desperate, I decided I had nothing to lose and tried it. I found a quiet spot in the shade beneath a tree, shut my eyes, and quieted my mind. Within a couple of minutes an answer came to me as if someone were speaking quietly within my mind. "You are dehydrated. You have had nothing to drink for days. Drink four glasses of water and your headache will be healed. Then, keep drinking." I was startled to have such a clear "message" in such a short time. I realized I had avoided the presweetened iced tea served at every meal and so had had nothing to drink other than a morning cup of coffee for days! I never would have associated a headache with dehydration. I did as instructed and within a half hour the headache had disappeared. The next day I went on with my class and continued to drink water.

Listen to your body. Have compassion for your body. Take care of your body. Fill your own cup. Trust that as you care more for yourself, your compassion for others will naturally overflow.

IMMERSE YOURSELF IN WATER

Purity and cleanliness are simple virtues. These first words of the first rule for health were my invitation to go back to the basics. Water is the most basic element of life, since 90 percent of the human body is composed of water. "Outside bathe daily" was the first directive of the first rule. Formerly a shower person (it's quicker), I discovered the pleasure and soothing relief of soaking in a hot bath. I strongly recommend taking some gentle time several times a week to soak away your pain and tension. On other days, take a longer shower and mindfully allow the water to flow over you. If you have the opportunity to swim in a clean river, a lake, or the sea, this will have great healing effect. The negative ions of ocean waves are especially restorative. Each summer, my women's mentoring circle, which started a decade ago, has a retreat at a private lodge on a river in the Pacific Northwest. We bask in the warm sun on the deck, prepare tasty, nutritious meals for one another, float in the emerald green river, and sing river songs.

GIVE YOURSELF A PERSONAL SPA

Europeans have long known of the curative powers of hot and cold waters and have many spas specializing in the use of healing waters for all kinds of ailments. One of the most wonderful gifts of grace you can give yourself is to create your own immersion ritual—a personal spa treatment.

Supplies you will need are:

- Epsom salts
- Small bottles of fragrant essential oils intended for massage (lavender, bergamot, or grapefruit are stress relievers)
- A body brush or loofah sponge
- A squeeze bottle filled with olive oil, sesame oil, or grapeseed oil, scented with one or two drops of essential oils
- An inflatable bath pillow
- Candles for tubside
- A glass of cool water or mineral water with a slice of lemon, lime, or orange

Begin by creating private, uninterrupted time for your spa treatment. You will need at least thirty minutes. If you need to arrange child care, do it, or wait until your children are asleep.

First, fill a clean tub with hot water, two cups of Epsom salts, and a couple of drops of one or two essential oils (you can get these at most health food stores and pharmacies). My favorites are lavender and basil, which I find both relaxing and invigorating. You can also purchase ready-made scented bath salts or foaming bath. Light some scented candles and turn out the lights.

Before you step into the bath, use a dry brush or loofah to scrub your body, cleansing surface skin and stimulating circulation. Brush down your neck, arms, chest, torso, buttocks, and legs, and in a circular motion around each joint. Move slowly and mindfully.

Step into the bath and lean back against your bath pillow or a rolled-up towel behind your neck. Feel your muscles relax. Breathe in peace as you breathe in the steam, and as you exhale, release all tension and worries. If your mind wanders to tasks, gently bring it back to the sensations of your body.

As you immerse yourself, the Epsom salts help to purify your body of the lactic acid that builds up in tight, painful muscles and joints. I was taught by an osteopath to follow a hot soak with a cool shower to wash away the impurities and residue of salts from the skin.

When you emerge from your bath, pat yourself dry with a soft, clean towel. Next comes the massage. The Ayurvedic method originating in India, which you may prefer, is to do the oil massage *before* the bath, but I prefer it this way. Using a small plastic squeeze bottle of olive, sesame, or grapeseed oil scented with a drop or two of fragrant essential oils, pour some into your palm, and begin with your face. Make sure the oils are the type to be used directly on the skin rather than the kind to heat over a candle!

I promise you won't smell like antipasto; the gentle fragrance you have added to the oil is enough to keep you from smelling like olives or sesame. The oil will seep into your thirsty skin, and takes about a half hour to be fully absorbed. You may want to wear a robe or warm-up suit for a while so that your street clothes don't absorb any oil.

A Virtues Massage

I recommend a spiritual practice to take this purification practice to a deeper level. As you massage each part of your body, thank it for something that it has done for you, or appreciate it for a virtue: the beauty or friendliness of your face, the discernment and clarity of your mind as you massage your head, the responsibility of your shoulders, the love of your hands, the generosity or compassion of your breasts or your chest, the flexibility of your knees, the purposefulness or beauty of your legs, the steadfastness of your feet. The very cells of your body have absorbed and stored memories of abuse and words of negation. Replacing them with positive words releases the remnants of shame at a cellular level. This practice of self-care cleanses you of old attitudes toward your body and your being. Chapter 4 delves further into the power of language to expand your experience of grace.

EAT LIFE-GIVING FOODS

The first rule also prescribed eating "pure, water-based foods. . . . Dark greens, legumes, rice, root vegetables. A little meat. Cut oils by two-thirds."

"Water-based foods" are fresh fruits and vegetables. They are simple foods, free of additives. Fruits and vegetables flush out the system, serving as natural diuretics. Eating these foods releases A and B vitamins, acting as natural mood elevators. "Dark greens" include raw greens like collards, kale, bok choy, spinach, or swiss chard. These are ideal for steaming. We also need to consume dark leafy lettuces, which contain the most nutrients. Other vegetables that are delicious when steamed for ten minutes are asparagus, cabbage, broccoli, and cauliflower. I find that adding sliced onions to the steamer sweetens the vegetables and makes them even more flavorful.

Natural, organic foods are widely available now, and it is well worth taking the time to explore new ways of eating that are more healthful than the fast foods that deplete us rather than nurturing us. "Fast food" is a true anathema to one seeking a pace of grace. When we fail to drink sufficient water or eat nourishing food, instead consuming empty calories and indulging our cravings for addictive (and possibly allergy-related) high-fat, high-sugar, and high-sodium foods, we tend not to sleep well. We constantly struggle against lethargy, fatigue, and irritability. Simple changes increase the flow of water within our bodies and enable us to be more energized, more joyful, and more rested. We are able to be more truly present to others and appreciative of life. It all works together.

EAT SMALL AMOUNTS FREQUENTLY

If you feel fatigued, you probably also have secondary hypoglycemia or low blood sugar as well. If you do not eat foods that sustain your blood sugar level, you will begin to feel faint, fuzzy brained, shaky, and hungry. Some people also experience unexplained irritability or even rage. Commonly we mistakenly go for a glass of orange juice or something sugary to boost sugar, but you will find that within an hour your blood sugar has dropped even further. This is because we need a gentle pace of grace in the buildup of blood sugar, which can be achieved only with protein and complex carbohydrates rather than sugar.

If you are suffering from a high amount of stress, you can bet that your blood sugar is stressed too. There are two things you can do to greatly alleviate your symptoms: (1) Eat frequent, small, high-protein meals, and (2) Exercise every day. Your goal is to smooth out the spikes in blood sugar that drop you into fatigue. Blood sugar levels spike and then drop *steeply* after caffeine or sugar, even in the form of fruit juice.

You need to eat about five times a day in moderate amounts, with protein at each serving. Yogurt, soy beans, tofu, and low-fat cottage cheese are among the foods one can have that are low in fat and high in protein. You can also eat a boiled egg, some tuna fish or salmon, or peanut butter on half an apple. Legumes, which for me were an entirely unexplored possibility until I received the Ten Rules, are extremely nutritious, low in fat, high in protein, and very satisfying. Savory lentil soup or hummus (made from garbanzo beans) with crisp veggies for dipping make delicious meals or snacks. Keep a pace of grace in the way you feed yourself. It will smooth out your blood sugar and give you a sense of sustained, peaceful energy. For recipe ideas, see www.paceofgrace.net.

REDUCE OILS AND FATS

I confess that at first, cutting oils by two-thirds as suggested by the first rule for health was very difficult. Not all of you will need to be that drastic, but the fat content of my diet was far too high. Fatigue sent me the message that I needed something to warm my body, and sugar and fats are what I craved. I found that as I acted on the other rules for health, especially drinking six to eight glasses of water a day and exercising moderately, the craving for high fats and sugars lessened. My blood sugar became more stable. I also returned to my habit of eating small, frequent meals and found that helped immensely as well.

EAT HEALTHY OILS

Not only is cutting down on oils healthful, but information has now come to light that some oils are more healthful than others. Organic canola, sesame, pumpkin seed, walnut, olive, and flaxseed oil all have the much-needed health-giving omega-6 and omega-3 fatty acids (John Finnegan, *The Facts About Fats*). One way to make "better butter" is to heat a mixture of half butter and half oil (any of the above will work) in the microwave and place it in the fridge. It will make a delicious and healthful spread. I say this because I for one refuse to give up butter altogether. It is one of life's small pleasures, especially on seedy toast in the morning.

Take Proper Supplements

Until I received the Ten Rules for Health, even though I had studied nutrition as part of my practice of holistic psychotherapy, I had no idea how effective supplements could be in healing serious physical and mental symptoms. Learning more about supplements and herbs was life changing for me, by dispelling the depression that often accompanied fatigue and turning around a painfully crippling condition of arthritis. Finding the right supplements literally freed me to move with a true pace of grace.

The third of the Ten Rules had to do with vitamins and homeopathic treatment. (I'll present the second Rule about breath in the next chapter.)

Rule 3: Proper Vitamins

Increase B, C, and E. Speak to a homeopath and listen to what she says.

Unfortunately, our agricultural practices in many parts of the world, including North America, have leached the land of nutrients. This is one of the main rationales for complementing our diets with vitamins and dietary supplements. The supplements I take include a good multivitamin and sufficient amounts of B, C, and E, as well as an antioxidant such as coenzyme Q-10, and glucosamine sulfate with MSM.

This is another of those instances in which no formula fits everyone, but everyone needs some dietary supplements. Use your intuition and good information about what you need for your own health to thrive. Go to an expert you trust to consult about a vitamin regimen and nutritional supplements that suit your specific needs. You may well find, as I did, that the use of vitamins, herbs, and homeopathy under the guidance of a health practitioner you trust could make an enormous difference in your health.

Drink Herbal Teas

Drinking herbal teas is one of the simplest, most pleasant ways to give your body healthful supplements. My habit of drinking ginger tea each morning turned out to be a marvelous protection from colds and other viruses going around. A natural antibiotic, it aids digestion as well. Before I even go to my prayer corner, I prepare a cup of ginger tea. I break off a two- or three-inch piece of fresh ginger root (which you will find in most supermarkets), peel it, slice it in two, put it in a cup of water and microwave for three minutes or bring to a boil on the stove. When I am at home, I sip on it during my reflection time and then replenish the water in my cup throughout the day.

Lift the Depression of Fatigue

If you ever hit burnout, whether as the result of an energy disease, an accident, or an overextended lifestyle, you may find yourself experiencing one of the most literally depressing symptoms of all—fatigue. Fatigue levels fluctuate, but some days you feel you can hardly move. A fatigue day is one in which even breathing feels like too much effort. You simply have no "juice" or energy to do anything. A thickness settles on your chest, like a large immovable cat.

In the early days of post-polio, I was having a particularly bad day of fatigue. I was weeping with exhaustion. In desperation, I phoned the post-polio support line. The woman who answered said she called days like this her "bog" days. What an apt expression. It helped just to have a name for it. Yet she had no suggestions except to just ride it out.

I found that on these severe fatigue days, I automatically went into depression, a feeling of generic sadness and hopelessness, and an inability to make my mouth smile. As my caring and connection to my body deepened, I became more aware of the sensations I was experiencing. It was like tuning in a radio station that had been fuzzy and finding that I could now hear it clearly. One day I was "listening to my body" and made an observation. On a "bog" or fatigue day, even after the physical sensations of heaviness and exhaustion had lifted, the depression remained, like a lingering mist that moved off too slowly. I then experienced the emotional fatigue of having to climb out of the secondary depression. I decided to take Saint John's Wort, a natural antidepressant herb, which can be taken in homeopathic, tablet, or tincture form, to see if it made any difference in preventing these protracted depressions. Although it took a couple of weeks to take effect, I found it made an enormous difference. I no longer experienced the "depression shadow" after a fatigue day. I also found it significantly calmed anxiety and prevented the discomfort of disconnected thoughts bouncing around like a Ping-Pong ball in a tile bathroom, which was a symptom of mental fatigue. I confess that shortly after I began taking it, my doctor recommended it as well.

I no longer need to take Saint John's Wort on a regular basis because I have learned through practicing the Ten Rules for Health that if I keep my pace of grace, stress and fatigue can be nipped in the bud. Yet it was a remarkable help at a time of crisis. Sometimes, we need extra help to break the cycle of fatigue and anxiety, then we can go with a new flow of grace.

Reduce Pain with Supplements

I found another important way that naturopathic and homeopathic supplements work well with allopathic, prescribed medication to sustain health and manage pain. As we age, pain is one of the most difficult challenges we face. Pain in muscles and joints is exhausting. It takes enormous energy to cope with it day to day, and it greatly increases both tension and fatigue. It can really dampen our joy and steal our sense of grace.

In the months after the onset of post-polio, I developed severe osteoarthritis. In my experience, joint pain and osteoarthritis seem linked to loss of muscle tone and strength. When my muscles deteriorated severely during the onset of post-polio, it put extra strain on my joints. It was as if the weight-bearing wall of a house had crumbled, straining the frame to the breaking point. I ended up needing a knee brace for a while, then a cane. The pain in my left knee and right hip became so excruciating that I could hardly move my left leg. I had to keep it very stiff, and had to lean on a cane to walk. Aspirin didn't touch the pain, and I was afraid to take anything stronger. After six months of hobbling and having to navigate stairs one step at a time, my thigh had visibly atrophied. I never thought I would be sad to see a thinner thigh! And I felt as though I had aged a decade.

My doctor recommended an anti-inflammatory drug that had just come on the market called Vioxx, and he gave me several samples. I am one of those people who normally suffer the severe side effects of any drug, but I tried the medication. I had absolutely no negative reactions, and my pain subsided miraculously within one day! I knew this was a new drug, along with Celebrex, being promoted as a wonder drug for arthritis. I took Vioxx for a while and gradually my leg muscles grew stronger and my atrophied thigh regained its shape. Then I learned about glucosamine sulfate.

Glucosamine sulfate and MSM are commonly recommended over-the-counter vitamin supplements to regenerate cartilage in the joints. A pharmacist I respect tells me that we should take glucosamine throughout life, to keep rebuilding the cartilage that wears thin as we age. Make sure to take it with lots of water just before or after a meal. I have also found that bromelain and turmeric, used in curry, are natural anti-inflammatories, and they help to stop and then prevent inflammation of the joints. I was glad to learn about this because the ultimate damage to organs such as the liver from using drugs such as Vioxx has not been tested over time.

After I started taking glucosamine, I no longer needed Vioxx on a regular basis and would take it only occasionally, once or twice a month, which my physician said was fine. Not all drugs are this flexible, so please don't be so casual about other prescribed medications. Do check with your own physician *any* time you want to change the dose or usage of a prescribed drug. Sometimes stopping abruptly can be damaging. Consult a physician, naturopath, or homeopath whom you trust to determine what medications or supplements are right for you.

For two years I suffered with pain in my knee and hip, having no idea that arthritis was reversible. I had needlessly submitted to the pain. One of the hardest challenges for me was being forced to sit while speaking at a conference instead of walking around the stage, which is my normal style. I might as well have had my arms and legs bound with rope. The first time I was able to stand again to give a keynote talk, I shared the moment with the audience and received a thunderous ovation of support. Now I no longer need a brace or a cane and am virtually pain-free, as long as I stay faithful to the Ten Rules and steadfastly maintain a pace of grace. I'm even dancing again.

Restore Your Balance

"Go to a homeopath and listen to what she says" was also part of Rule 3. Homeopathy is a gentle yet powerful healing method that helps to rebalance the elements in the body. It operates somewhat like an inoculation, using an infinitesimal amount of a substance that causes the symptom to set up a healing response within the body. I went to see a friend of mine who is a homeopath. She had known of my work with The Virtues Project for years and had attended some virtues workshops herself. She said something that struck me to the core. She explained that the body's natural response is to create balance—homeostasis. Tactfully, she added, "You have had a very, uh, active life, in fact, one of excess and intensity. The balancing state to excess is paralysis." I felt a little shock of recognition in my solar plexus. Paralysis was, of course, the state in which I found myself at age eleven when I contracted bulbar polio. The primary site of paralysis was my throat, which was completely paralysed. I was unable to swallow, eat, or speak and had trouble breathing. When post-polio hit, I noticed I was having trouble swallowing and that talking for any length of time absolutely exhausted me.

I find that taking arnica, or Traumeel, which is a combination of various homeopathic remedies including arnica, several times a day is very powerful in alleviating pain from any kind of tissue or muscle damage. I find it acts immediately! When my mother-in-law fell and broke her shoulder, she found that the painkiller her doctor had given her was causing other problems such as dizziness and upset stomach. I recommended she take Traumeel, and she found that it immediately reduced her pain. I talked with her the first morning after she started taking it, and asked, "From one to ten, how is your pain now?" She was amazed to realize that she had passed the night without pain and now it was at a "one." The day before she had been grimacing in pain.

You can take homeopathy as needed, and stop it without a problem. Doses above 30X should be taken only on the advice of and under the supervision of a homeopath.

BE ALERT TO ALLERGIES

In my private practice as a psychotherapist, I wondered what caused chronic depression and other energy-depleting symptoms in my patients. I suspected that allergies played a part, and I became interested in the innovative approach of clinical ecology, which was then a very new field. Clinical ecology appealed to me as a holistic psychotherapist. In the 1970s it was a relatively new field of medicine that looks at the entire environment, from food to air quality to the gases and chemicals we are exposed to, as a source of allergens and health hazards.

I collaborated with a physician who specialized in clinical ecology. He would refer patients to me whose physical symptoms seemed to have a psychological origin, and I would refer to him my patients whose mental and emotional symptoms I intuited were linked to a physiological problem. Sure enough, the people I was seeing with chronic depression, when tested for allergies sublingually and subcutaneously (under the tongue and skin), were discovered to have severe allergies to basic foods such as wheat, eggs, corn, dairy, and chocolate (yes, I consider it a basic food group). Ironically, we tend to crave the very foods to which we are allergic. Unfair as it seems, it is true. Many of my depressed clients found that eliminating a certain food—or limiting themselves to having it only once a

> *If physicians don't become the nutritionists of the present, nutritionists will become the physicians of the future.*
> —clinical ecology saying

week or so—released them magically from chronic depression and fatigue.

Sixty-seven-year-old William came to me because he was feeling so exhausted from years of poor sleep that he was contemplating suicide. After a few sessions exploring his personal history, it was clear to me that there was no psychological reason for his depression. He didn't strike me as clinically depressed, and he had horrible reactions to antidepressants prescribed for him over the years. I sent him for a clinical ecology workup. To his amazement, he had a severe and unsuspected corn allergy. Together we discovered that corn syrup or cornstarch was in many of the foods he ate regularly. He was an International House of Pancakes man, breakfasting several times a week on pancakes and syrup. When he asked the server to let him know the ingredients in the syrup, he found it was 100 percent corn syrup! He began to bring in his own pure maple syrup and continued enjoying his breakfast outings. He began sleeping through the night. He got excited about exploring healthier eating patterns, and in our few final sessions, instead of talking symptoms we discussed vegetable steamers and simple recipes. At our last session, we celebrated his amazing new energy and zest for life. With this simple key to sustaining his mental health, he no longer needed a psychotherapist.

Release Your Cleansing Tears

One of the most healing things we can ever do for ourselves is to have a good cry. Releasing our purifying tears gives us a peaceful heart. This came home to me once when I was working as the spiritual care director at a hospice. I entered a room where several family members were anxiously gathered around the bed of their dying mother, who was weeping. One of her daughters was rapidly patting her arm, crooning, "You're doing fine, Mum, you're just tired." Her son was trying to interest her in a music tape he had brought for her. Mum continued to moan softly as tears coursed down her face, and she seemed to be in another world. Suddenly, the chaotic tension in the room was broken when a nurse breezed in to give the patient her medication. She took one look at the grieving woman and said something I will never forget. "Yes, Marie, you cry those tears. Those are healing tears." Then she breezed out again. The family calmed down immediately, and the energy of the room shifted into peaceful companionship. Once Marie had cried for a while, she opened her eyes and smiled tenuously. Her tears were a river gently leading her back to herself. She was then able to connect with her family.

LET FEELINGS SURFACE

As you apply health practices that allow the FOG of Fatigue, Overwhelm, and Guilt to lift, don't be surprised if you start to feel more deeply. As we attune more lovingly and mindfully to our bodies, not only do our symptoms clear up but our emotions show up. Feelings from which we have disconnected with our rushed, overstressed lifestyle tend to rise to the surface of our awareness. When we keep a gentler pace and reel in our attention to notice what is going on in our bodies, perceptions formerly as obscure as scenery rushing past a window in a moving train suddenly appear more clearly, including grief we have postponed.

A powerful way to open yourself to a deeper, more abiding sense of grace is to give assent to tears, and in fact to pay tender attention to whatever you are feeling. Don't fight your tears. Let them flow.

The pace of grace mindset is a powerful support when strong emotions come up. There are some simple methods to help you release your feelings in a way that adds immeasurably to your health. The key is to give yourself permission to experience your feelings, own them, then release them. When you do this, you will reemerge into a lighter, more vital place. I promise you, you will feel more alive and your relationships will benefit from your increased vitality.

HONOR YOUR FEELINGS

I've always been fascinated by the realization that when we empty our cups of those overdue tears, we open up a whole new range of emotions, including our virtues of hope, enthusiasm, discernment, and joy.

Sometimes illness is a *substitute* for grief, a vehicle for expressing our inaudible emotional pain. Almost always, it is a cry for help. See me. Hear me. As physical health improves, the heart and soul become very vulnerable. Allowing our grief and respecting our tears is an essential part of the healing and purification process. When we own our feelings, and have a safe way to express them, our health can improve dramatically.

When we were doing some virtues work in New Zealand, a Maori man in his thirties came up to me and asked if I would spend some individual time with him. He said he had had three heart attacks in the last year. My first question was, "What's breaking your heart?" His eyes got wide and then filled with tears. "I can't let my brother go." His younger brother had committed suicide and he simply could not accept it. Nor had he cried about it. All he felt was a chest-crushing anger. As I listened to him and invited him to speak to his brother, he was able to get in touch with his tears. We also designed a ritual for releasing his brother's spirit. On the next full moon, he went to the beach near his home, built a small raft, and sent off some of his brother's belongings. He wept, said good-bye, and prayed for his brother's safekeeping in the spiritual world. Even after our brief talk of about an hour, I noticed that his coloring had changed, he wasn't so pale, and he looked happy.

If you are struggling with an energy-depleting illness or otherwise feeling overwhelmed, you are bound to experience grief for what you've lost: your free-dom and mobility, life as you knew it, the ability to work, and confidence in your body. As your grief surfaces, don't judge yourself as weak. Have compassion for your pain. It is helpful to have a companion or a counselor to help you release your grief. You need not descend into depression. In fact, releasing tears *allevi-ates* depression, as long as you don't remain in a state of grief for too long. The baptism of your own tears will help you to heal.

Feelings often act as gatekeepers for virtues. As a mother, I instinctively knew that my children needed to cry their tears and have space to express their feelings. I found that when they were able to release hurt or distress, they could quickly summon their own courage, or peace, or whatever virtue they needed.

One time, I drove to a Laundromat with my two-year-old son. While lifting him out of his car seat and grabbing the duffel bag filled with laundry, I inad-vertently slammed the car door on his finger. He screamed, and I immediately dropped the laundry and sat down with him in my arms to comfort him. I just listened to his crying and looked at his swelling finger. "That really hurts, sweet-heart, doesn't it?" He nodded and his sobs subsided in volume but continued. I decided we would be more comfortable in the Laundromat, so I took him in and sat with him in my lap as he continued to cry quietly, his chest still heaving. The laundry could wait. While we were sitting there, three different strangers approached and either chucked him on the chin or said inanities like "Don't cry, little boy." One woman tried to stuff a lolly in his mouth! I said, "He's hurt himself and just needs to cry right now. Thank you anyway." They all went off with a disapproving look, as if thinking I was being somehow negligent to let him cry. When a huge blood blister formed under his little fingernail, I said, "We need to go to the doctor, sweetie. Your finger is really hurt." Again, he nodded. Although the waiting room was full, the doctor's receptionist took one look at Craig's red, swollen finger and said, "We'll squeeze him in." Craig was quiet and calm by the time we entered the treatment room. The doctor came in, took one look at his finger, and said, "Oh, this will need to be lanced."

"Will it hurt?" I asked. He nodded and his eyes widened, as if to say, "Why are you asking this in front of the kid?"

"Can you give him a local anaesthetic?"

"No, not where this is located."

"Then I'll need a minute alone with my son, please."

The doctor looked shocked. "Look, I'm really busy this morning."

"I really appreciate your fitting us in when you're so busy. It's very kind of you. This will just take a moment," I said, giving him my best mother bear glare. He backed out of the room.

"Craig," I said, "the doctor needs to fix your finger with a needle. At first, it will hurt a lot, but then it will feel better." Craig put his head down on my shoulder and cried silently for a few moments. My tears joined his.

A few minutes later, the doctor stuck his head around the door. "Now?" he asked. "Yes, Doctor, he's ready now." Then Craig turned around in my arms and held out his finger toward the doctor. I will never forget the look of amazement on the doctor's face.

The more we replace the habits that keep us out of touch with our emotions— such as rushing, overdoing, and addictive eating—the more present we will be to our feeling reality. We derive enormous benefits from being more in touch with our feelings. We can't suppress one emotion without suppressing all emotion. As feelings awaken, we experience a fuller range of emotions—not only sadness, but also joy. When we honor our feelings as part of our reality, we also receive the spiritual gifts they carry—the virtues contained within them.

I have witnessed this over and over during the process of companioning, when listening deeply to someone and making it safe for them to cry healing tears or express anger. Melissa, a timid, soft-spoken woman who attended a retreat I was facilitating, had never been permitted to grieve for an uncle who died when she was six years old. He was her favorite relative and had lived close by since her birth. Her family did not allow her to attend the funeral, and kept sending her to her room whenever the death was being discussed, probably wanting to protect her. After he died, they simply never mentioned his name again. To her, he had just disappeared. At the retreat, when she finally gasped out her anger at being kept in the dark, she wept and keened in the arms of several retreat participants. Afterward, she was radiant as the women in the circle acknowledged her for her courage, her love, and her loyalty to her uncle who had been so dear to her. For weeks after the retreat, her husband of thirty years commented on how she had changed, how outgoing and courageous she was. "What happened to you in that retreat?" he asked. "I finally let those old tears out," she said. "It was magic."

CLAIM THE GIFTS IN YOUR FEELINGS

Claiming our feelings allows us to transform them into the virtues that reside within them. For example, when I claim my fear, I can open myself to the gift of trust. When I claim my anger, I recognize the gift of my sense of justice. When I claim my loneliness, I can receive the gift of friendship.

I first learned this wonderful secret from a First Nations healer, Bett Tsa'megahl, who said that each of our feelings carries a spiritual gift. The "Gifts of Feelings" shows the virtues that come to life when we have the courage to claim and own our feelings. This is a template for discovering the grace that resides in our inmost feelings.

Much of the time in the early days of my post-polio, I lay flat on my back. I needed a large dose of compassion for myself to keep from sinking into the emotional flatline of depression. I needed time to grieve, time to accept what was happening, to adjust to doing so much less. In the past, I had nodded sagely whenever I heard the statement by self-help guru and author John Bradshaw that "We are not human doings, we are human beings." When I was suddenly taken out of action, I discovered I didn't believe it for a minute! Recognizing how entrenched I was in the unconscious sense that my value was what I could *do* was itself another shock, given that I had spent years learning and teaching about the virtues of our being. Once I fully experienced the early stages of grief—denial, anger, bargaining, and sadness—I was able to move into acceptance—a powerful virtue. Acknowledging and claiming our feelings allows us to receive the gifts within them—the virtues at their core. The personal practice of these virtues allows us to act rather than react, to stand strong rather than be blown about in the winds of our feelings or desires. Rather than being at the mercy of our feelings, we are free to act with mercy or justice or friendship. Other precious gifts seemed to flow, once the block to my emotions had been removed. I developed more subtle awareness. I felt infused by joy in noticing a ray of afternoon sun illuminate the tree outside my window. I observed the beauty of my husband's hands. I could sense when he was feeling a bit sad, and I would companion him gently. Physi-

> **The Gifts of Feelings**
> *When I claim my Pain*
> *I receive the gift of Compassion*
> *When I claim my Anger*
> *I receive the gift of Justice*
> *When I claim my Loneliness*
> *I receive the gift of Friendship*
> *When I claim my Guilt*
> *I receive the gift of Forgiveness*
> *When I claim my Shame*
> *I receive the gift of Humility*
> *When I claim my Fear*
> *I receive the gift of Trust*
> *When I claim my Solitude*
> *I receive the gift of Faith*
> —Bett Tsa'megahl

cal sensations were more intense and pleasurable. I tasted my food and enjoyed it more. I don't believe I could have received such gentle gifts without being forced to slow down into awareness. I told a friend, "While I was flat on my back, I was able to see Heaven more directly."

I encourage you to keep a pace of grace as you take steps to purify your body and experience your emotions in a purer way. Be gentle with yourself, and expect surprises.

And let him that is athirst come. And whosoever will, let him take the water of life freely. —Revelation 22:17

⤛≡◉ EXERCISE GRACE ◉≡⤜
Do a Three-Day Purification

Choose three normal days—including one day off. Make self-care your first priority each day, regardless of what else is happening. Think of this purifying regimen as an experiment. Observe its effect on your mood, your interactions with others, and your sense of well-being. Incorporate the following practices into your regular routine:

1. Immerse yourself in water, with a fragrant bath or a slow, mindful shower.

2. On your day off, add a personal spa treatment with dry brush and fragrant oil massage. As you massage each part of your body, acknowledge a virtue in it for which you are thankful.

3. Drink pure water. Fill a pitcher or bottle with at least six glasses of pure water and drink continually until it is empty. Always have water on hand in your car. Remember to drink *before* you become thirsty.

4. Eat life-giving, water-based foods (fruits or vegetables) at every meal. Take your time to eat mindfully, and really taste your food. Eat healthful snacks between meals.

5. On your day off, plan your day to incorporate something you would truly enjoy. Listen to your body. What do you need? Find a way to get some solitude. Is this a day to lie on the couch for hours with a good book? Do you feel like being creative with paints or a craft? Going to a place of beauty? Make sure your plans are restorative and restful, and keep a pace of grace.

6. Each morning, journal for about ten minutes. Write about your experience of self-care the day before. What was easy or difficult? What difference did it make in your day? Then, reflect on how you are today and what you need in order to have a graceful day. Plan your food, drink, exercise, and rest. Write questions such as:

    - How do I feel today?
    - What do I need today?
    - What do I want to eat?
    - What would a pace of grace look like today?

SUMMARY OF CHAPTER 2: PURIFY YOUR BODY

- Fill your own cup first. Dare to be luxuriantly selfish.
- Listen to your body. Be a compassionate caregiver.
- Respect the mind–body connection. When you take care of your body, your emotional and spiritual health benefit too.
- Immerse yourself in water both externally and internally.
- Give yourself personal spa treatments, including a Virtues Massage.

- Drink pure water. Keep yourself hydrated!
- Eat pure, life-giving natural foods.
- Eat small amounts frequently. Keep your blood sugar stable.
- Be alert to allergies. Rotate your diet to avoid allergy overload.
- Use supplements, herbal teas, and homeopathic remedies, and medication when you need it, to help manage pain and alleviate fatigue-related depression.
- Welcome the feelings that surface as you purify your body.
- Claim the virtues—the gifts within your feelings.

The next chapter is about the purifying practice of breathing.

THREE

Breathe Easy, Breathe Deep

Cleanse thou the rheum from out thine head and breathe the breath of God instead.
—Jalal 'u' Din Rumi, thirteenth-century Persian mystic and poet

Strange as it may sound, becoming ill with post-polio gave me a chance to breathe. For the first time in years I became mindful of my breathing, often pausing to feel the intake and outtake of my breath. Breathing mindfully is one of the simple privileges most of us take for granted as we rush around getting things done.

I was struck down by polio at eleven, while spending the summer at an international religious retreat center in Eliot, Maine, called Green Acre—for me the happiest place on earth. I played with children from around the world and snuck out of children's classes to listen to world-class speakers orating on God, prayer, the future of mankind, and other fascinating topics. Every summer, my mother, my two younger brothers and I would stay at a cottage deep in the forest, or sometimes in a room at the inn overlooking the Piscataqua River. My father drove up from New York some weekends. One day I was playing on the spacious lawn with the other children and suddenly I dropped to the ground with a sharp pain in the back of my neck. My throat felt tight and painful, and I was unable to swallow the tea my mother spooned into my mouth to revive me. It just came out of my nose and wouldn't go down. A doctor was called and I was rushed to the nearest hospital in Portsmouth, New Hampshire, and placed in a quarantined ward with two other children, both of whom died before my eyes.

One night, when my fever peaked, the medical team was hours away from placing me in an iron lung. The paralysis of my throat muscles blocked speech, breath, and swallowing. I was fighting for breath and had to be fed intravenously. The most immediate concern was that my kidneys had grown sluggish and seemed to be shutting down entirely. It was at this point of toxic overload that most children with bulbar polio died, but I was one of the few fortunate ones who mysteriously took a turn for the better.

The night of the crisis, an angel came to my bedside in the form of Helen

Canterbury, a local nurse who was as round as she was tall, with hands like small hams. She was an old friend of my parents whom we had met at Green Acre when I was still a baby. Helen must have slipped or bullied her way past the quarantine, for she sat beside me all night whispering about waterfalls, streams, rivers, and tall glasses of lemonade. Finally my kidneys found all this talk of water irresistible, and the crisis passed. At dawn, I was able to urinate, my breathing became normal, and I was able to take my first sip of water. I remember my throat muscles were so slack that some of the water went up my nose, but little by little my body remembered how to sustain itself with air, food, and drink. My voice returned gradually and was several octaves lower, and has remained so for the rest of my life.

Forty-four years later I received the Ten Rules for Health to help me through my second crisis with polio. I noticed that whenever I swallowed, my head automatically turned to the side, a habit I had for years while recovering from polio as a child. I had to remember to chew more carefully to avoid choking. And I needed to remember to breathe, to build strength in my lungs.

The second rule reawakened my awareness of the breath of life, which, like water, is an essential element of health:

Rule 2: Breathe (Pranha)

Learn Yoga. Walk or exercise every day for ten minutes, then fifteen, then twenty. No more. Breathe fresh air every day. You haven't breathed deeply in years.

It was true. I had become so overwhelmed by the part of our work that was anathema to me—the hundreds of e-mails coming in each day, and growing demands to manage communication around the world, with all the accompanying administrative tasks—that I was continually holding my breath, shoulders hunched up to my ears, trying to plow through the day. When I am doing my heart's work of writing, speaking, teaching, or working with people, I breathe much easier.

Do you find yourself moving through life at a breathless pace? How often are you conscious of taking a breath, of breathing fresh air deep into your lungs? As I pondered the Ten Rules, I recognized how true it was that I hadn't "breathed deeply in years," and had subsisted on shallow breathing. If we are driven—moving constantly on automatic pilot, and very task-focused—we take breathing for granted. More accurately, we forget to breathe.

Pranha, the word used in the second rule, is a term in Yoga for "breath of life." It also means vital energy. Increasing the flow of breath several times a day greatly enhances our vitality. In some big cities, such as Singapore, merchants have opened oxygen bars, even at the airport, to help people "refill" and purify the air in their lungs. Rather than "subsistence breathing," consider breathing deeply on a regular basis. It is one of the great secrets to having abundant energy for what you want to do with your life. Take this strategic step for healing, whatever your malady.

Take a Breather

Whatever you are doing and wherever you are, take time every hour or at least every two hours to refresh your air supply. Doing so will replenish your energy flow throughout the day.

Dr. Andrew Weil's highly acclaimed books *Spontaneous Healing* and *8 Weeks to Optimal Health* recommend the regular practice of deep breathing. He instructs us to curl our tongues up against the roofs of our mouths (a Yoga position that allows full circulation of energy throughout the body), inhale through the nose for four counts, hold the breath for seven counts, and exhale through the mouth for eight counts, making a soft blowing noise when we exhale, keeping our tongues in the Yoga position. This is a simple routine we can do several times a day very unobtrusively no matter where we are. It fills our lungs with life-giving air.

Exercise with Grace

One of the most valuable lessons I learned from my illness was to set a pace of grace with exercise. Gentle exercise such as Yoga is often the best choice for people whose lives are already too stressed. Exercise need not be seen as yet another arena for performance, but as a practice of nurturing ourselves. Rather than throwing ourselves into exercise the way we do with the constant pressure of activities during a busy day, let us use exercise as a breather, a way to pause in the day and refill ourselves.

Even when we are in severe fatigue, ten to twenty minutes of gentle exercise and exposure to fresh air can rejuvenate us. Gentle ways to regenerate tired muscles include restorative Yoga, walking, swimming, mild water aerobics, Tai Chi or other movement methods, and in some cases moderate use of weights.

Practice Restorative Yoga

When I saw that learningYoga was listed as the first instruction under Rule 2 I was worried. Because of the severe fatigue I was experiencing at that time, I couldn't imagine having the energy or the strength to join a class, much less drive myself there. At that point, in the first few months after the onset of the illness, I was experiencing a severe return of the original symptoms of bulbar polio—muscle weakness, stiffness, pain in my kidneys and hips, tightness of the lower back, and severe fatigue. I had had to give up driving because I would have a startle reflex when another car came along, and at times my reflexes were too slow to make a turn at the right time. To my relief, when I rang Gay Meagley, a Yoga instructor in our community, she offered to give me private sessions in my home.

Gay taught me "restorative Yoga," a series of gentle exercises that anyone can practice, including a way to cleanse or "wring out the kidneys." After doing the "Kidney Twist" for a week, the pain in my kidneys had disappeared and I noticed an increase in my energy.

I want to describe some of the restorative Yoga exercises here and highly recommend that you use them if you are energy-challenged or if you find yourself at a point of fatigue during the day. They will help you to refresh your energy at your daily low point—typically early to mid-afternoon:

    1. Full rest position

Have with you a towel or Yoga mat and a small pillow. Lie on the floor with your legs up on a chair, knees bent, your bottom close to the chair, and allow your legs

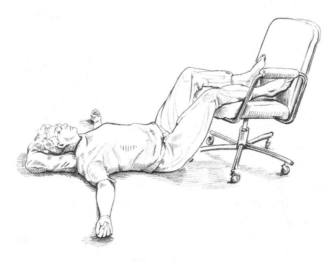

to fall open naturally. Place a pillow under your head or a rolled-up towel under your neck. Close your eyes and breathe. Let your abdomen relax. Breathe from your belly. The blood will flow to your brain and your lungs, and you will find this as restorative as a power nap.

 2. Downward Flow

In this exercise, get on the floor, with your bottom as close to a wall as possible. While lying on the floor or on a bed, raise your legs up against the wall, bending your knees slightly if you need to, heels resting against the wall. Gradually inch your legs wider apart, without causing strain to your hips. Then bring your legs back to center, about a foot apart. This exercise also allows the blood to flow into your brain. Breathe deeply a few times while in the position, then rest.

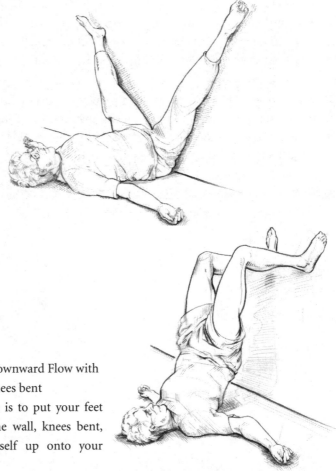

 3. Downward Flow with
      knees bent
An alternative is to put your feet flat against the wall, knees bent, and lift yourself up onto your shoulders.

4. Kidney Twist

Lie on the floor on your stomach, facedown on a pillow, legs straight. Roll onto your left shoulder, moving your left arm to the right to grasp your right thigh as you move it up to a bent position. Then, twist onto your back and put your right arm out to the side. Keep your left leg out straight underneath your bent right leg. Hold for several seconds. Do not strain yourself, just turn over gently. Then return to facedown position and roll to the other side, repeating the sequence. Repeat three times. Breathe deeply as you do this.

5. The Bridge

Lie on the floor with your bottom very close to a chair with legs. Grasp the legs in your hands, put your feet on the seat of the chair, knees bent, and boost yourself up onto your shoulders, keeping your body quite straight. This is very helpful for tight muscles in the shoulder and neck, as well as circulating blood and oxygen to give you a "brain boost."

If you do not have floor space at your workplace, or would not feel comfortable getting on the floor, you can practice the following sitting exercises, using your chair as a tool.

6. Open Heart Shoulder Stretch

Sit forward on the edge of your chair, feet flat on the ground, knees bent. Reach your arms above you and lock your fingers, palms up, stretching gently and breathing deeply. You can also do this in a standing position.

7. Hanging Waterfall

Sit forward on the edge of your chair with your legs wide apart. Drop down from your waist and hang loosely, allowing your hands to rest on the floor palms up. Allow the weight of your head to fall forward and gently allow your spine to be stretched.

8. Twist

Sitting forward on the edge of your chair, place one hand on the arm of the chair, the other hand on the back of the chair, and gently twist your body toward the back of the chair. Then switch hands and twist in the other direction. This stretches your lower back. Remember to breathe deeply while doing this. If you have a chair with no arms, just place your hand on your opposite thigh while one arm holds the back of the chair.

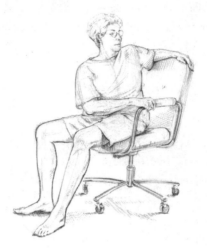

9. Downward Dog

You need a stable chair to do a standing version of the Downward Dog. Place both hands on the seat of the chair and walk your feet gradually backward until you are leaning forward in an inverted V with your buttocks up in the air. This stretch is good for all your joints and muscles. Bend your knees slightly.

⊷⟨⟩ The Virtue of Discernment ⟨⟩⊷

How many a sign there is in the heavens and the earth which most men
pass by and ignore. —Qur'an 12

Discernment is quieting our minds and sensing the truth about things. It is being contemplative and vigilant in seeking to understand what is true. We are able to make distinctions between what is real and what is an illusion. We open ourselves to spiritual guidance. We trust our inner vision to recognize what is right for us in this moment. We observe, decide, and act with wisdom.

Signs of Success

I am practicing Discernment when I . . .
- Think clearly and calmly
- Resist making impulsive decisions
- Perceive what is really true
- Seek inspiration
- Make wise decisions
- Don't try to impose my will on reality

Affirmation

I am discerning. I use my inner guidance to perceive what is real and true. I cultivate my wisdom.

EXERCISE WITH MODERATION

We need to remember to exercise as much as our bodies need but not more. We can treat exercise as addictively as anything else. The key is to know what is right for your body. My guidance in the second rule was very helpful. For me, ten minutes a day, then fifteen, then twenty, was just right. There have been days when I can walk for an hour or more, but if I do that several days in a row I end up in bed. Post-polio is a relentless teacher.

Kate, a woman in her forties with two young children who lives with the fatigue and pain of fibromyalgia, told me, "My garden is a source of great joy to me. Before fibromyalgia hit, I spent hours digging, planting and weeding. It was a meditation for me and brought me out of the busyness of life, back to myself."

I once told her, "Kate, for you it is 'Goddening'—your connection to Spirit." Kate gave up this soothing, sacred activity for a while after fatigue took over her life. One day she decided it would do her good to get out in her garden again. She walked out into the early-spring sunshine and hoed, plucked, and planted for a half hour. "Moderation was the key," she said. "I am able to spend thirty minutes, and because it gives me joy, it is restorative for me."

Individuals with muscle weakness should consult their health care professionals to make sure that the exercise they do is not going to cause further fatigue. Gentle swimming, walking, and isolated muscle exercises can often do a world of good. Being content with whatever we are given, including our energy level, is one of the virtues we need to cultivate. It is a danger to the health of our bodies and our souls to live without it.

The challenge for someone who is in a state of severe fatigue is to exercise just enough but not too much, by practicing the virtue of moderation in an extremely mindful way. This is a true application of a pace of grace. It is critical to discern the delicate balance between too much and too little exercise. I cannot emphasize this enough. Many people who have been ill succumb to the temptation to overdo when they begin to feel better. Kate once confessed to me she was in bed for a week after forging ahead for hours to finish a gardening project. "I just kept my head down and ignored my body that day." We so want to be "normal" that the temptation is always there to give up the discipline of a pace of grace, falling back into denial and excess. It's all about energy conservation. If you withdraw more energy than you can sustain, you will deplete yourself and it will cost precious time to return to the level of energy you had before you went on your energy binge.

If a person already struggling with fatigue overdoes exercise, the resulting fatigue can mean the loss of a day or even a week of energy. I found that if I walked too long, I would be unable to move off the couch the next day. Yet if I failed to have *enough* exercise, true to the "use it or lose it" principle, I would lose muscle strength and my muscles literally atrophied.

The subtlety of body economics and energy conservation is a great teacher. An unexpected gift in learning to perceive this delicate balance is that it refines our virtues of discernment and mindfulness, so essential to the spiritual life. The power to make distinctions, to weigh difficult decisions, to separate the wheat from the chaff, to perceive the subtle distinction between purity of motive and ego, is awakened through mindfulness of the body.

Invite Inspiration

When we breathe, oxygen purifies our system, releasing toxins and supplying vital nutrients to circulate throughout the body through our blood supply. A spiritual meaning resides in breathing as well. By taking time each day for inspiration, for daydreaming, for contemplation, we invite a flow of pure awareness to sustain our souls.

Judi, my beloved friend and co–spiritual director for years, has a rich prayer life, with many different techniques for connecting to Spirit. For quite a long time, breath was her preferred form of prayer. As she inhaled, she held a simple mantra in her mind, such as "Emanuel" (God with us). As she exhaled, she would repeat it. Judi discovered that her lung capacity actually expanded during the months she knelt on her prayer stool to do breathing prayer.

A management consultant giving a keynote talk about leadership said something that really lodged in my soul: "The most creative leaders I know can often be found with their feet up on their desk, leaning back and just staring into space. Sometimes it is in a moment of doing nothing that the greatest ideas come to us."

The word "inspire" literally means to breathe in. Being inspired is being moved by the awareness of God. It is filling oneself with divine inspiration. Cultivating a habit of breathing deeply allows us to live more reverently and consciously. Stopping to breathe allows us to center ourselves mentally and spiritually. It is a spiritual practice of recovering our peace in the midst of the chaos around us, a quiet prayer, a moment of grace.

. . . learning to be content with whatever happens, with however much or little you receive. When you learn to relish each moment in your life, know that you have become steadfast in knowledge.
—Swami Chidvilasananda

⋙ EXERCISE GRACE ⋘
Breathe the Breath of Life

- Breathe deeply several times a day.
- Breathe deeply by swimming, walking, or doing Yoga for at least ten minutes, more if your body is happy with more.
- Do the deep breathing exercise three times a day. (Inhale for four counts, hold for five counts, exhale for six counts.)
- Take a "breather" about six hours after you awaken. Rest when you feel tired, by using one of the restorative Yoga positions (for example, Downward Flow with legs up on chair or wall).
- Take some time each day for inspiration, whether it is staring off into space or with a more formal routine of reverence as described in chapter 12.

SUMMARY OF CHAPTER THREE: BREATHE EASY, BREATHE DEEP

- Center yourself physically, mentally, and spiritually throughout the day by breathing mindfully and deeply.
- At a regular time each day, exercise for ten to twenty minutes, depending on what your energy level is.
- When your energy is low or you have fatigue, use restorative exercise such as Yoga or Tai Chi to help you strengthen your muscles and regulate your breath.

- Cultivate your virtues of moderation and discernment to find your true balance point of just enough exercise, not too much and not too little.
- Watch out for denial and the temptation of overdoing. They will cost you valuable time and energy.
- Open yourself to inspiration every day.

Caring for your body is an act of compassion opening you to a healthier, more gracious life. It can also serve as preparation for a deeper level of transformation—an even more rigorous commitment to the purification of your inner life. The next chapter offers simple steps for purifying your thinking and your language to enhance the flow of grace in your life.

⋆⟶⊙ FOUR ⊙⟵⋆
Purify the Language of Your Life

As a man thinks in his heart, so is he.
—Proverbs 23

After twelve-year-old Billy and eighteen-year-old Kenny died, I was the only one left on the isolated polio ward. At first, I felt totally bereft, unable to console myself in my customary way—by singing. At the age of eleven I sang all the time. I had perfect pitch, and was often chosen as a soprano soloist in school concerts. When my voice was suddenly cut off, something remarkable happened.

Lying in my bed, unable to move and incapable of making any sound at all, I was submerged in silence, like a deep pool within a cave, illuminated by soft emerald green light. I felt safe in this private inner world. It protected me from the daily pain the nurses administered with searing hot towel treatments and manipulations of my legs. Even though my nerves were affected so that I couldn't voluntarily move my legs, my skin was excruciatingly sensitive. I learned to drift down beneath layers of silence where the pain couldn't touch me.

Later, when I was working with traumatized children in therapy, I discovered that they too had this safe place inside, and that when I could help them tap into this secret wellspring of strength, they were able to heal their own anxieties and fears very quickly. Years later, working at the hospice, I often witnessed a light of awareness dawn in people who knew their time in this world was brief. Veils fell away as they got closer to death. Perhaps they were entering that sacred space within and seeing life more clearly.

I remember James, a businessman in his sixties with terminal cancer, who revealed to his wife and children what he appreciated about each of them for the first time. I witnessed their tears of joy as they received the gift of his affirmation. James confided in me later, "I have been a terribly critical man, I know my children have felt that. But now, I see who they are somehow. I don't know why I always dwelled on what I wished were different about them." He died ten days later, leaving a true legacy of confidence and love.

> *In the city of Brahman is a*
> *secret dwelling,*
> *the lotus of the heart. . . .*
> *As great as the infinite space beyond*
> *Is the space within the lotus*
> *of the heart.*
> —The Chandogya Upanishad
> (Hindu teachings)

Whether we are experiencing an illness that forces us to live more mindfully or making a conscious decision to escape a lifestyle of stress, when we practice purifying health practices, we shift our inner sensibilities. We become more aware of the subtler themes and dynamics of our lives. As our health improves, an expectancy grows that life can, and indeed should be, good. We seem more able to live from a peaceful inner core.

Hope, once retrieved, has its own momentum. It stirs in us a desire for a more intentional and grace-filled life. This opens us to a new Teachable Moment—the opportunity to go to a deeper level of transformation, by purifying our inner lives as well, reflected in how we think, speak, and act toward others and toward ourselves. One of the most sustaining practices of a pace of grace lifestyle is the choice to be more gracious in our relationships.

As I followed the Ten Rules for Health, purifying my system with clean food, water, and air—and crying when I needed to—I gradually recollected that profound sense of peace and clarity I had known as a child. As long as I kept my pace of grace and was faithful to the Ten Rules, I could keep myself from reentering the FOG of Fatigue, Overwhelm, and Guilt.

I became more careful and deliberate about the words I used and the emotions I entertained. Thoughtless remarks and even a slight negative thought felt out of sync with my tender new sense of peace. Having lost my life as I had known it and then recovered it with the redemptive practices of the Ten Rules, I didn't want to waste a moment in negativity.

PURIFY YOUR LIFE OF NEGATIVITY

Reflecting on the deeper meaning of purification, I recalled a Teachable Moment I had had years before, which helped me to purge my marriage of a long-standing power struggle. The problem started shortly after our wedding with a traumatic experience that triggered my fear of losing my husband.

A few months after our wedding, my husband and I took off on a seminar tour around the United States, including a group retreat in a remote campsite in the Colorado Rockies. One night, as we lay on a sagging mattress in an unheated cabin, I was awakened by violent shaking. My first thought was that it was an earthquake. A moment later, I realized it was Dan, burning with fever and shaking so uncontrollably that even though I was holding him in my arms, he fell off the bed. I lugged the mattress onto the floor of the cabin, where we remained the rest of that long night. The emergency physician who saw him the next day told us that the results of his tests suggested melanoma, a deadly form of cancer. Even after the crisis was over and the diagnosis turned out to be false, I was left with a deep fear of losing him. I had always lived with a lurking sense of early abandonment, and Dan's illness restimulated that childlike terror. So I began a power struggle with my husband—one he wanted no part of—about his health and nutrition practices. I became obsessed with his diet. Being a meat-and-potatoes guy who thinks of vegetables as garnish and a half pint of Ben & Jerry's Cherry Garcia as a minimum daily requirement, he resisted my every effort to reform him. One day when I cried and pled with him to change, he told me, "Linda, you have lots of influence with me but no control." Yet I battled on, like Don Quixote tilting at windmills.

Several years later, we were visiting a relative, and I found myself complaining bitterly about my husband's intransigent ways. Early one morning of the visit, while I was praying and meditating, a car alarm went off in the neighborhood. Being a believer that when one is in a prayerful state everything has meaning, I asked in prayer somewhat jokingly, "Is there something I should be alarmed about?" Immediately, I heard, "Yes. Every word of negativity is an act of distrust in Me." I felt shocked and admonished by these unexpected words. It dawned on me that I had been indulging in the worst sort of negativity by judging and criticizing my husband because he refused to conform to my expectations. Like many of us, I unwittingly considered it my prerogative to backbite about those closest to me. I immediately stopped talking about him in a critical way and began to reflect on what I could do to change my attitude.

The alarm incident was a turning point that purified our relationship of needless pain and useless misery. I recognized that my typical state of disappointment was a deeply engrained habit of negative thought and criticism I had inherited from generations in my family. Instead of doggedly continuing the struggle, we relaxed into enjoying one another and have agreed to disagree about nutrition. I am happy to prepare what he likes to eat as long as I nurture myself at the same time.

Since this Teachable Moment, my husband and I have negotiated many small changes to make our lives together more pleasant and peaceful, but I have now come to accept his basic nature, eccentricities and all. He continues to neglect his health—according to my standards—but he's still here, and I've decided to relax and enjoy him. A friend of mine with a lilting southern accent once prophesied, "Linda, I'm shuah yo' husban' will enjoy many years of poor health." Of course I have many imperfections as well, which he has *always* tolerated and accepted for more than twenty years, without a word of complaint, not being prone to criticism.

Eliminate Needless Pain and Useless Misery

Our relationships with our intimates are meant to be our safe harbor, but how often are they the source of our greatest pain? I believe much of it is needless pain that can be healed by a commitment to the virtues of kindness, tenderness, peacefulness, compassion, and contentment.

A woman who attended a recent virtues workshop confessed to me that she and her husband were engaged in a long-standing conflict and competition. They had tried various techniques and counseling over the years, but nothing seemed to help. "We just can't seem to stop arguing. It's become our basic way of communicating," she said. Her husband, who was not attending the workshop, came in on the last morning of the workshop to ask when she wanted him to pick her up at the end of the day. When I saw them together, I had a strong intuitive hit about their marriage. I went over to her during a break and said, "Your husband is your mirror image. You even look alike. Your destinies are intertwined. He needs your tenderness. And so do you." Her eyes filled with tears of recognition.

As a psychotherapist, I have often observed habits of negativity causing needless pain and useless misery in the lives of my clients, friends, and relatives. These habits are particularly destructive with our intimates. I call them the "Troubled C's" of relationships:

- Control—attempting to control another's actions
- Criticism—thinking and speaking negatively, focusing on flaws
- Contempt—judging others as worth less, putting them down
- Contention—engaging in frequent arguing, fighting, and conflict

Many of us engage in lateral violence within our families. This is a term I have learned in my work in community healing with Native Americans and First Nations in Canada, which means turning one's shame and anger sideways toward members of our own tribe, our own people.

Many of us commit a form of lateral violence with those closest to us by perpetuating negativity and putting each other down. Criticism, gossip, and backbiting is very common in our families. It is practically a form of entertainment, but in truth it is a kind of spiritual violation. In the very place where we are meant to be safe, we feel exposed and demeaned. Backbiting deflects and distracts us from working things out with each other face-to-face to resolve our inevitable conflicts. Instead of healing hurts when they arise, we tend to nurse them over time, creating wedges between us.

Don't Put Each Other Down, Lift Each Other Up

Virtues are in the eye of the beholder. The power of acceptance can transform a negative power struggle into a balm of peace and tenderness. I was in a hotel spa one day when an elderly gentleman entered the steam room. My first thought was that I was grateful for the spa rule to wear bathing suits at all times. We struck up a conversation and I found him to be a delightful person, very gentle, interesting and humorous. Suddenly, a blast of cold air hit us as the door opened, and a woman hissed, "Where have you been? I've already had my swim. As usual you just have to keep me waiting. Get out of here, now!" Her tone didn't hide her contempt and disgust. As the door closed again, he sighed and said, "I'm just an old fool. I'm always too slow for my wife." I thanked him for his friendliness and told him how delightful our conversation was. He smiled sadly and left. I thought then that nothing—nothing!—is worth that loss of dignity, respect, and love between two people in a marriage. His wife had many options, including doing her own thing, allowing him his own pace, reminding him gently, or making a simple, positive request like "Darling, would you be willing to have your swim now? I'd like to get ready for our day." I assumed she had come to this point of contempt through many frustrations over the years, yet there are other ways to deal with them that don't destroy the spirit. She was destroying his confidence with her critical words and at the same time choosing to destroy her own peace. I have seen this pattern many times in couples. Control, criticism, and contempt become second nature. The balance of control becomes the fulcrum of the relationship. People don't think about it consciously—they just react—yet they are making the choice to be unhappy. It is a choice that can calcify into a habit of thinking, speaking, and feeling. It is deeply destructive of joy.

John Gottman, author of *Why Marriages Succeed or Fail*, cites contempt and criticism as the leading predictors of divorce. In his research on couples, he has a 90 percent accuracy rate in predicting divorce based on observing these habits. I believe that you have to choose between control and love. You cannot have both.

REPLACE NEGATIVITY WITH VIRTUES

I have absolute confidence that we can heal the Troubled C's of control, criticism, contempt, and contention. Just as the darkness can be dispelled when we walk into a room and turn on the light, we can replace negative habits of thought and communication with positive ones. We can begin thinking in light of the virtues of

- Acceptance—seeing each person as whole, noticing the virtues the person does have. Giving up the desire to control and change them and instead entering into a loving relationship with them as they are.
- Appreciation—feeling and expressing positive regard and gratitude for one another's nature and actions, both what we are and what we do.
- Assertiveness—asking for what we need in a respectful and peaceful way, setting clear boundaries and telling the truth as we see it, about what is just.

Failing to accept and appreciate one another as we are causes needless pain in our relationships. Negativity, like a thick cloud blocking us from the sunlight, keeps us from experiencing all the love and acceptance we are capable of. This is merely a habit, which we can choose to purify by creating a gentle shift into peacefulness.

It is said that we can replace any negative habit by a positive one with three weeks of continual practice. Demeaning thoughts and words can be replaced by thoughts and words of appreciation and encouragement. We can ask ourselves three simple questions: Are these words true? Are these words necessary? Are these words kind? With this simple step, the grace of a relationship will open like a flower.

Thich Nhat Hanh, a renowned Buddhist monk and peace advocate, in his book *Peace Is Every Step*, speaks of the word "suchness," used in Buddhism to mean the essence or particular characteristics of a thing or person, its true nature. He says, "Each person has his or her suchness. If we want to live in peace and happiness, we have to see the suchness of that person. Once we see it, we understand him or her, and there will be no trouble. We can live peacefully and happily together."

A couple I have known all my life, Janet and Manny, have managed to sustain their joy. As they grew old together, they still laughed, smiled, and gazed lovingly at one another, and touched each other affectionately. I once asked Janet, "What's the secret of your marriage? You seem so happy." "We are happy, and have been for over fifty years," she said. "I don't know if it's a secret, but I never tell him how to drive."

PURIFY YOUR THOUGHTS WITH VIRTUES

As the physical purification practices of the Ten Rules cleared my mind, I began to cherish positive language in a deeper way as a touchstone for purifying my own thinking. I sought to build a new life more reflective of the gentler virtues. Being highly goal-oriented all my life, I had mastered determination, perseverance, purposefulness, excellence, and enthusiasm. What I now needed in greater measure were acceptance, gentleness, moderation, and grace. I found that as my attitude shifted toward these virtues, it was far easier to use gentle language.

If the shift in our attitude is genuine, rather than another subtle attempt to control or manipulate others, our relationships will automatically change—because the dynamic itself has changed. To illustrate this, press the fingers of one hand against the fingers of the other, making a tent of tension. Now curl the fingers of one hand, removing the pressure from one side. The fingers of your other hand automatically relax and change their position. The dynamic of a negative relationship cannot be sustained without your participation. When you change, the relationship changes.

Remaining locked in negativity is spiritually lethal. Criticism and contention are contaminants that spoil the natural grace and joy that are possible in

⤙ The Virtue of Peacefulness ⤚

Blessed are the peacemakers, for they shall be called the children of God.
—Matthew 5:9

Peacefulness is an inner sense of calm that can come in moments of silent gratitude or prayer. We become very quiet and look at things so we can understand them. We face our fears and then let them go, trusting that things will be all right. Peacefulness is giving up the love of power for the power of love. We treat others as we want to be treated. We solve conflict by sharing our truth and listening to others with compassion and justice. Peace in the world begins with peace in our hearts.

Signs of Success

I am practicing Peacefulness when I . . .

- Create inner peace, with a regular time to pray or meditate
- Give my worries to God and ask God's help in solving them
- Use peaceful language, even when I am angry—speak gently
- Avoid harming anyone
- Appreciate differences
- Give up the love of power for the power of love

Affirmation

I am peaceful. I use peaceful language and find peaceful solutions to any problem that arises. I find my inner peace and let it carry me gently through the day.

every relationship. The virtue of acceptance can heal negativity. When we accept the "suchness" of our children, our spouses, and our parents, with all their quirks and sometimes maddeningly unchangeable ways, we can relax and enjoy a more peaceful and pleasant life. What if one day you got up and decided to choose gratitude for what you *do* have and release resentment about what you don't have in your relationships? This is not to say that you give up on asking for what you need and want or that you ignore your sense of justice. If your partner is not carrying his or her weight, ask assertively for what you need. This is far more successful than constant nagging and negativity. Acceptance doesn't mean giving up on what is important; it means embracing people as they are.

Be a Peacemaker

Times such as these, when we are more keenly aware of the value of life, are good times to reassess what we are doing to sustain joy and hope in our relationships. I personally believe that every thought, word, and act of peace adds to the peace of humanity. Each is a stone tossed into the pond of the human spirit, and the ripples go out, touching each one of us.

When we feel hopeless or afraid, we can always find a virtue to actualize, a positive action we can take to create peace in our lives and in the world. In the aftermath of the September 11 tragedy, I was very touched by the actions of Americans across the country to stand in unity and solidarity with Moslem Americans. In one Midwestern town, a woman learned that her Moslem neighbor was afraid to leave the house wearing her chador, or head scarf. She donned a scarf herself in the Moslem style and walked with her neighbor to shop for groceries. Soon so many women in town were wearing chadors that the streets were full of color.

When a Moslem mosque in Boston held an open house, hoping people would come to learn about their true beliefs, the entire congregations of a Christian church and a Jewish synagogue walked down the street en masse to attend.

These acts of kindness and courage awakened in me a longing to do what I could to build peace. I began to examine my own life for habits of lateral violence—judgments or backbiting in my thoughts or speech. I began to replace every thought and word of negativity with a thought or word of peace. I confess I had been very critical and vocal with my husband about certain political leaders. I instantly stopped and began instead to wish them well and pray for their wisdom and courage.

We can spread peaceful thinking throughout this planet. The notion of critical mass is powerfully supported in some research about "the hundredth monkey." Scientists discovered a remarkable phenomenon while studying the behavior of monkeys over a period of weeks on several islands. To observe the animals more easily, the scientists tossed food onto the beach so that the monkeys would emerge from the jungle. The monkeys would sit on the beach, picking sand off the fruit and eating it. One day, one of the monkeys decided that instead of picking the sand off of a banana he would wash it in the sea as well. By the time the hundredth monkey on one island imitated this practice, the monkeys on other islands, who never saw the practice, instantly began to adopt it. Can you imagine the impact on the collective human spirit when one of us engages fully in the work of transformation? Every act of peace is a step toward critical mass.

I have immersed myself in the practice of virtues for the past decade, and I can tell you that even when attempting to live very mindfully, we have lapses. The important thing is to notice it when it happens, observe and listen compassionately to our own deepest concerns, and then choose the virtue in that Teachable Moment that will give us a positive path back to a relationship of grace. This came home to me one morning when I reflected during my prayer time on an old frustration in my marriage. "It's not the way you think it is," I heard in meditation. From this, I discerned that my image of the perfect marriage was overblown, that I was once again expecting my husband to meet all my needs, thereby overburdening the relationship. No one can be everything we expect. When we are honest about it and able to detach from the popular Western conception of marriage as a means of sating all of our needs, we recognize that it is more truly a spiritual adventure. It is God's laboratory in which we get to test, strengthen, and grow our virtues. Nothing pits us against ourselves spiritually like sustained intimacy.

There is a unique joy in long-term, loyal relationships. We *can* achieve sustainable intimacy if we are willing to sacrifice the dream of a perfect love for the simple joys of an unconditional love.

Focus on What's Right

In practical terms, how do we break the cycle of lateral violence? How do we replace a lifetime of negative thinking and speaking? We can use a powerful key to transforming habits of negativity and replacing them with grace. This ancient key has always been available but is rarely used. It enables us to transform the way we think, speak, and act, to become more affirming, appreciative, and accepting.

One of the most practical ways to purify our thinking and stop speaking negatively is to start focusing on what's right. This is a spiritual discipline that we need with our children, who are deeply sensitive to our shame about their inadequacies. We need it most with the people in our own families. When we are able to focus on their positive qualities, life takes on a new sense of grace.

I often begin a Virtues presentation, whether it is for an hour or a week, by making three promises to the audience. "In our time together," I say,

"First, I promise you will learn a new language.

"Second, you will know how to change the world.

"Third, I will teach you some magic."

The magic is a simple water trick symbolizing the purification of old habits, such as criticism, dishonesty, bullying, and apathy, by replacing them with virtues of acceptance, honesty, friendship, kindness, and excellence. I begin by filling a small clear glass with water from a large pitcher, saying, "When we are born, we have the pure potential for all the virtues, such as love, kindness, justice, truthfulness, integrity, and creativity.

"We start to lose that purity when we are called names such as 'lazy,' 'stupid,' 'mean,'" I say as I pour coffee into the glass of water.

"Our sense of our own goodness is clouded by criticism and then by actions such as biting another child, cheating on an exam, bullying others, criticizing the people we care about." By now the water is totally dark.

"One day, you decide this isn't how you want to live. You want to live by the virtues—the best within you. There is something you can do immediately, today, to change yourself and the world around you. You can use the magic of your virtues to replace bad habits."

As I pour fresh water into the glass, under which is a large bowl catching the overflow, I describe the power we have to replace negative habits with virtue: "If we have been bullying others, we can begin today to magically transform our behavior by being the best friend anyone ever had, by being an encouraging leader. We can go home and clean the kitchen without being asked, and that act of help-fulness will instantly change the atmosphere at home. We can think, speak, and act with peace, and the ripples of those actions will spread through our families, our schools, our communities and the world."

My final point comes from a pearl of truth found in the world's sacred scriptures about the virtue of purity: "We have the power to purify our lives at any time we choose, but this time that purity comes not from the innocence of a baby, but from the strength of our choices—the power of our will." I love to see the big-eyed expressions of the bullies in a student audience or the smiles on the faces of people for whom this simple truth about their own power resonates.

I personally find it devilishly difficult to *stop* doing something I am used to doing, even when I know it isn't how I want to behave. After all, in my family, the habit of critical perfectionism is generations old. I find it far easier to start a new habit than to stop an old one. In the years I have been writing, speaking, and at-tempting to live by the virtues, I have learned to give loving attention to the growth of my character. I have developed an intimate relationship to the virtues, and I find them to be an inexhaustible source of grace. There is nothing in life we cannot solve if we have the will and the skill to call on our virtues.

These great treasures have been with us since the dawn of time, yet it is only in bringing them to the forefront of our awareness that we can tap into this great inner reservoir of spiritual power. When we do, they become the ear with which we hear, the eye with which we see ourselves and others, and the language that shapes our thoughts and our words, the dialect with which we communicate all that matters.

CULTIVATE THE DIVINE VIRTUES

Our family initiated The Virtues Project out of a desire to give children a sense of the meaning of their lives. We had no idea at the time how illuminating our exploration into the virtues would be and what profound implications it would have for every age and stage of life. As we researched the world's diverse sacred traditions, we received a whole new perspective on the power of the virtues and their central place in the human spirit.

In all the sacred texts as well as the oral traditions of the world's indigenous peoples, the virtues are named as the qualities of the Creator and the characterristics of the soul. They are the link between the human and the Divine—the Divine spark within all of us, the image of God reflected in our souls. Courage, love, generosity, justice—these timeless virtues are the very meaning of our lives. In our ceremonies marking the significant passages of life and death, we turn to the virtues to describe the meaning of our lives—the service, or kindness, or generosity contributed to the world by one who has died, or the excellence, hope, and idealism of a new graduate, or the promise of love, faithfulness, and joy marriage holds for a bride and groom. In all the sacred traditions the virtues are at the very core of belief.

VIRTUES ARE UNIVERSALLY VALUED

The indigenous people of many cultures transmit their traditional values from one generation to the next through their oral histories, which focus on the virtues of courage, honor, generosity, unity, reverence, and endurance. All the stories told by the grandmothers and grandfathers contain virtues. *Black Elk Speaks*, for example, by the great spiritual leader of the Oglala Sioux, contains his prophecies about the coming together of the four races of humankind in unity.

Every hero embodies bravery, perseverance, or sacrifice. In our recent work with the Yapese community in the Western Pacific, we learned of the sacred tradition of the navigator, a privileged role for which certain men were chosen. The navigator, after rigorous purification rituals, was given a special woven palm bracelet and then went to sea, guided only by the stars. The virtues of this honored tradition were courage, patience, and endurance, which form the foundation for the culture of Yap.

The centrality of the virtues holds true in all the spiritual and philosophical traditions. The two great ideals of ancient Greece are virtue (goodness) and beauty. Plotinus (AD 205–270) expresses how virtue allows us to reflect the image of God:

> *To make our soul good and beautiful is to make ourselves like unto God: because God is beauty.*

Virtues are the central theme as well in the Bhagavad Gita (Lord's Song), which religious scholars consider the primary sacred text of Hinduism. Virtues such as dedication, detachment, devotion, and service are emphasized throughout the Vedas, Vedantas, and Upanishads as well. Chapter 3 of the Bhagavad Gita is entitled "The Book of Virtue in Work." The text describes the purpose of work as a wedding of meditation and action, inviting the believer to work reflectively, selflessly, and generously.

> *. . . thy task prescribed*
> *with spirit unattached perform,*
> *since in the performance of plain duty,*
> *man mounts to his highest bliss . . .*
> *let each play his part in all he finds to do,*
> *with unyoked soul.*

The virtues are the essence of our being, and at the heart of our faith. They are who we are in our purest identity and the purpose for which we were created.

In the Sikh faith of India, virtues are described as the purpose of communion:

> *By communion with the Naam (the word of God), one becomes the abode*
> *of all virtues.*

—Guru Nanak, *Jap Ji* (the daily prayer of the Sikhs), stanza 11

In the Torah of Judaism, also contained in the Pentateuch, the first five books of the Old Testament, there are countless virtues described, some in lyrically poetic terms. For example, the Proverbs of Solomon, son of David, contain exquisite descriptions of the virtues of loyalty, faithfulness, wisdom, understanding, and self-discipline, among many others:

> *Do not let loyalty and faithfulness forsake you; bind them around your*
> *neck, write them on the tablet of your heart.*

—Proverbs 3:3

The prophet Micah describes the essential relationship with God as related to the love of virtue:

> *With what shall I come before the Lord and bow myself before God on*
> *high? . . .*
> *He has told thee, O mortal, what is good;*
> *and what does the Lord require of you,*
> *but to act justly,*
> *and to love virtue,*
> *and to walk humbly with your God.*

—Micah 6:6-8

Virtues are the essence of the Christian Gospels as well. Jesus said that the Kingdom of God was within us. He revealed the Beatitudes as a guide for how to live by our Divine essence. He describes the virtues as the blessings of God:

> *Blessed are the poor in spirit (humble), for theirs is the kingdom of heaven.*
>
> *Blessed are those who mourn, for they shall be comforted.*
>
> *Blessed are the meek, for they shall inherit the earth.*
>
> *Blessed are they which do hunger and thirst after righteousness, for they shall be filled.*
>
> *Blessed are the merciful, for they shall obtain mercy.*
>
> *Blessed are the pure in heart, for they shall see God.*
>
> *Blessed are the peacemakers, for they shall be called the children of God.*
>
> *Blessed are those who are persecuted for righteousness' sake, for theirs is the kingdom of Heaven.*

—Matthew 5:3–10

In the teachings of the Buddha found in the Hitopadesa and Dhammapada, said to be compiled in the third century BCE, we find a reference to virtues as the essence of the sacred traditions. *Hear the essence of thousands of sacred books: to help others is virtue, to hurt others is sin.*

Buddha spoke of the positive power of a life of virtue:

> *Better than one hundred years lived in vice, without contemplation, is one single day of life lived in virtue and in deep contemplation.*

As we continued our search through the scriptures, we were thrilled to discover this vast mine filled with the gems of virtues, the spiritual wealth linking people of all cultures. In the process, we discovered a common language that every community around the world instantly recognizes as their own. It was particularly poignant to me after September 11, 2001, to receive standing ovations from Moslem audiences in Kuala Lumpur. To me, it seemed a wondrous thing that North Americans would be welcomed so trustingly and wholeheartedly by government leaders, university faculty, students, and parents. There is a moment I have come to anticipate with every group, from prison inmates to corporate executives, when light dawns in their eyes and tears fall from their eyes. This is the moment when they realize that the virtues are the gifts within them and that it is possible at any moment to choose to live a life reflecting these great qualities. I was deeply touched when I saw that look in the eyes of Moslems in Malaysia.

In the Qur'an, the Holy Book of Islam (AD 640), the prophet Mohammed exhorts humanity to submission to the will of God, righteousness, faith, generosity, prayerfulness, trustworthiness, patience, justice, obedience, and forgiveness.

> *Whoever submits his whole self to Allah and is a doer of good he will get his reward with his Lord; on such shall be no fear nor shall they grieve.*
> —Qur'an 2:112

> *. . . who master their anger, and forgive others! God loveth the doers of good.*
> —Qur'an 3:28

The Baha'i Faith, which was founded in 1844, describes the cultivation of virtues as the central purpose of religion. The virtues are so essential that without them we can receive no value whatever from religion:

> *It is religion . . . which produces all human virtues, and it is these virtues which are the bright candles of civilization. If a man is not characterized by these excellent qualities, it is certain that he has never attained to so much as a drop out of the fathomless river of the waters of life that flows through the teachings of the Holy Books, nor caught the faintest breath of the fragrant breezes that blow from the gardens of God . . . —Abdu'l-Bahá, Secret of Divine Civilization*

Bahá'u'lláh, founder of the Baha'i Faith, also describes the virtues as the fruits and the purpose of religion:

> *Regard thou faith as a tree. Its fruits, leaves, boughs and branches are, and have ever been, trustworthiness, truthfulness, uprightness, and forbearance.*
> —Baha'i Compilation on Trustworthiness, 1

> *The Purpose of the one true God, exalted by His glory, in revealing Himself unto men is to lay bare those gems that lie hidden within the mine of their true and inmost selves.*
> —Gleanings from the Writings of Bahá'u'lláh

In the Book of Mormon of the Church of Jesus Christ of Latter-day Saints, virtues are central to the life of the believer.

> *And now I would that ye should be humble, and be submissive and gentle; easy to be entreated, full of patience and long-suffering; being temperate*

in all things; being diligent in keeping the commandments of God at all times ... And see that ye have faith, hope and charity, and then ye will always abound in good works.
—Book of Mormon, Alma, 23–24

> Use a sweet tongue, courtesy, and gentleness, and thou mayest manage to lead an elephant by a hair.
> —from *The Gulistan of Sa'di,* Sufi mystic, 1258, ACE

Over the years that I have been learning about and consciously practicing the virtues, I have come to treasure them as the most sacred gifts in my life. They are mysterious and powerful, both within us and beyond us—angels that can assist us and qualities within our own souls that seem to grow miraculously whenever we act on them. They are the purest expression of human will, because to develop them we must consciously cultivate them. While they are innate in all of us, they don't come to us by chance. They grow as a muscle grows—by being exercised. They awaken as we put them into practice. I have often been at a moment of choice, such as to complain or to accept, to detach or to push my will, and find I am refreshed and lightened each time I choose the way of virtue.

We had a huge "Aha" moment when we realized that virtues could be spoken as a language! The prime minister of the Solomon Islands said to us, "You have brought forth the virtues buried in the Bible and turned them into a language to use every day."

Language is the vehicle for thought. Focusing our thoughts on virtues is the natural antidote to the negativity that blocks us from true intimacy and harmony with others. Rather than criticizing someone for something they *don't* have, we can call forth the virtue they *do* have and invite them to practice it. We can ask others for what we do want rather than condemning them for doing what we don't want them to do. Speaking the Language of Virtues evokes cooperation, whereas criticism provokes resentment and resistance.

USE VIRTUES LANGUAGE TO ENCOURAGE

A general manager at an Australian resort said that after attending a Virtues seminar he got far better results with an employee who was consistently late by speaking the Language of Virtues. He had been in the habit of shaming the fellow almost daily by asking, "Why are you always late?" or threatening, "You know there are plenty of people who want your job." All he would get was a head-hanging response and a mumble. One morning, shortly after the workshop, he said, "Louis, I need to talk to you. I appreciate the fact that you're a hard worker. I know I can rely on you to do your job well. It's important for you to be reliable about time too. What would help you to be on time every time?" Louis then explained that his wife was very ill, and he now had to care for their two young children and get them to school in the morning. After commiserating with him, the manager asked, "So, how can we help you to be responsible for your kids and reliable about the job too?" Louis arranged to have another worker cover for him the first hour of each day. In exchange Louis worked an extra hour at the end of the day when his children were in an after-school program. With a new schedule to accommodate his family's needs, he was indeed on time every time, and seemed to take even more pride in his work, and in his reliability.

Use Virtues Language to Affirm

When we affirm and acknowledge a person's virtues and hold them accountable in the context of their virtues, we are actually helping them to awaken and strengthen their own soul qualities. We disconnect from virtues whenever we shame or blame each other or ourselves. The way we speak and the words we use have great power to discourage or to inspire growth. When the language of our thoughts and words is infused with virtues, it transforms our relationships and gives them a whole new positive energy. It prevents emotional burnout as surely as good health practices prevent physical burnout. It allows us to replace shaming and blaming with personal responsibility and respect. It is the language of encouragement, a path to grace.

Language need not be merely a reaction to our experience—it can *shape* our experience. Words are generative. When we speak gentle, compassionate, thankful words, our feelings follow. Our expectations change. The way we see others and the world becomes more positive.

When doing a Virtues workshop for a television network, I was struck by the story of a woman who worked with Jim Henson as a puppeteer, or, to be more accurate, a "muppeteer." She had tears in her eyes as she shared with the group that her parents had labeled her as shy and how that had become the script for her life. She believed this label led her to find work behind—and beneath—the scenes, and she continued to this day to find it challenging to make friends. "Now that I see the pattern, I realize I can cultivate my friendliness. Sharing this story with all of you is my first step," she said, smiling.

USE VIRTUES LANGUAGE TO CORRECT

We can purify our language from words and attitudes that put others down and literally dis-grace them by speaking affirming, tactful language that empowers them. Even when you correct someone, tact is far more effective than verbal abuse.

We met a baker in Western Australia who had been dragged to a Virtues workshop by his wife and left quite pumped up. He came up to my husband and me on the street the next day looking very excited. "It works!" he said. "What works?" my husband asked. "That virtues language! Last night I went to work in my bakery. I'm the worst boss in this town and I thought I had the laziest employees, but last night I tried an experiment. When my helper dragged over a large bag of flour, I said, 'Thanks for being helpful, Henry. My back is a bit sore tonight.' He looked really shocked and said, 'What did you say, boss?' So I said it again. Then all night he was running around doing whatever he could think of and asking me, 'Anything you need, boss?' And all I did was use one virtue—one word."

USE VIRTUES LANGUAGE TO THANK

Words of thanks and appreciation when they include the virtues we see in others are deeply affirming. "It took courage for you to speak up to your boss today." "Thank you for being so considerate about driving when I was tired." "It was helpful of you to set the table. I appreciate it." If we merely say "Thank you," we are focusing on our own virtue of thankfulness. When we specify the virtues in others for which we are thanking them, we are affirming *their* positive qualities. It is a much greater gift in that moment of gratitude.

GIVE UP SHAMING AND START NAMING VIRTUES

Are you aware of the power you have to affect others, particularly those closest to you? We are exquisitely sensitive to what our intimates say to us. Any word of criticism is like a particle of dust in the eye. When we act more tactfully or lovingly toward one another, we inspire a more positive response. Likewise, if we use harsh, critical, negative words all the time, they not only reflect inner negativity—they breed negativity.

When your words are weighty, weigh your words. Stop and think about how you want to say something, find the virtue to which you are calling someone or thanking them, and you will be speaking the language of love and encouragement, the language of grace.

In many families, children are constantly criticized, often with the intent of making them "behave." At a gathering I attended, a young mother watched worriedly as her nine-month-old daughter hoisted herself around a table in pursuit of a small candle. The mother kept moving it out of her reach, but the child persisted, diligently following the light. Her mother whispered to me, "She's really stubborn." I said, "She's really determined and persevering. It will serve her well." I offered the baby my wooden necklace to chew on and she immediately gave up the pursuit of the candle.

Instead of saying to children who are fighting, "Stop that fighting right now," we can call them to the virtue of peacefulness. "How can you solve this peacefully?" Instead of shaming a child or an adult by calling them "lazy," "stupid," "mean," or "shy," we can call them to responsibility, respect, kindness, or friendliness. To a teen mouthing off at us, we can say, "I'll listen to anything you say as long as you say it with respect."

ACT with Tact: Appreciate, Correct, and Thank

Tact is a gentle virtue that can grease the wheels of all our relationships, make life more gracious, and allow us to tell each other the truth in a way that helps us to hear it. This is a practice within the first Strategy of The Virtues Project: Speak the Language of Virtues. Managers can apply this strategy to give forthright yet affirming performance feedback. We can also use it as a way to encourage excellence in a child doing a chore at home or an adult doing a service for us. Teachers are using it on report cards to note a student's strength virtues and their "growth virtues"—areas needing improvement.

ACT is an acronym for Appreciate, Correct, and Thank. Dale Carnegie, who wrote the classic book *How to Win Friends and Influence People*, originally coined the term "positivity sandwich." He taught that you can tell anyone anything if you sandwich it between two positive comments. It not only saves face, it encourages openness to change. I find this an abiding idea to simply and powerfully practice the virtue of tact.

> *There's a fullness of time for things . . . You have to know when to prod and when to be quiet, when to let things take their course.*
> —Sue Monk Kidd,
> *The Secret Life of Bees*

The ACT with Tact approach is helpful when we want to give in-depth feedback to someone, for example when they are doing a job or there is a need to correct behavior. It is very useful in performance appraisals, whether talking to a child about a chore they have not yet completed or to an employee one is evaluating. It is also the kindest way to fire someone.

I once had a personal assistant who reminded me of a bouncy Newfoundland puppy—full of enthusiasm, but she kept breaking things. Mostly she broke her promises. I learned that any working relationship needs a trial period, allowing us to become engaged before we get married, so to speak. When her three-month trial period was up, she came up to my desk for our meeting, her head hanging.

"I know what you're going to say," she said, her mouth quivering slightly.

"So, you know this isn't working out as we had hoped?"

"Yes."

"I'd like to give you some feedback about our three months together." Her head hung lower and she looked as if she was steeling herself for a blow.

I said, "First of all, I want you to know what I have appreciated." She looked up. "Your courtesy when you answer the phone has been excellent. You have a lovely voice and a professional, friendly manner. People feel welcomed and you give a very positive, warm impression. Also, you have really created orderliness with the filing system."

She was bright-eyed by now and seemed more able to cope with what I was about to tell her next.

"What you needed more of to make this job work is trustworthiness and assertiveness."

"Really?" she said. "How?" She was all ears.

"Do you remember when I worked half the night to prepare a FedEx package to go to a client before leaving for Denver? When I got home, you had done

> *Do you see the glass as*
> *half empty or half full?*
> —Unknown

a grand job sorting the files, but the package was still there. I have to be absolutely able to trust that my priorities are your priorities. This has often not been the case."

She said, "I know. I just get so caught up in the details. And I know I need to work on assertiveness. Can you tell me more about it?"

"You always say yes to me when I ask you to do something, then sometimes it is beyond what you can do, and it just doesn't get done. I needed you to be more assertive about what was possible, so I could trust what you were able to take on."

"That is so true. I have always had a problem saying no."

She moved as if to get up, but I said, "Wait, I want to tell you what I am really thankful for—your love. I know you love me, and you love The Virtues Project. It has been a pleasure to be around you."

She began to cry at this point and said to me, "Linda, will you write that down? On my good days, I'll look at the virtues I need to work on, and on my bad days I'll look at the good things you said to me. And thank you for being so kind. That is the best firing I've ever had."

She and I have remained friendly to this day and always have big smiles for one another when we see each other in our small town. I have had occasion to call her new place of employment, which has her cataloguing stock and answering the phone. Her voice is as warm and professional as ever.

When correcting a child, look for what's right first, then call the child to the virtue needed and end with something positive. When a child is cleaning her room, if half of it is messy and half clean, comment on the orderly half. "This side of the room looks so tidy and orderly. What would help you to put the rest of the room in order in the next fifteen minutes, so we can go out and have fun?" They might say "a timer" or "some music." Then end the conversation with "Excellent job." What a difference from "Aren't you finished yet? You're slow as molasses. If you don't finish soon we're going to the lake without you." When we begin and end with a positive comment, people can hear just about anything.

Make Simple, Positive Requests

One of the habits that prevents us from sustaining grace in our relationships is complaining and making demands instead of asking for what we want. Simple, positive requests allow others to save face and help them to be open to what we are asking for.

We have been encouraged by various schools of thought to believe we should unburden our feelings to others, and recite to them the ways their negligence has hurt us, and that then suddenly their compassion will rush to the fore and they will repent. It doesn't tend to work that way. Complaining merely distends the hurt.

Complaints are heard as criticism, and one's automatic response is to defend against them. Statements such as, "Why are you always working? Why can't you spend more time with me? I wonder if you love me anymore," or "I'm sick and tired of your working so much. Don't you care about me?" are not likely to inspire greater intimacy. If you turn it around by transforming a complaint into a simple, positive request, it is far more likely to attract a positive response. "I'm starting to really miss you. You're working very hard these days. Is there a way we could spend more time together?" Sometimes taking a simple action, such as getting tickets to the theater or planning a surprise weekend, is far more powerful than a long harangue about not being together enough. If intimacy is your goal, it is far more effective to attract than attack.

Marshall Rosenburg has a wonderful expression in his groundbreaking work on Nonviolent Communication. "Would you be willing . . . ?" I love this. It is courteous, it is gracious, and it is assertive. It allows us to ask for what we do want rather than condemning others for what they're not doing to please us.

There is another, even more personal level of transformation in the way we use language that can greatly enhance the quality of grace in our lives. It is changing how we talk to ourselves.

Replace the Internal Critic with the Gentle Observer

In purifying the language of our lives, we need to heal our criticism of ourselves. As we change the way we think and speak about ourselves, we automatically become more gracious to others. If you catch yourself using shaming or negative self-talk, stop and replace it with a virtue or a positive intent. A friend of mine used to use terms like "I'm going in circles" and "I can't think straight." Now she stops herself and says, "I need to discern what I want to do" or "I'm working on clarity."

BEFRIEND THE JUDGE

The inner critic or judge can block us from experiencing a fuller sense of grace in our lives. We are often our own harshest critics. I've caught myself when I receive the evaluations after a presentation scanning through the positives and latching on to the one negative comment, then chewing on it and overinflating its importance. Negativity is ego-syntonic. It fits our negative self-image, received in childhood from the negative labels and attitudes we received from our parents and teachers.

Many of us have internalized the early criticism that was dished out in large doses—sometimes with the best of intentions—meant to improve our character. Think about the words you heard about yourself when you were a child. I have asked this question of people all over the world and have heard the same litany of "stupid," "lazy," "good for nothing," "useless." I'm not surprised to find that the harshest labels of all that I have heard from workshop participants were those given to prison inmates when they were children. They were literally cursed by the adults around them, and they lived according to the words used to describe them. Once when I asked a group of inmates to call out their childhood labels as I stood at a flip chart marking them down, I felt as though the paper was going to burst into flames.

As children, we are utterly dependent on the adults in our world to describe us to ourselves. The vocabulary of shame becomes the script for our sense of ourselves, and we spend our lives either acting it out or resisting it and desperately, compulsively trying to prove it wrong. I have met highly intelligent and perceptive men and women in prisons from the United States to Australia who were scripted to be destructive of themselves and others.

A man born in Iran wept in one of my workshops as he told how he had come by the name "Destroyer" at the age of five and had been riddled by guilt and shame for the rest of his life. His father had at last saved enough money to build a bathhouse beneath their home so that the family would no longer need to go to the public baths. Parviz ran down the stone steps to where his father was standing looking at the completed construction. "Daddy, Daddy, I want to take a bath!" he called. His father said, "You stupid boy! It will be hours before the water fills the bath." Parviz's heart had been wide open, and his joy was shattered by this angry response. He ran up to the nursery and hid under the cradle where his baby sister was sleeping. He accidentally tipped over the cradle, and the baby fell out and began to scream. His father, followed by all the adults in the house, thundered up the stairs, and screeched at him, "Destroyer!"

From that day, anytime he entered a room, they called him by this soul-crushing label. Parviz was in his fifties when he attended this Virtues workshop and began to heal his image of himself, replacing the label of "Destroyer" with the affirmation "I am a gentle man of peace." He had in fact become very passive in his life for fear of hurting anyone. Once he discovered the truth of what had happened, he was ready to balance his peacefulness with justice and confidence. How different his life would have been if his father had recognized this special moment of closeness, had acknowledged his son's enthusiasm and invited him to be patient. They could have stood together with great pleasure watching the bath fill with water.

One of the reasons we put such pressure on our intimates to affirm us is that we fail to do it for ourselves. It is simple to change that lifelong habit of negative self-talk and be more gracious to ourselves. I have found that the Language of Virtues has truly allowed me to re-parent myself and to experience an attitude of acceptance and affirmation.

I have come to understand that we cannot deny or eliminate the inner judge, but we can befriend it. We can listen when a shameful thought comes up, ask "What do you need?," translate it into a virtue and offer it the comfort of our willingness to change for the better. This melts the inner abuse we have been dishing out to ourselves for so long. Once, I was talking with a friend who was in the habit of shaming and blaming herself continually, taking up where her parents left off. I asked her what she would name her inner judge. "'Attila the Hun' works," she said, laughing. "How can you befriend this part of yourself?" I asked. "I guess I could call her 'Hon,'" she said. My own inner critic is named "Mack," which stands for Mack truck, my inner pushy broad that craves control. When I befriend her instead of resisting her, she relaxes. I wouldn't want to give up her sense of determination altogether. She has been key to my survival.

DO NOT ACCEPT SHAME FROM OTHERS

> *No one can make you feel inferior without your consent.*
> —Eleanor Roosevelt

I remember a client of mine named Ellie who came to me with crippling anxiety. She was unable to keep a job, her teenage children ran roughshod over her, and her husband continually tormented her with caustic digs, such as "You can't even set the table right." Her every other sentence was "I'm sorry." "I'm sorry I'm late," she'd say when coming into my office two minutes past her appointment time. "I'm sorry," she said once when she bumped into the chair before seating herself. She kept her body in a sorry state, walking with hunched, rounded shoulders, as if she didn't want to take up any more space than she had to. Her mother had devalued her, shamed her over and over, and always demanded that she say how sorry she was. Ellie learned that her life of apology was a continuation of the shame her mother carried within her and had passed on to Ellie. Through weekly "homework" of using *only* affirming language toward herself, she saw gradual yet definite change. When she walked in one day with her head high and her shoulders back, I saw the confidence that had taken root in her soul. She described a moment of pure assertiveness when she said to her husband, "Either say something kind to me or don't say anything at all," and had walked out of the room. He was openmouthed at this remark but had actually begun to come around and speak to her more courteously.

SPEAK RESPECTFULLY ABOUT YOUR BODY

As we purify the negative habits that block us from a fully gracious life, we need to show love and respect for our own bodies. They are a gift to us, wondrous in their mechanics and their supple responses to how we treat them. One of the most powerful ways to create health is to purify the language we use about our bodies. Our words go deep. Our bodies "hear" every word we say. Our very cells respond to words of appreciation and love or to words of contempt and disappointment. The Virtues Massage in chapter 2 is one example of a way to replace shaming words by naming virtues. Another is to be very mindful about the words we use about our bodies. One of my friends who is amply endowed refers to herself as Rubenesque, referring to the voluptuous, full-bodied women in Peter Paul Rubens's paintings. These words contradict the shame many women in Western culture carry for not fitting the pale, young, anorexic image of what is desirable. If we are thin, we think of ourselves as "skinny." If we are full-bodied, we are "too fat." We need to appreciate the meat on our bones and the curvaciousness of our bodies, whatever shape we are.

> *Who cannot love herself*
> *cannot love anybody.*
> *Who is ashamed of her body is*
> *ashamed of all life . . .*
> *Who cannot respect the gifts*
> *given even before birth*
> *can never respect anything fully.*
> —Anne Cameron, author of
> *Daughters of Copper Woman*

The trend these days to undergo radical surgical makeovers in which women are literally eviscerated, sucked out, injected with Botox, reshaped and given new breasts, and men are given artificial abs, indicates to me a profound rejection of the self in its real and natural state. My massage therapist says, "It's an insult to God." Personally, I love and admire the wrinkles on the faces of an aging man or woman. To me, this is part of their beauty and a sign of their wisdom.

GIVE UP PERFECTIONISM FOR TRANSFORMATION

Authentic spirituality means giving up perfectionism for the rigorous process of developing ourselves one thought, one act, one day at a time. A man doing service in Africa for his faith community received a telegram from its international headquarters appointing him to a very revered and important position. He wired "Not worthy." The next wire he received said, "Become worthy."

We experience joy and exhilaration when we hold the virtues close as the source of our true personal wealth. The virtues allow us to stretch our courage and to experience the healing balm of forgiveness balanced by the spiritual diligence of right living. A man riddled with guilt and earnestly desiring to change went to see a great spiritual master and asked him, "Lord, how can I change myself? I am so flawed and sinful." The master looked at him with tenderness and said, "Little by little, day by day."

If you realized how powerful your thoughts are
you would never again think a negative thought.
—Peace Pilgrim

⊷⟫ EXERCISE GRACE ⟪⊶
Think Positively

Make a commitment to purify your thoughts and words of negativity for a period of five days.

1. On the first day, without judging, but just gently observing, notice how many times a day you think or say a negative thing about a coworker or family member, or anyone, including yourself. Record this on a page in your journal.

2. On the second day, take time to reflect on what qualities in others you find upsetting. As Carl Jung, the great psychoanalyst, taught, these may well be the shadow qualities in yourself that trouble you.

3. On the third day, commit to immediately replacing a negative thought with a positive one. Look for a virtue in the person who is annoying you.

4. Refrain from backbiting and gossip. If someone makes a critical remark to you about another person, either change the subject, courteously excuse yourself, or tactfully tell them you'd rather not talk about someone who isn't present.

5. Use encouraging words every day. Mention something you appreciate about your intimates, even if it is something they are wearing, or thanking them for being helpful in some way.

6. On the fifth day, reflect and journal about the different ways this positive thought campaign has affected you.

SUMMARY OF CHAPTER 4:
PURIFY THE LANGUAGE OF YOUR LIFE

- When we purify our bodies, we receive the gift of a clear mind.
- We can purify our lives of needless pain and useless misery by releasing ourselves from negative habits of thinking and speaking.
- We can choose to engage in the "Troubled C's" of control, criticism, contempt, and contention or act on our virtues of acceptance, appreciation, and assertiveness.
- When we accept the "suchness" of our intimates, we are able to give up the love of power for the power of love.
- Be a peacemaker. When we change our own part of a dynamic, the relationship changes automatically. With our thoughts, we can change the world.
- We receive great spiritual value by giving up the dream of a perfect love for the joys of a loyal, unconditional love.
- Focus on what's right.
- Focus your energies on cultivating the Divine virtues. All sacred traditions describe them as the purpose of life and the gifts of the soul.
- Use the Language of Virtues to encourage, affirm, correct, and thank.
- Give up shaming and start naming virtues.
- ACT with Tact. When you want to give someone feedback, offer them a "positivity sandwich" of appreciation, correction, and thanks, and they will be able to hear what you have to say.
- Make simple, positive requests. Let people know what you *do* want rather than criticizing them for what they are not doing.
- Replace your internal critic with a gentle observer. Rather than trying to cast out the inner judge, befriend it and listen to its message as a Teachable Moment.
- Resist taking on the shame or pain others give you.
- Use only respectful, loving words about your body.
- Give up perfectionism for transformation, little by little and day by day.

The next chapter is about the healing power of forgiveness, a purifying virtue that restores our energy and heals our relationships.

FIVE

Forgive

When Peter came to him, and asked, "Lord, how often am I to forgive my brother
if he goes on wronging me? As many as seven times?" Jesus replied, "I do not say
seven times but seventy times seven."
—Matthew 18

One of the most powerful ways to purify our lives is to release resentment and learn to forgive. When I was lying flat on my back in the early days of post-polio, one of my spiritual challenges was to forgive myself for my overdone life. I could feel my internal critic stirring up inside my mind, ready to blame and shame. Yet I felt a Divine tenderness surrounding me, like a warm breath, and I wanted to emulate it. "What do you need, Mack?" I asked my inner critic one day, remembering to befriend it rather than resist it. "I need to trust you to take care of your body and not slide back," I heard. This Teachable Moment was a sweet reminder of the power I had to make changes, and having received the Ten Rules for Health, I experienced a faint stir of hope that I could indeed turn around this debilitating illness. I hadn't heard of remarkable recoveries for others with post-polio and assumed the condition was degenerative, yet I had received the Ten Rules for Health and my intention was to do all I could to follow them.

I also knew how stressful and draining guilt could be, having become accustomed to it as an insistent bedfellow for many years. I no longer wanted to awaken with a knot of tension in my stomach about all I was not accomplishing, and my illness humbled me into realizing I no longer could carry the world on my shoulders—nor did I want to. Workaholics often feel this way, and it is one of the illusions that need to be purified in our search for a pace of grace.

I realized that a part of the purification practice of the first three rules for health was not only about cleansing my body but also my mind, not merely about breathing more deeply but breathing more easily. So I began to consciously practice self-forgiveness. "I forgive you, Linda," I would write in my journal. "I know you had good intentions in working so hard. You were so diligent. Now it's time to be more peaceful and moderate." This gentle forgiveness brought up my tears of grief. I have often found that anger or judgment is a barricade to sadness. It's best to purify ourselves from it by letting those tears flow, as explained earlier. I found it remarkably soothing and encouraging to forgive myself, giving me the boost I needed to make amends for my years of self-neglect. Without it, I believe I might have just given up.

BE ACCOUNTABLE, NOT GUILTY

In the FOG of Fatigue, Overwhelm, and Guilt, my experience is that guilt is the most insidious theft of grace in our lives. It is like a parasite eroding our self-esteem from within. It absorbs huge energy and blocks our hope. One of the simple principles of a sustainable, virtues-based life is that we no longer pander to guilt and shame as a lifestyle. We no longer resist changing ourselves because of the hopelessness at the core of guilt. Carrying guilt over something that occurred in the past is self-indulgent. It keeps us frozen in a paralysis of will, feeling unable—but in truth being unwilling—to change. Some of us wear the persona of the penitent, allowing our wounded honor to fester beneath our hair shirts, yet we do little to actually change our lives. Holding on to guilt clenches our muscles and grinds our teeth. It has a profound effect on our physical as well as spiritual well-being. Chronic guilt literally cripples us.

I remember the Holocaust survivors I worked with in a mental health clinic in New York in the 1970s. These young urban Jewish women, whose parents and grandparents had perished at Auschwitz and other concentration camps during World War II, were carrying "survivor guilt." They continually sabotaged their own happiness by withholding intimacy from their husbands and depriving themselves of pleasure. Guilt had become their way of life. Only when they realized that they were not only imprisoning and "ghettoizing" themselves but also their husbands and children did they realize that they could replace their guilt with loving responsibility in order to live in present time. By having the courage to take off their hair shirts and live fully, they were taking a stand for freedom. They were reclaiming their lives from the original perpetrators rather than allowing them to continue their oppression into another generation. Part of their therapy was to forgive themselves for experiencing joy. I saw more tears when we undertook this part of their treatment than when they were recounting the worst details of their history.

I imagine that all of us carry guilt about something we regret in our lives. Holding on to it prevents us from moving with the flow of the spiritual current.

We miss so much if we remain stuck in guilt. It is like clinging to a dead limb while the river of life holds the promise of new adventures and beautiful sights just around the bend. It takes an act of courageous will to detach, to let go, and dare to forgive ourselves.

PRACTICE IMPECCABLE INTEGRITY AND UNFAILING TENDERNESS

A virtues-based approach to life recognizes that the journey of our lives is all about change and growth. We are given countless Teachable Moments in which to grow our virtues, to reflect more truly our Divine nature, to become more one with God. The path of a spiritual being is one of impeccable integrity and unfailing tenderness, for ourselves and all the world. The balance of righteousness and tolerance, justice and forgiveness is our holy ground. As we live the virtues more deeply, they call us to true balance. "I'm so hard on myself," I hear from people. "I beat myself up all the time." Whenever I hear people use critical language about themselves, "stupid idiot" being a common favorite, it reminds me of my old habit of doing the same. With the Ten Rules I have become so much more self-accepting, and I am immeasurably happier, more in the flow of grace than I have ever been before. I only wish that I had known—and acted on—this awareness earlier in my life, but never mind. I forgive myself.

When we focus on our virtues, we no longer act like victims of our own deficiencies. What a huge relief to experience the shift in our spirit by recognizing that we are innately worthy and that at any time we can meet our current life lesson head-on. Self-forgiveness is essential to the process of spiritual growth. We can always choose to cultivate a virtue that will amend even the worst sin.

SELF-FORGIVENESS HEALS

I once had an unforgettable encounter with the redemptive power of forgiveness in an Australian women's prison. I was invited to give a workshop on The Virtues Project, and about a dozen inmates attended. One of them, I'll call her Jackie, swaggered into the room, joking and poking at the others, and gave off the aura of the alpha leader. She seemed brittle beneath her too-loud laughter and defiant stare.

After I briefly explained what the virtues are—the gifts of spirit and character within all of us, which at any time we have the power to choose—a woman named Helen spoke up in a meek, quiet voice. She said, "Oh, I don't have any of those. I have zero self-esteem." I acknowledged her courage for being the first to speak. She looked a bit stunned, and we moved on to the first virtues exercise.

I then demonstrated how to acknowledge someone for a virtue, and invited them to do an introductory exercise in sharing circles to explore their own virtues—both their strength virtues and their growth virtues, the ones they needed to cultivate. As each woman finished sharing, the others in the circle acknowledged her for a virtue they saw in her. Helen raised her hand again, and I noticed her eyes were filled with tears. "Miss, I *do* have virtues! My mates said I had self-discipline because I always get to my job in the laundry on time. It's true! And you said I have courage. If I have those virtues, then maybe I have others. I can't ever say I have no self-esteem anymore." The group cheered.

I then introduced an exercise called a Virtues Pick. This explores how virtues apply to everyday life. I asked for two volunteers to model the exercise with me in front of the group. Jackie was the first to volunteer. Then another woman came forward to sit with us facing the group. Each of us randomly chose a card with a virtue on it and a description of how to practice it. We then shared how it spoke to our lives and received virtues acknowledgments from the other two. I modeled the first pick by sharing some challenge in my life, reading the card aloud—I don't remember what it was—and explaining how it spoke to me. Then Jackie and the other woman acknowledged me for virtues they saw in me. The group remained in hushed silence watching us. The second woman did her share. Then it was Jackie's turn. Her face became flushed as she shared her story and the hardness left her voice. She was a "lifer," with no chance of parole. She had become very drunk one night and executed the four sexual abusers in her family—uncles and cousins who had abused her as a child and had started molesting her young daughters. The Virtues Card she received was Forgiveness, and as she read aloud what it said about self-forgiveness, the tears coursed down her cheeks. She looked up, smiled radiantly and said, "I don't know if I can ever forgive myself, because what I did was unforgivable, but this gives me hope that maybe God will forgive me one day. And now I know what I'm going to do with the rest of my life!" She pointed to the poster of the fifty-two virtues I had put on the wall, and said, "I can't raise my own kids, but I can do something to be of service to every woman who comes through the door of this place! Service, that's my virtue." When the workshop ended, she ran off down the hall to talk to the warden about a regular Virtues program for the inmates.

⇥ The Virtue of Forgiveness ⇤

To those who do wrong out of ignorance, then repent and correct themselves,
your Lord is indeed forgiving and kind. —Qur'an 16:19

When we are forgiving we overlook the mistakes others make and love
them just as much as before. We can even forgive ourselves when we do
things we are sorry for. Forgiving ourselves means we stop punishing ourselves or feeling hopeless because of something we did. We move ahead,
ready to do things differently, with compassion for ourselves and faith that
we can change.

Signs of Success

I am practicing Forgiveness when I . . .
- Remember that everyone makes mistakes
- Take responsibility for my mistakes
- Share my feelings without taking revenge
- Stop giving uncaring people the chance to hurt me
- Correct my mistakes instead of punishing myself with guilt
- Accept God's forgiveness

Affirmation

I am forgiving of myself and others. I can learn from my mistakes. I have the
power to keep changing for the better.

TRANSFORMATION IS THE ONLY AMENDS

We cannot change the past or undo the actions we deeply regret, but we can make amends in the present by changing what we do now. We can practice restorative justice in our lives. Instead of making excuses, we can make amends. Instead of shaming ourselves when we make a mistake, we can take responsibility to clean it up. We can call ourselves to humility, not humiliation.

One of the most powerful justice exercises I have witnessed is reconciliation between a victim and offender. The victim of a violent crime, such as the murder of a son or daughter, craves hearing the remorse of the perpetrator. I have been deeply moved to see the forgiveness and even affection that flows between the two when the perpetrator admits their sorrow and regret for what they did. One woman I know of is still writing to a man who is in prison for twenty-five years for killing her daughter. She has become his lifeline and his mentor.

Our inner lives and private character are the essence of our true reality, not the events around us. It is not what happens but how we respond to it that makes all the difference. As Stephen Covey says in *The 7 Habits of Highly Effective People*, between the stimulus and the response there is always choice. Our natural joy is released as we live more and more in the awareness and practice of our virtues, as we flex those spiritual muscles and do what we know is right.

If we have made a big mistake, then we need to make major reparation. Disunity with others is one of the greatest drains on our spiritual energy. An unresolved conflict or unforgiven act, particularly with our intimates, severely depletes us. Chronic power struggles are the most draining of all. By taking responsibility for our own part of a problem, and clearing it up with someone, we can refresh and revitalize the relationship. One of the slogans of The Virtues Project used in schools is "We don't make excuses. We make amends." When we have made a mistake, transformation is the only amends. Thinking about what we can do to restore trust when we have broken it and then consciously becoming trustworthy has the power to restore lost love.

This is a true story about a repentant man who was full of sadness and regret for something he had done. He went to a spiritual master and asked, "How can I know if God has forgiven me for what I did?" The master replied, "You'll know you are forgiven when you no longer do it."

You may recall the saying that there are three kinds of people: those who let things happen to them, those who wonder what happened, and those who make things happen. The virtues are the keys to changing our lives for the better, even when we find ourselves in a state of hopelessness. When we choose to live by our virtues, life always offers hope.

I met a young woman of twelve in the Seattle Youth Detention Center who had shot a stranger two years earlier as the required initiation to join a gang. After I gave a brief Virtues workshop for the young women in her cell block, she came up to me with shining eyes and said, "Now I know how I'm going to live. I knew I needed a new lifestyle when I get out of here, but I had no idea what it would be. Now I know—the virtues! They belong to me, right? Like you said, they're inside me. They're mine. That's how I'm going to live!"

Taking responsibility to transform our actions is the key to making us eligible for forgiveness. Our decision to do things differently, with the help of prayer and our virtues, is the only meaningful way to respond when we have done something we regret. The only way to purify our lives of a mistake is to make it right. Whether we do this with the knowledge of the person we have wronged depends, as they say in the Twelve Steps program of Alcoholics Anonymous, on whether to do so in an active way would cause further harm. We can always do it by committing to change our behavior whether they know about it or not.

Keep Relationships Clean and Clear

One of the most cleansing, purifying practices I know is to clear up misunderstandings before they fester. I think of it as preventive forgiveness. A word of caution, however. This takes great trust and tact, and some people are not up to hearing anything that could be interpreted as criticism of their actions. They prefer to chew on conflict, build walls, and engage in bickering and backbiting. It's a habit they may not have the will to break. However, with relationships that are meaningful to you, I believe it is worth trying. If you have wronged someone, go to them and say, "I need to clear something up with you. I realize I may have insulted you yesterday when I made a flip remark. I just want you to know I respect you and I meant nothing by it." Modeling this habit of clearing up your own mistakes makes you eligible to go to them when you feel upset about something and say, "What would be a good time to talk? I need to clear something up with you." When they are ready to talk, tell them with as much tact as possible what is bothering you, remembering to make a positivity sandwich. "I really value our friendship and appreciate what a loyal friend you are. I've been bothered about something you said the other day, and want to clear it up with you. What did you mean by . . . ?" When they have said their piece, end with thanks. "Thanks for being honest (or understanding or helpful). I feel better." This is one of the ways to actively practice preventive forgiveness, sustaining the grace and unity in our relationships. It is also a way to restore justice.

When you do not feel that it is safe to clear things up directly with someone, and that it might complicate the situation further, listen compassionately to your own concerns, get to the heart of the matter yourself, and then forgive the person. Let it go. I have found that if I continue to harbor a petty grievance or a sense of resentment, the best solution is to do some act of service for the person involved, even if it is a simple prayer. It actively shifts my energy and refills me with a sense of grace.

Compassion Leads to Forgiveness

When we see people as wounded rather than malicious, we can forgive them. Dr. Bill Plotkin, in his powerful book *Soulcraft*, says that in our past we receive a sacred wound, which is often the source of our greatest virtue. Every person has an experience of betrayal or loss, usually in late childhood, which takes them deep within themselves and shapes their decisions about their lives. It causes them to come face-to-face with their own will to survive and thrive, and holds the possibility of great strength. For me, it was the moment of truth within the pain of polio at eleven, when I decided to accept what I couldn't change about my mother's inability to love me, and got on with my life. The notion of the "wounded healer" is certainly true of me. My loneliness as a child attracted me to helping others heal their pain. It carved a deep place of compassion within me for the loneliness and struggle of others, and led to my becoming a psychotherapist and later a community healer. I know firsthand that when I truly understand someone's pain, I can feel love and compassion for even the most dysfunctional and destructive individual.

As a psychotherapist in a mental health clinic, I once worked with a woman who had held her three-year-old son's hands under boiling water. He was no longer in her custody. Despite my fierce mother bear protectiveness of innocent children, I found the mother to be an innocent in her own way. She was mentally challenged and unable to connect to a sense of self-discipline or restraint. She couldn't distinguish between a mild punishment and torture. My recommenda-

> *There is a limit at which forbearance*
> *ceases to be a virtue.*
> —Edmund Burke

tion was for the child to remain in foster care, but I continued to see her for many months, to help her strengthen her coping skills.

Balance Forgiveness with Justice

What if the abuse is at the center of an intimate relationship? Are we meant to keep turning the other cheek? To live a healthy life, we must balance forgiveness and justice. Sometimes forgiving someone first requires that they stop their behavior and restore justice. Although I am a believer that a committed relationship is the most fertile soil for the growth of our virtues, and that the work of purifying our relationships is an ongoing opportunity for our soul work, this doesn't mean that we should remain in an intractably toxic or hurtful relationship. Peace at any price does not support the spiritual growth of anyone.

If you are in a relationship with someone who is unwilling to do the soul work of intimacy, first ask yourself these questions:

- Are you honestly doing all *you* can to change the dynamic?
- Are you engaged in power games or using peaceful ways to change things?
- Are you playing your own part to cultivate the virtues of love and acceptance?
- Are you assertively asking for what you want and need?
- Are you clear about your own boundaries? (Chapter 10, "Set Clear Boundaries," delves further into this topic.)
- Are you forgiving what should be forgiven?

If your partner is merely paying lip service to change but not actually changing, you may find yourself increasingly restless, uncomfortable, and unhappy. You may find that regardless of what you do, your relationship continually revolves around the abuse cycle: verbal, physical, or emotional abuse, followed by apologies and promises to change, then the breaking of the promises with a repeat of the abuse. If you continue to forgive this pattern, you are not helping anyone. It is time to establish justice. Decide what you can do to stop the abuse. Remember to watch what people do, not what they say.

If your efforts for change do not budge the continuing cycle of abuse, you need to admit that in some way you are colluding with your partner's delinquency. Spiritually, you are doing him or her no favors. The key is, is your partner willing to share the responsibility for change?

My friend Julie was in her second marriage to a man with ice-blue eyes whose face was as angelic as his character was devilish. She confesses that she

> *Strive ye then with all your heart to treat compassionately all humankind—except for those who have some selfish, private motive, or some disease of the soul. Kindness cannot be shown the tyrant, the deceiver, or the thief, because far from awakening them to the error of their ways, it maketh them to continue in their perversity as before.*
> —Abdu'l-Bahá

knew before they married that he had "a cruel streak." When they had been dating for four months, he started seeing another woman behind her back and continually accused her of being paranoid and unconfident. He also would make hurtful remarks to her, pushing her most tender buttons. Like so many of us, Julie did not listen to her intuitive knowing but sacrificed her self-esteem on the altar of wishful thinking and familiar pain. Her ego became hooked on winning the prize of Peter's affection at any cost. She took his philandering as a challenge, one she would continue to endure throughout their seven-year marriage and after the birth of their two children. Once she became enmeshed in this pattern of rejection and disappointment followed by tearful reunions and empty promises, it took masterful determination to extricate herself from it. Peter and Julie had matching distress patterns. Peter fit the bill for Julie's familiar pattern of seeking love from her rejecting father, and Julie's increasing demands fit Peter's historical comfort zone of resisting the efforts of a dominant and seductive mother for whom he played the role of the surrogate husband. After months of marital counseling during which Peter skillfully evaded change, Julie began the painful process of disentangling herself from the marriage. She could no longer bear to be with Peter, and she realized that staying with him would be a form of spiritual suicide.

Joyless, destructive relationships are a huge energy drain. Essential to our spiritual and emotional sustenance is having affirming, positive people in our lives who are committed to their own health and well-being as well as to ours. A relationship that fails to sustain hope, one that is characterized by chronic irritability, criticism, control, contention, and contempt is soul destroying. If every effort you make to bring about change fails, perhaps you need to make some courageous choices to purify your life of a toxic relationship. Sometimes purification requires the release of a relationship that simply cannot sustain us.

FORGIVENESS CAN HEAL

I remember a man at the hospice whom I was companioning as he was dying. He had been estranged from his brother for more than forty years, and he felt helpless and hopeless about it. Although he thought about nothing else, he did not feel he could actually contact his brother. I asked him what would be the best thing that could happen. "We would be together again. But I don't think he will forgive me." "You really care about your brother. What would give you the courage to let him know?" I asked him. Within forty-eight hours, his brother was at his bedside, wrapping him in a long embrace. They both wept and shared their forgiveness of one another. How we waste time with hopelessness.

In my late thirties, after years of grief and anger about my unsatisfying relationship with my mother, I felt it was time to grow up and forgive her. For three days, I sat in my bedroom for several minutes at a time repeating over and over, "Mom, I forgive you, I forgive you." These words brought a flood of tears each time. The first day, I didn't mean a word of it. By the third day, I felt a softening inside, and was amazed to find that the anger was no longer there. Although I said nothing to my mother about this, I noticed on our next phone call that she was inexplicably warm to me. She actually asked me some questions about myself. I am convinced that she felt the shift in her own soul. When we forgive someone, both hearts are healed.

> *The most powerful emotions are expressed when*
> *the unconditional love of God is accepted by the*
> *broken, needy and sinful person.*
> —Brother Donald Bisson,
> a Christian spiritual retreat director

⤙⟴ EXERCISE GRACE ⟴⤙
Dare to Forgive Yourself

You may want to do this exercise in a healing circle or in solitude. I have found it very powerful when done with large groups, whether with children or adults.

1. Write on a sheet of paper, without anyone else seeing it, some action you deeply regret.

2. Allow yourself to feel your grief about it. If you feel the need to cry, let your healing tears fall.

3. Make a fire in a fireplace or a safe container. Crumple up the sheet of paper and throw it in the fire. Watch it burn.

4. As it burns, say the following prayer: "Creator, I ask that You forgive me (us) for this action. I humbly send it to Your loving care. Help me to transform this action. Make it my teacher. With Your transforming power, help me to replace it with a new way of being."

5. In your journal or on a second sheet of paper, which you will keep, write down an affirmation in the present tense, which will serve as your commitment to a new behavior or virtue to replace the old action. For example, the sin I burned was something I regretted doing to control my sons. My commitment was "I now trust you to live your lives by your own process."

6. Act immediately on your commitment. This may mean saying the affirmation for several days, or taking some gentle action to reflect it. Notice the shift in your spirit!

SUMMARY OF CHAPTER 5: FORGIVE

- Learn to forgive yourself. Hope will help you to change.
- Don't hold on to guilt. It stops you from moving with the flow of grace in your life.
- The path of a spiritual being is one of impeccable integrity and unfailing tenderness for yourself and others. Stand in these balancing virtues.
- You can always cultivate a virtue to amend even the worst sin.
- Transformation is the only true amends. Don't make excuses, take responsibility for changing behavior.
- You know you are forgiven when you no longer indulge in the behavior you regret.
- Keep your relationships clear by cleaning up your mistakes and clearing up misunderstandings when others are open to it.

- Understanding that we all have "sacred wounds" helps us to find compassion and forgiveness.
- Balance forgiveness and justice. It serves no one to allow the cycle of abuse to continue.
- When we forgive someone, both hearts can be healed.

The next chapter focuses on purification of financial practices as a way to free our energy and build our health and prosperity.

SIX

Heal Your Finances

To those leaning on the sustaining infinite, today is big with blessings.
—Mary Baker Eddy, founder of Christian Science

I awoke one morning, a few months after I began practicing the purification practices of the first rules for health, with a sense of peaceful, vibrant energy. I could practically feel the blood flowing through my veins. I smiled as I washed my hands and face, and moved gently into my morning routine. I prepared a cup of steaming ginger tea, sat in my prayer corner to watch the sun rise, and to journal, pray, and meditate. I then did ten minutes of Yoga, followed by a ten-minute walk on the forest path a few feet from our house. I breathed deep of the clean pine-sweetened morning air. As I was preparing a breakfast of multigrain toast, yogurt, and fruit, I realized how deeply alert I felt. It was like waking up after a long sleep troubled by dreams of aimless, anxious running through chaotic streets in a strange city, then being flooded by relief at being safe at home in my own bed. I was at home in my body for the first time in years.

That day, I felt ready to go deeper into the gentle process of reflecting on how I had lost control of my time and my energy, and I began to think about something that until then I had not had the strength to face—money. I opened a credit card bill and groaned.

That week, with the help of my gentle inner observer, I took a long look at the habits that seemed linked to my overdone life.

DO FINANCES DRAIN YOU OR SUSTAIN YOU?

Just as I had exhibited a "starve and binge" pattern in my eating, I noticed a similar pattern in my relationship to money. I realized I needed to purify myself of this unsustainable habit as well. I had to admit that I was carrying what felt to me like a huge load on my back, of accumulated personal and business debt, like a bag of boulders weighing me down. What seemed perfectly natural according to the world—spending beyond my means by using credit cards, for example—had enormous impact on my levels of fatigue and stress. I had developed a pattern of living simply and frugally for months, and then suddenly having a shopping binge or offering to pay for a vacation for our children. This would happen roughly once a year, just enough to keep me in the red on an ongoing basis. My discomfort was proportionate to the level I owed on my line of credit, which my banker happily continued to extend. I never intended to get into this predicament. It happened as a result of some bad business decisions and some unexpected losses, yet one of the threads running through it was a belligerent denial and naïve belief that somehow it would pass, without having a plan for how I would responsibly bring it about.

As I reflected on this repeating pattern, breathing deeply to soothe the anxiety rising in my chest, I recognized that anger was at the heart of this pattern— anger arising from working too hard for too little. Didn't I deserve it? I had to swallow hard when I thought about the six-figure advance I had received for my first two books, which frightened me so much I had turned most of it over to a well-meaning group of businesspeople to expand our project. The money was gone within a year with nothing to show for it. This was the same year I came down with post-polio. I realized that the stress from this mistake was probably one of the factors that made the onset so severe. I had a very hard time forgiving myself for seeing this windfall as a terrifying responsibility with which I thought I had to expand our project, rather than a gift of grace to allow me to relax. If only I had been thankful instead of fearful.

Also, for two years in a row, when we had worked in developing countries, they were unable to pay us after we had completed projects of several weeks. We ended up paying our own airfare and hotel bills as well. We do a good bit of pro bono work each year, but this time it was unintentional, and we did not have reserves for such unexpected losses. Combined with my occasional fits of indulgence, the debt load had grown out of proportion to our income. So much for moderation and grace. It horrified me to think of the many people I knew who had declared bankruptcy. I did not want to go there.

Later that week, I had a moment of startling clarity as a crimson dawn filled the sky. I had been journaling my thoughts each day, seeking to understand what kept me stuck in this pattern and what virtues were involved. I knew that justice was one of them and that I needed to set clearer boundaries with our clients. I also recognized that by my episodic overspending, I was fundamentally saying to

God, "You're not giving me enough." It was as if my trust in God was fragmented, and my issues about money were cordoned off in a place where I felt alone and abandoned— that old familiar song. I recognized that I had slipped into what Jesuit Donald Schell calls "functional atheism." Where was my trust in God's grace to provide what I needed? The angry, defiant adolescent in me, who grabs her credit card and elbows her way past reason into a shop, needed to take a step back and repent—rethink this behavior—in the light of grace. It had destroyed my peace for too long.

As I prayed for understanding, two virtues came—contentment and thankfulness. I experienced them as strong, gentle spirits presenting me with a gift to hold in each hand. I had a deep sense that they truly had the power to lift me out of my lifelong cycle of overrestraint followed by overspending. Somehow, I would find a way to break the cycle.

As I finished my reflections that day, I recorded in my prayer journal my commitment to dissolve debt, create sustainable abundance, and practice contentment with what God provides, ending with an affirmation, "I am free and clear." I was excited and hopeful as I rose from my prayer chair. I immediately walked into my office and wrote "free and clear" on a colorful label and placed it on the bottom of my computer monitor. Now it literally frames whatever I do. I now practice responsible abundance.

SPEND SUSTAINABLY

One aspect of energy conservation is to use all of our resources sustainably—not only our time and energy, but also our money. Being unclear about expenses, running up debts, and not keeping financial papers in order are major energy drains that deplete our health. In the feng shui concepts of energy conservation, financial healing is essential. Clearing up our finances and living by a budget with firm boundaries around spending restores energy on a deep level. Taking steps to heal our financial state is a spiritual act of responsibility—enabling us to respond ably, and providing a sweet, righteous sense of well-being.

In the United States, one of the richest countries in the world, financial sustainability is elusive. Overspending is rampant. In 2002, both corporate and personal bankruptcies smashed all previous records. In the corporate world, 186 public companies with a staggering $368 billion in assets filed for bankruptcy in

> *The will of God will never take*
> *you where the grace of God*
> *cannot sustain you.*
> —Anonymous

2002, according to the tracking service BankruptcyData.com. The *New England Economic Review* stated in July 2000 that credit card borrowing, delinquency, and personal bankruptcy were then at an all-time high.

Although spending beyond our means is standard for millions of us, it is neither a financially nor a spiritually healthy way to live. It is anything but a lifestyle of grace. According to Suze Orman, author of *The Laws of Money, the Lessons of Life*, the average American has $8,000 in credit card debt with a typical interest rate of 18 percent. If they paid only the minimum payment each month, it would take fifty-four years to pay off, and cost $23,000 in interest payments alone. When we chronically overextend financially, it drains us rather than sustains us.

I find it ironic that we call our credit cards by the opposite of what they are. They are debt cards. The more we use them, the greater our debt. We don't really *have* the money in our "credit limit." And if we are making minimum payments, we pay for what we buy twice or several times over. In *The 9 Steps to Financial Freedom*, which I found profoundly helpful, Suze Orman says we have one or both of two choices when we find ourselves in a financial fix: increase our income and/or decrease our spending. It sounds simple, but it is a radical change for many of us.

When we compulsively overspend, we are acting from dissatisfaction and resentment. We are saying, "My life is not enough. I am not enough. God is not giving me enough." We are squandering our true wealth, which is a sense of contentment with what we have. A major part of this comes, I believe, from allowing the current materialistic culture of excess to dictate how we measure our worth. We not only need to take practical steps to disrupt this illusion about what matters, we need to change our inner lives at the same time.

I sought the wisdom of a good financial advisor to help me develop a plan for financial sustainability. After a long talk with my banker, I obtained a consolidated low-interest loan. I also knew that unless I changed my inner attitude, unless a shift occurred within my spirit, the cycle could repeat itself endlessly.

I found three practices very helpful in healing my inner financial pain:

1. Reevaluating my sense of wealth and worth
2. Practicing thankfulness every day
3. Creating a pace of grace in my spending

Reevaluate Your Wealth and Worth

Money is not just money. It is meaning. In Western culture, to have too little is a source of shame and creates a sense of failure and literal worthlessness. Having a great deal of money or material goods signifies that someone has "made it." Ubiquitous advertisements barrage us with messages about the things we need to live well. Before they can read, our children are in danger of becoming compulsive consumers. I recall a friend whose three-year-old threw a tantrum and refused to go to nursery school unless she was wearing her "alligator shirt" replete with the Izod emblem.

Our culture tells us that success is defined by fame and wealth. People of my generation cut our teeth on "rags to riches" stories as well as stories of the men flinging themselves out of windows on Wall Street the day the Great Depression started. Inner-city kids have been murdered in recent years for a pair of Nike sneakers. What is wealth, really? What are your true valuables? Even obscene amounts of money do not guarantee financial sustainability. Despite salaries in the millions, many entertainers and sports stars spend so excessively that they go bankrupt.

I also know people with relatively low incomes who live very well in their frugality. One of my relatives, whose income is at the U.S. poverty level, always seems to have enough saved to loan to family members. When it is time to buy a car, she has saved the money needed for the down payment and has studied *Consumer Reports* to make sure she is getting the most for her money. She has a beautiful wardrobe lined up neatly in her walk-in closet, courtesy of the Sears catalogue, lives in a lovely home, and always has what she needs. We always joke that she does poverty well. Her line is, "If I'm so smart, how come I'm not rich?" "You are," I always say.

I recently visited a friend of mine in the multimillion-dollar house she and her husband built when they retired. As she and I walked into the garage to drive to the store, I looked at their Lexus and late-model SUV and said to my friend, "Do you realize that you and your husband are among the wealthiest people in the world? Probably the top ten percent?" She looked genuinely puzzled and answered, "No, not really." My friend's money had not bought her happiness. I knew too that she treasured our friendship, which has lasted since the first day of high school, as one of the most precious things in her life, as do I.

I took a good look at my life and revised my picture of my own wealth. I began to see what a wealthy woman I am. A friend said to me, "Linda, I know you don't have much money now, but you live the way people wish they could if they had money." As I focused on the wealth I do have, I realized it was a simple thing, really, to allow contentment and gratitude to flood the dry areas of my soul that seemed linked to a sense of scarcity in the areas of money and love. It was like turning my face up and feeling a warm summer rain start to fall.

BE THANKFUL FOR WHAT YOU HAVE

One of the things that helped me to set my financial house in order was to practice gratitude for what I value in my life, beginning with my family and friends, then contemplatively looking at the other things in my life for which I am thankful and literally counting my blessings: the laughter I share with my grandchildren on our adventurous walks, the achingly beautiful view of ocean and mountains from our island home, the fact that I am a published author—a fact that still astonishes me when I walk into a bookstore and see my books on the shelf—the people whose lives I have been privileged to touch, the amazing resilience of my body, the opportunity to travel the world, and the intimate connection my husband and I have with people of many cultures.

I learned much about the virtues of thankfulness and contentment from the women in a Fijian village. I remember my surprise at the response of a friend when I enthusiastically showed her my photos. She was looking at a picture of me standing with some of the villagers outside a small tin-roofed house. We were all smiling with joy. "Oh, those poor people," she said. "What do you mean?" I asked. "Look at their clothes and that house." I laughed and told her that these villagers were in fact quite wealthy. They owned their land, had no mortgage payments, and had all they needed in abundance. They thought that *I* was poor. "Why?" she asked. I told her how the village had given me a Meki, which is a full Fijian welcome with traditional dances, gifts, a Kava ceremony, an opportunity to present The Virtues Project, and response speeches by the elders, followed by a lavish banquet. After the formal ceremony, the women led me to a house with a long woven mat spread on the floor. They had placed ample dishes of food along the full length of the mat, and we all sat around the food together and feasted. Every dish was more delicious than the last. Coconut wrapped in fresh edible leaves, papaya (which they call pawpaw), Lady Finger bananas sweeter than any I had ever tasted, plates piled with taro, fresh fish in coconut cream, and sweet, golden pineapple for dessert. As I sat with the women, we talked and laughed.

Each time I tasted a new dish, I told them how delicious it was. I said, "Now that I have tasted this delicious food that you have right here in your own garden, I'll have to live here now." An elder with very few teeth in her mouth put her head back and roared with laughter. Then she became serious and asked me, "Don't you have pineapple in your garden?" "No, Auntie, I have to buy pineapple flown to my land from another country." She shook her head sadly. "Do you have bananas in your garden?" "No, Auntie, I have to buy them flown in from South America." They asked me about each dish and shook their heads in disbelief at my poverty. They then looked at each other and seriously invited me to move to their village. To me, these are wealthy people. They need few clothes, have no heating bills, as it is always hot there, and can swim in the Pacific any time they wish. They have abundant leisure time. They call the coconut tree the "tree of life," and they use every part of it—the roots for medicine, the fronds for shade, weaving of mats, roof material and baskets, the coconuts for food and for drink, and they use the oil on their bodies. They have plenty of food, and everything they eat is grown in their gardens, harvested from the sea, or raised in their local farms. They think of themselves as wealthy, for good reason.

KEEP A PACE OF GRACE IN YOUR SPENDING

One of the simple ways I found to eliminate the tension that would develop from the "starve and binge" pattern—overrestraint leading to overspending—was to find ways to nurture myself better, to practice generosity in simple, moderate ways. This approach miraculously prevents discontent. I think of it as "responsible abundance." I now budget for small, regular indulgences that give me great pleasure rather than building up the sense of deprivation as I used to. I give myself gifts of love and appreciation, such as buying a pair of ten-dollar hand-crafted earrings at an open-air market, attending a concert, having a massage, having a picnic beside a lake or river, going to a thrift shop and finding a huge knee-length sweater to wrap around me in winter.

I now have a practice of giving myself small gifts from nature to celebrate

⊷≈⊳ The Virtue of Thankfulness ⊂≈⊷

I have learned to be content with whatever I have. —Philippians 4

Thankfulness is being grateful for what we have. It is an attitude of gratitude for learning, loving, and being. It is also being thankful for the little things that happen around us and within us every day. It is an openness and willingness to receive each of God's bounties. To be thankful is to have a sense of wonder about the beauty of this world and to welcome all of life as a gift. Thankfulness is a path to contentment.

Signs of Success

I am practicing Thankfulness when I . . .
- Have an attitude of gratitude
- Show appreciation for what others do for me
- See the difficulties of my life as opportunities to learn
- Am receptive to gifts
- Appreciate what I have instead of envying others
- Count my blessings every day

Affirmation

I am thankful for the many gifts within me and around me today. I celebrate each moment by opening myself to beauty and to learning. I expect the best.

meeting a goal. When I completed the manuscript for *A Pace of Grace*, I went for a walk on a nearby beach and found a shell that looked like an angel's wing. Its shape was a perfect expression of grace to me. It now adorns my prayer table. My husband prepared a special candlelight dinner at home, which I appreciated far more than spending on a lavish dinner. These two ways of celebrating gave me a sweet, sustainable sense of satisfaction, with no regrets. When you have little money, you can choose to think of yourself as poor or steward it wisely and think of yourself as blessed.

PRACTICE FINANCIAL JUSTICE IN YOUR FAMILY

I'd like to share one last method that I feel is very helpful in alleviating the shame-based, impulsive spending that comes from a sense of deprivation.

Couples can increase the sense of grace in their relationship by practicing financial justice, particularly if one of them is the primary homemaker and the other is seen as the breadwinner. Breadmaker, breadwinner, what's the difference? Both contribute to the capital of the family. Those who work in the home should be compensated by the family income for the services they render. Think of what it would cost to pay for a nanny, a cook, a chauffeur, or a cleaner. This person should receive a salary that both partners agree is a reasonable amount, and be paid regularly and predictably. No one should ever be demeaned by having to go to a spouse for a handout.

No matter how much or how little money you are bringing in as a family, every person should have some personal spending money to use any way he or she sees fit. Even a very modest portion of the family income is better than having to go to another adult to ask for money. Even if the primary provider is out of work, develop an informal agreement that a small amount of money will be made available for him to spend freely. It's a question of dignity. If you are single, the same principle holds true. Give yourself freedom within boundaries to spend something without having to account for it.

When my husband, Dan, and I were newly married, we had some financial challenges after relocating. Dan proposed that whoever got a job first, the other receive part of that salary, first for the work done inside the home and second for a portion to be allocated to "personal spending." This way, neither of us would feel beholden to go to the other to beg for money. We developed a percentage policy that to this day has saved us from much potential conflict. It is the rule of "Yours, Mine, and Ours." We pool a certain amount of what each of us earns into a joint account for mortgage, insurance, groceries, and other family expenses, maintaining the freedom to spend or save the rest as each of us chooses to. Each of us is responsible for our own expenditures, and I know this practice has saved us from an enormous amount of potential conflict.

TEACH YOUR CHILDREN TO SPEND WISELY

In an age when materialism constantly threatens our children's value system, we must teach them to spend wisely. A successful executive in India whom I met on my travels told me how he sets positive financial boundaries with his children. He never once said, "Money doesn't grow on trees." When his children ask for something they want to buy, such as the latest brand-name sneakers, he doesn't say, "You can't have the Gucci shoes, they're too expensive" or "We can't afford it." "That makes it sound like we're poor or that I don't care about them or that I am cheap. Rather, I say, 'Why buy a hundred-dollar pair when you could get a fifty-dollar pair now and another fifty-dollar pair in three months? Then you'll have two pairs.'"

Ellen, another parent who has clear boundaries, says, "Our clothing budget is three hundred dollars a month. It's up to you whether you want to use most of it on these shoes or get another pair more reasonably priced plus a pair of pants." My father used to say, "I'll buy you anything you need. Anything you want, we have to talk about."

I also believe children ought to do chores for free. They are full members of the family, and need to share the responsibility for the family home. Allowance should be freely given, rather than a payment for chores.

GRATITUDE: THE ANTIANXIETY REMEDY

In these troubled days, when the world no longer feels safe and when the economy is so uncertain, we have a special challenge to keep anxiety from overshadowing our lives. One of the ways to get on with our lives is through remembering to practice thankfulness throughout the day. It compels us to notice the beauty in small things, and to slow down into awareness of the gifts each day brings. I believe that when we are thankful, we create a magnetic attraction for abundance. When we are fearful, we attract further stress. The practice of gratitude is one of the best remedies to help us replace fear with trust. It is a matter of focus.

In managing my health, I find it invariably uplifting to practice gratitude every day. When I was still suffering with fatigue, I would appreciate things like the softness of the couch, the fact that I was warm and dry inside on a cold, rainy day, or that I had a good book to read, a hot supper, a friendly voice on the phone. Now I am thankful every day for the absence of fatigue and the energy I have learned to sustain through my pace of grace.

The practice of gratitude keeps a tender smile on your face, sustains your peace through the day, and serves as a magnetic source of peace for others. Others will literally be drawn to your peaceful presence.

Be content with what you have;
rejoice in the way things are.
When you realize there is nothing lacking,
the whole world belongs to you.
—Lao-tzu, Chinese mystic, founder of Taoism, 604–531 BCE

⊷⇒ EXERCISE GRACE ⇐⊶
Count Your Blessings

The following exercise will help you to initiate gratitude as a daily practice. Before you begin this practice, spend a normal day just noticing, without judgment, how many times you think a negative thought, focus on what is lacking, make a critical comment, curse what's happening, or express irritability and impatience. Just notice. Record in your journal at the end of the day what you observed, how you felt, and how your energy was affected.

Spend the next few days practicing gratitude. Begin with your journal:

1. Begin the day by reflecting on at least three things for which you are thankful. Dwell on each for a moment and let yourself imagine and appreciate each of them.

2. Ask yourself what will make this an enjoyable day of grace. Decide on how you want to structure the day or some action you can take to make it enjoyable.

3. Before you go to bed, journal three things for which you were grateful today.

4. Once each hour, notice something you are thankful for—the speed of your computer, the sandwich in your hand, the friend by your side, a laugh with a colleague, the sweet smell of your child after a bath.

5. Speak words of appreciation and encouragement. Use the Language of Virtues to acknowledge the kindness or helpfulness or courage of a child, a friend, an employee, a coworker, or yourself.

6. Record in your journal how these gratitude practices affected your emotions and your energy.

SUMMARY OF CHAPTER 6:
HEAL YOUR FINANCES

- Honestly assess your financial habits. Do they drain you or sustain you?
- Overspending is a sign of discontent with what God provides. It is a statement that you are not enough and your life is not enough.
- Clear up your finances. Make more money and/or spend less money.
- Reevaluate and revise your picture of your true wealth. What are the real valuables in your life?
- Practice thankfulness every day. Count your blessings.
- Establish a pace of grace in your spending. Practice responsible abundance. It will help you eliminate erratic, unconscious habits that lead to debt.
- Be generous to yourself. Indulge in small, lovely gifts.
- Practice financial justice. Establish a salary for the partner who works at home.
- Whatever you have, provide personal freedom to each person to spend a small percentage as they see fit.
- The "Yours, Mine, and Ours" accounting approach can prevent conflict.
- Daily gratitude helps to heal anxiety.

The next chapter focuses on how to sustain gratitude and develop a whole new possibility for abundance by transforming the space around you.

-◦⟹ SEVEN ⟸◦-
Create a Space of Grace

*Have nothing in your home that you do not know to be useful
or believe to be beautiful.*
—William Morris, designer

I can't tell you when the journey through the FOG of Fatigue, Overwhelm, and Guilt became fascinating to me. It just happened. Each day that I had the energy to move a little further in practicing the Ten Rules for Health, my awareness became a little clearer. It was like walking along a mist-shrouded forest path, coming upon occasional clearings where the brilliance of the light warmed my soul. In one of these clearings, where I reflected on what was stressing me and what was blessing me, I realized that the soul-satisfying process of spiritual housecleaning had deepened my capacity and my need for orderliness around me.

As I began to regain my strength and was able once again to think and work energetically, I discerned something niggling at my mind—I needed my home to *look* the way I felt. Once this thought broke through into awareness, I developed a craving for my home to be cleaner and clearer.

MAKE A SPACE FOR GRACE

All the abundance writers say that clutter obstructs wealth, and that one of the best ways to attract the new in your life is to clear out the old. They tell us to make space for a richer life, a better job, or a more beautiful wardrobe. For me, making a space of grace was an essential step in creating a more complete sense of grace in my life.

The mindful practice of virtues is our true wealth, and it brings bountiful returns as we live more kindly, speak more tactfully, and love more gently. It gives us a taste for the good life in its truest and most meaningful sense. As we live more consciously we develop a natural longing to have our outer environment match our growing sense of inner peace and well-being. Creating a space of grace becomes a need rather than a vague wish to someday clean up the place.

The Virtue of Order

Thus saith the Lord. Set thy house in order. —1 Kings 20

Orderliness means being neat and living with a sense of harmony. When we are orderly, we have a place for things we use and keep them there so that we can use them whenever we need to. It means planning something so that it works, doing something step by step, and staying on track, instead of going in circles. Being orderly makes it easier to accomplish things. When we appreciate the order of creation, we can see the beauty and harmony of all living things.

Signs of Success

I am practicing Orderliness when I . . .

- Have a place to put each of my things
- Put my things away in the same place every time
- Have a plan before I start any job
- Solve problems step by step
- Create a harmonious space that brings peace to my soul
- Appreciate the beauty and order of God's creation

Affirmation

I live this day with order. I do things step by step. I create beauty and harmony in my space and in my life.

Setting our home or work area in order not only reflects inner order and beauty—it *creates* them. When we are stressed or distressed by events beyond our control, including world crises over which we feel helpless, the act of creating a clean, gracious environment gives us a bower of peace—a sense that all is right with the world, at least in our small corner.

It may be that creating a space of grace around you may be the most natural starting point for a positive life change. Wherever you choose to begin the process of purifying your life of what is cluttering it and impeding your natural peace is a fine starting place.

One of the advantages—and disadvantages—of being ill is that we have a license to procrastinate, to postpone housecleaning and mundane tasks indefinitely. "Leave the dust," one post-polio phone buddy told me. "Your first priority has to be your health." Easier said than done as I coped with an occasional once-over performed cheerily by my husband, for whom vacuuming—or "super-sucking" as he proudly calls it—meant the job was done.

As my energy supply gradually refilled, I developed an acute awareness of the things that drained it—talking too long on the phone, waiting too long before taking a rest, and above all, the clutter in my house. It wasn't enough to have a room neat and relatively clean. I literally felt weighed down by the physical clutter lurking above my head in the attic and surrounding me in cupboards and drawers.

In the hectic pace of life most of us now keep, we have little time for basic maintenance. This creates further stress. Unpaid or misplaced bills, overstuffed closets, desk detritus, piles of papers and files, and unpacked boxes are among the countless energy drains we tend to accumulate in our homes. They become black holes of worry and guilt, continually leaking mental and emotional energy.

Ask for Help

As I began to move beyond survival mode, my craving for order, simplicity, and cleanliness kept increasing. I realized that clutter was a huge drain on my energy, a block to peace in my spirit. The battle with fatigue leaves one fragile, and I knew this was hardly the time to roll up my sleeves and dig into spring cleaning. Yet who else could make the hundreds of little decisions about what would be tossed and what would remain?

As I pondered how to move forward with the daunting task of clearing my house, a friend fortuitously mentioned a woman named Jane, who was an interior design consultant specializing in feng shui. Feng shui (pronounced fung shway) is the ancient Chinese art of balancing the elements in one's space for optimal harmony and energy flow. It offers methods of attracting abundance and sustaining peace. Although quite a complex system, feng shui contains some simple principles that I found easy to apply, even as a novice committed to not taking on a new body of knowledge.

Those few hours of consultation with Jane were one of the best investments I have ever made. As we walked through the house, she shared with me a fantastic secret—a vital key to recovering from an energy disease or an overstressed lifestyle—namely, identifying what blocks the flow of "chi," or energy, in our environment. It had to do with how the furniture was arranged, the number of items in a room, or on surfaces, the way colors were used, the setup of my home office. She pointed out that repainting the living room walls in a warmer shade of white, with rose rather than gray tones, would change the quality of light in the room and make it a warmer space.

A friend of mine who is order-challenged, particularly in her home office, invited a friend who is naturally orderly to come to her home and help her clear and reorganize. She paid her by the hour, and both women felt deeply satisfied by the results of just one day of using a fresh eye and a listening ear to discover the best system for my friend to use for her files and work area.

Because so many of us have full lives these days and still want and need an orderly environment, many professional organizers now offer services to help reorganize our homes, tool area, shop, or help us move. They can help us to shovel out and start afresh. (Online resources for helping you organize can be found at www.clutterbug.net/help/.)

CLEAR A NATURAL PATH

Jane showed me a few easy actions that immediately increased the flow of chi in a room, such as rearranging the living room furniture. With her help, it took only a few minutes and it looked and felt like a new room. I could hardly believe how different the room felt when the light increased by moving a chest from in front of a window. By moving the couch facing our fireplace back a foot, we cleared the natural path to easily walk through the room. There were other simple things, like peeling off the busy wallpaper border of chickens on weather vanes, with which the previous owner had enthusiastically decorated the top and bottom of every wall. I had been plotting a huge "chicken barbecue" with my friends for two years, but my husband liked the chicken borders, especially their Wedgwood blue color. He had reluctantly agreed to replace them with another pattern in blue when we could find one, but at the moment we were at an impasse. So I had to be moderate, and if the truth be told, a bit surreptitious. I gleefully peeled off the chicken borders flanking our entryway and hallway passing the bedrooms. It took about ten minutes. I immediately felt an opening up of the space, as if a canal of energy had been blocked and was now released. Mercifully, my husband said nothing.

With her practiced eye, Jane spotted a round table, pressed onto us magnanimously by friends, which I had absolutely no place for, so had shoved into a corner and adorned with knickknacks, which I don't particularly like having around. The table was custom-made and quite valuable, pedestal-based, with a tooled leather top. I didn't feel it matched anything in our rather contemporary living room. Yet Jane's eyes lit up when she saw it. She showed me that it was the perfect size for a dining room table and needed only a beveled glass top to serve the purpose. She gave me the number of a glass supplier nearby, and a few weeks later we had a new and admittedly very handsome and unique dining room table.

I took copious notes as Jane talked, and of course created a nice fresh file for them and placed it in my Home and Family file drawer so I'd be able to find it later, when energy permitted further steps to reorganize my home. The greatest gift of her visit was that it upended my resistance and gave me hope.

BEFRIEND YOUR RESISTANCE

It is helpful to admit and gently acknowledge the resistance that keeps us from taking this step to clean and clear the spaces around us. When we recognize the Teachable Moment and call on the gentle observer instead of the internal critic, it makes all the difference.

We can come up with so many reasons to procrastinate or relinquish entirely the need to create order in our homes and workplaces. For those of us suffering with energy challenges—and I believe that is the great majority of us these days!—the notion of tackling the physical clutter in our lives can be utterly daunting. The very idea exhausts us. We just can't imagine finding the time or the energy to attempt it.

Another source of resistance is the denigration of the role of cleaning—linked in our minds with menial, devalued work. Individuals who are the most stressed and busy easily rationalize its place at the bottom of their priority list. Many men resist orderliness as a feminine trait, though I have known men—my father and my husband included—who keep their tools and work areas in pristine order.

We may understand in the abstract that order will sustain our energy and chaos will continue to drain it, depriving us of a sense of grace in our own homes. Yes, yes, yes. We've heard it all before. We associate it with the most boring aspects of life, with memories of being forced to "clean up your mess" by our parents when we were younger and had far more interesting things to do on a Saturday morning. I hated it when my parents blithely told me "A messy room means a messy mind." They probably tossed this off as a motivational comment while, in truth, this belief seeped deep into my sense of myself. It was time to reclaim my natural innate virtue of orderliness!

LET GO OF HOPELESSNESS

The judgments we have internalized about ourselves—our beliefs that we are inherently disorganized—are the most painful form of resistance to setting our house in order. A friend of mine had a defining moment that helped her cut through her clutter guilt. She works very long hours, driving hundreds of miles a week bringing services to the elderly in their homes. One Saturday morning, she was feeling an old familiar despair over the chaos of her cluttered home. Once again, she could not find the motivation or the energy to get off the couch and get to it, feeling that all she could do was to restore her energy by resting. She began to pray her shame and her hopelessness. She heard Spirit say, "I am the God of chaos too." She felt a quiet acceptance, which released her from her paralysis of will. Often a small shift in the spirit makes all the difference. Creating a space of grace around us is meant to be a guilt-free exercise, not sourced in shame, but in self-care.

My own limiting belief that I was inherently unable to cope with my own chaos—scripted by labels I received as a child—dissolved in a new awareness that creating order and beauty were a gift I could give myself. After Jane's visit, the lightness of mind and the sheer joy I experienced when walking into the clear, open feeling of my beautifully arranged living room overtook my resistance. I realized that in light of my new commitment to energy conservation, it would be very costly to neglect this aspect of life. I found that the returns in terms of renewed energy and well-being were enormous.

Cleaning and clearing our environment literally creates a space of grace. Beauty and order in our environment create a continual flow of the chi of well-being and peace, restoring our physical and spiritual energy. Being in a harmonious space with colors that nurture us and things we love around us, with the clutter gone, stimulates and affirms our internal sense of order and peace.

MAKE A START

The key to managing this project of purifying your space is to not take on too much at once. Unless you can afford a cleanup crew to come in, which would be wonderful, you are like most of us and have to do it yourself. Clear the clutter one small area at a time. It might be a drawer you open all the time, or the stove, or your bathroom. Make this one small area as clean and perfectly orderly as you want it to be, and let it serve as your beacon of hope. The day I came to terms with my need for a financially sustainable practice, one of the first things I did was to clean my stove top, which bothered me every time I used it. I spent thirty minutes scrubbing, inserting fresh shiny burner liners, and removing every spot and fingerprint from our microwave above the stove. When I finished, the stove and microwave were gleaming. Every time I walked into the kitchen, it was a reminder of my power to make changes for the better.

BEGIN WITH SURFACES

I found that there were levels to the cleaning and reorganizing process. I thought of level one as the surface of things, and level two as what is inside drawers and closets. The best starting point is a room in which you spend a lot of time. Begin by clearing the most visible space, such as tops of dressers rather than drawers or closets. Being able to walk into the room and see a new, harmonious order creates the encouragement needed to tackle the less visible levels of detail.

Don't just sweep it all into the top drawer either. Place all the things that are "out" and need to be sorted in bags or boxes to deal with later. Then, spend some contemplative time arranging the room just as you want it. Play with the arrangement. Sit back and reflect on how you need it to be. I spent an hour listening to slow jazz and gazing at the things I had on my mantelpiece. I took away several things and found that there were five things left, which seemed the right number. Each was very special: a raku bird, gifted to me by the staff when I left my job as spiritual care director at the hospice; a small Native American vessel with a phoenix carved on it my husband had received as a gift; a silver mobile of gulls that moved gently with each air current; and two other gifts received in our travels. I was surprised to realize that all of them were birds. The painting over our mantel is of two soaring gulls over sunlit waves washing onto a beach, gifted to my husband and me by our beloved friend Carol Evans, a Canadian artist, who said she thought of us when she painted it.

Just having the room clean and clear, despite the still bulging cupboards on either side of the mantel, gave me peace. I was going for the first level of order, and trusted I would get to the next when energy allowed.

Organize with a Pace of Grace

I have learned that the fear of tackling the chaos creates far more wasted energy than getting to it. Once I had some small successes with feng shui, and my living room looked beautiful to me, I was filled with righteous enthusiasm for this once daunting task. I also realized that I had to keep a pace of grace with it, or I'd end up flat on my back. I looked again at the Ten Rules for Health and a small phrase in one of the rules stood out. The seventh rule was:

Rule 7: Pursue Peaceful Activity

Cut television down. It depresses you. Read what comes to you. Listen to music, clear and clean in small ways, watch the fire, write letters to your friends.

"Clear and clean in small ways" sounded doable and the best way to start with what I now call level two cleaning. I love a clean, sparkly bathroom so the surfaces usually shine. However, the drawers are another story. I began with the drawer I use most often, the top bathroom vanity drawer, in which I keep things I use every day. It was overstuffed, and I habitually rummaged to find things—very "dis-feng-tional," as my husband and I have come to call it. Every time I opened that drawer, it emitted little whiffs of shame and guilt, but this time I was ready for it. First, I put on the earphones to my portable CD player and turned on some cleaning music—what I need for cleaning inspiration is modern gospel singers, such as BeBe and CeCe Winans or Mary Mary. I was immediately energized. I took everything out, placed them in categories, and tossed out the small bottles containing infinitesimal amounts of old lotion and anything else I wasn't using. I washed and dried the drawer thoroughly, and then placed things that belonged together in each section of a newly purchased plastic divider tray. This job that had hung over me like Poe's pendulum for about three years took me twelve minutes! The drawer has remained clean and orderly, and was a wonderful first choice for my cleaning safari, providing a daily reminder that order is indeed possible. It is amazing how one success sustains energy and hope for the rest of the job.

BEAUTY BEGETS ORDER

I remember the best gift my mother ever gave me. When I returned from camp at thirteen, she had a surprise for me. She had completely redecorated my room. She had painted the walls white and had sewn a lavender floral chintz bedspread, with a pale lavender dust ruffle, and matching dressing table skirt and curtains. She said, "Linda, you're a woman now and you deserve the beauty of a woman's room." Other teens might prefer to decorate their own rooms, but I found my mother's act of nurturance stunningly meaningful. Until that point my room had been in total chaos and clutter. Afterward, I kept it clean and neat.

My friend Pam offered to help her daughter realize her dream of a room all in blue, with a seascape theme, complete with waves on her walls. Together, they planned each detail.

When we discern and create our own vision of beauty in a room, the desire to keep it in order follows naturally.

David, a retired physician living with chronic fatigue syndrome, turned a tiny room in the wonderful old house he shares with his wife, Susan, into his personal haven. He built a wooden bed in the shape of a boat. On it is an antique quilt in reds and blues. A simple border of ships adorns the walls, and he handpainted a starry night sky on his ceiling. He has boyhood treasures arrayed on his dresser and a neat bookshelf with his favorite books. He naturally keeps his sanctuary immaculate. Su has a bower of her own in an upstairs room full of light, decorated by her own award-winning quilts. They both sing the praises of having their own rooms, and tiptoeing up or down the stairs when they want to be together.

CONTAIN TO SUSTAIN

I will be forever grateful to Julie Morgenstern, the organizing guru, whom I first saw on television during this time when I was seeking ways to purify my life and my environment. She spoke of a simple formula for creating and sustaining order called SPACE—an acronym for Sort, Purge, Assign, Containerize, and Equalize. I went out and got her book, *Organizing from the Inside Out*, to read more about it. She offers very practical, step-by-step recommendations on how to tackle even the most daunting mess. This is the first approach I have ever found to be both simple and sustainable. A closet I treated with Julie's advice has remained clutter-free for several years.

It works like this:

1. **Sort** things into three piles: Throw away, give away, put away. Have large plastic bags or boxes for the first two.

2. **Purge** by throwing away and giving away what you no longer want to keep. Keep only what is useful or beautiful. If you haven't worn an outfit for ten years, it is probably time to detach from it. Lighten your load, and simplify your life.

3. **Assign** each item a place—a home to which you will consistently return it. This discipline, whether it is a regular assigned spot in a suitcase, purse, briefcase, or a drawer, a hook for keys, or a file holder for homework, is hugely helpful in finding what you need quickly.

4. **Containerize:** This is the fun part! Once you have selected the things you want to keep, give some thought to containers—baskets, plastic tubs, decorated boxes, filing cabinets, hooks for the back of closet doors for hats, color-coded files, hanging file containers. I especially love the word "contain." It's a comforting word and a gracious practice. It keeps your house in order.

5. **Equalize** means to do daily maintenance to *keep* things in their place. It is taking ten minutes at the end of your workday to clear off your desk and put files away, so you come in to a clear desk in the morning; putting your personal items back in the same place in your briefcase or purse every time; using the container you have assigned for homework, keys, and other things you need quickly in the morning. All these practices of orderliness create peaceful pleasure.

Before I began using the SPACE plan, my purse used to drive me mad. It had eight different compartments, but I could never remember what went where. When I started disciplining myself to assign the same things to the same places after deciding what lived with what, I could find my keys and sunglasses blindfolded.

Choose the Right Containers

For me, finding the right containers is a delightful part of the process of reorganizing. Choose containers that you will enjoy looking at. Take your time to shop for them. When I first shopped for containers, I went mad over clear plastic tubs. I found them just right for storing sweaters, purses, winter gloves, and scarves on a closet shelf. However, I discovered that for my office shelves, they were distracting. Seeing all my office supplies piled together on the shelves, albeit neatly within their containers, was overwhelming. If there is anywhere I need a sense of simplicity, it is my office. I realized I needed things put away in drawers or in baskets on shelves to give me a sense of peace.

My husband eventually bought me stackable opaque plastic boxes that I covered with decoupage—pictures cut from magazines or attractive wrapping paper pasted onto the boxes. I also brought out my South Pacific shell collection and used my hot glue gun to attach them to the fronts of the boxes. This enjoyable, peaceful activity continues to serve as gentle recreation and an ongoing beautification process for my office.

Grace Your Children with Containment

My children grew up without very clear boundaries about neatness. I had been so shamed about messiness by my own parents, I went into "opposititis" with my two sons, not wanting to burden their wee souls. There was one boundary I did have though, and amazingly they seemed to revel in it. They were allowed to build "forts" in the living room with all the pillows and blankets in the house, plus assorted bits of furniture, on the condition that everything be put back in its place immediately when playing fort was over for the day. Yet I did not apply this awareness to their bedroom, which was always a disaster area. I even allowed them to draw on the walls, because "any day now" I was planning to put in new wallpaper. When I married Dan, a graduate of West Point and an inherently tidy man, they were ten and thirteen. At one point we were renting a house that was up for sale, knowing it was a temporary arrangement. The owners told us it had to be clean and orderly each day so that it could be shown to potential buyers.

Dan drew up a contract for all of us to sign. We had a rule that the Inspector (Dan) would confiscate anything left on the floor after 8 A.M. and place it in a closet. To retrieve the item would cost extra chores, or money that would go into a family fun fund. The boys found this idea delightful. Dan then did something that touched me. Knowing my older son had difficulties with Attention Deficit, Dan bought him two gifts that helped make the morning cleaning simple for him—a wicker trunk, into which he could easily scoop all his detritus, as well as a duvet that made it easy to make his bed. My son felt so proud as he stood ready for inspection. The house was immaculate on a daily basis. This was far from soul-destroying. This simple practice of self-discipline was a gift to all of us, and quite a Teachable Moment for me as a mother. Giving children the means to contain their things is an excellent way to help keep their own space orderly and peaceful.

MAKE FILES, NOT PILES

One of the most daunting sources of Fatigue, Overwhelm, and Guilt for me was the failure to file. My new mantra is: "Make files, not piles." When I do, a sweet righteous feeling of self-confidence fills me. I love having client information, legal documents, and bills at my fingertips. I call my habitual accumulated mass of general unknown entities "the lump." It consists of small items jumbled in a pile with important legal papers or unopened letters. When I allow the lump to grow, FOG accumulates along with the mess. Not being able to find things is chronically time-consuming and creates stressful anxiety. When I take the small amount of time required to neaten as I go at a pace of grace, it brings a quiet joy to the work.

MAINTAIN ORDER AT A PACE OF GRACE

I have found that only when I keep a pace of grace can I successfully equalize, as Julie Morgenstern calls it. Taking just ten minutes to put things away and clear my desktop makes a world of difference the next morning. When I am rushed, I have a much harder time putting things away. The occasional times I am unable to keep my pace of grace because of being too tightly scheduled, I pile things into a tray. However, as soon as possible, I return to my pace of grace and replace things in their assigned home. I *want* to do it, and enjoy doing it, because I know it makes all the difference to my peace of mind. I really applaud Julie Morgenstern for her discerning principles for simplifying the way we relate to our things. It has made a world of difference to me.

> *God is in the details.*
> —(A popular saying used by the architect Ludwig Mies van der Rohe, attributed to Gustave Flaubert, a nineteenth-century French novelist)

FIND YOUR RADIANT POINT

At a conference in Salt Lake City in 1994, I met a woman who had a foundation called the Glory of Home. She told me of the power of the "radiant point." This point is something we possess that fits our lives perfectly, and is the standard of beauty against which we measure all other things in our homes. It could be an outfit that we love to wear, a leather folder, or a piece of pottery. Her recommendation was that gradually we align all our other possessions with this radiant point, bringing everything to the same standard of value and letting go of anything that we do not love as much or find as useful. That notion has never left me. We are quietly energized by things we love. Holding an ideal to keep only what is useful and beautiful around us is a goal worthy of effort.

HAVE A SHOPPING SPREE IN YOUR CLOSET

One day I was packing for a trip and feeling restless about my clothes, dissatisfied with my outfits for the trip. I was also in austerity mode and didn't want to go out and just buy more. Too often I buy something hurriedly, and then never wear it after putting it on at home and finding it doesn't really look right in my own mirror.

I decided to go shopping in my closet. I arranged everything by colors and discovered I had some delightful new mix-and-match outfits I had never put together before. I cleared out what I hadn't worn for a year and put it in my giveaway bag.

This process exhilarated me. I felt rich and fortunate to have lovely, color-coordinated clothes, some of which were years old—my "classics." Just opening my closet door gave me a flush of pleasure rather than the old clutter shame. Taking time to clear and classify is an excellent way to create new order in your closets. Level two cleaning is deeply satisfying, like a righteous secret.

Your Living Space Can Be Simply Beautiful

Moving is an excellent time to clear out what is less than useful or beautiful from your possessions. When you arrive at your new home, you will have a new incentive to create order, knowing that you are putting away only what you consider truly yours.

I find it so pleasing to the eye and the heart to live sparely. One of my deepest pleasures has been to visit my friend Boo at her wilderness cabin in northern British Columbia each summer. Boo furnished the cabin with only what she needed. She kept it spare, yet there were touches of beauty in the special driftwood pieces she found to grace the window ledges. Beneath the row of windows facing the lake is a window seat along the full length of the wall, graced by a colorful cushion in a bright print. Beneath the window seat she stored homemade wooden boxes with rope pulls that could easily be slid out from under the window seat. In each box were related items—tools in one, paper goods and balls of string in another, candles and so on. She never wasted anything, and she stored them as treasures that she could lay her hands on when she needed them. The order and simplicity of the cabin itself gave me as much pleasure as the mountain vistas reflected in the lake outside the cabin windows.

Creating a space of grace restores our energy and gives us a bower of strength and calm. The very practice of order is balm to our souls. When we clean, clear, and beautify, we experience a sustained sense of grace. We are actively removing the message that our lives are overwhelming, unmanageable, and out of control. Clearing our surroundings is an essential part of a sustainable life, because beauty and order calm the soul and allow energy to flow.

Order and simplification are the first steps toward the mastery
of a subject—the actual enemy is the unknown.
—Thomas Mann

⊷⊜ EXERCISE GRACE ⊜⊷
Create a Perfect Room

First, choose your favorite room—one that you feel would nurture your spirit most if you arranged it exactly as you need it to be. Let it become your touchstone of beauty for the rest of your home. Make a simple plan for redesigning your room and take a first step.

- What does your space tell you about yourself?
- Which of your personal virtues would you like your space to represent?
- What colors do you need in this space?
- What about your space restores your spirit?
- What can you do to make it what you need it to be?
- What help do you need for this to happen?

SUMMARY OF CHAPTER 7: CREATE A SPACE OF GRACE

- Disorder can be very draining. Creating order sustains energy.
- Get the help you need to set your house (or work area) in order.
- Clear a natural path through your living and working space. It will open up the chi, or energy, in the room.
- Dispel your resistance by detaching from your belief that you are innately disorderly. Reclaim your natural orderliness.
- Make a start. Begin with outer surfaces. Put one small area in perfect order or cleanliness. It will inspire you to keep at it.
- Keep a pace of grace as you peacefully reorganize. Enjoy it!
- Make your space beautiful. Order will follow. Dare to be creative.
- I recommend Julie Morgenstern's SPACE formula: Sort, Purge, Assign, Containerize, and Equalize. Have fun choosing just the right containers.
- Give children containers. It will motivate them to keep their own spaces in order.

- Make files, not piles. Take the time to clear your work space each day.
- Find your radiant point, your ideal outfit or something of beauty to be the standard of what you would like to have in your closet and your home.
- Take a shopping trip in your closet. As you reorganize, keep only the things you love.
- Simplicity can be beautiful. Often, less is more.

Now that we've explained the many ways to purify ourselves, in Part Two: Pace Yourself we'll explore healthy ways to relate to time as a means of conserving our energy and sustaining a true pace of grace.

Pace Yourself

Every day is a good day.
So it is revealed in every culture,
every faith . . .
We humans are set up to take
life, death, and everything for
that matter,
day by day.
There's something about a day—
just long enough to gain
wisdom in;
just short enough not to over-
whelm us with its immensity.
A day is the perfect unit of and
for faith.
—Aaron Zerah,
The Soul's Almanac

EIGHT

Create a Pace of Grace

Moderation is the silken string running through the pearl chain of all virtues.
—Joseph Hall

Every day is a good day. Wouldn't it be lovely if before sleep each night we could say wholeheartedly this has been a good day? When we are suffering from fatigue, overwhelm, or guilt, it is hard to trust this simple possibility. Before I gleaned the gifts of my illness, I confess that at the end of each working day it felt more like I had been running in a marathon and had once again failed to finish. After post-polio hit, I had days of fatigue after which I simply felt used up for no particular purpose, which was even more depressing. I remember lying on the couch one day when it seemed almost too much of an effort to breathe. I could not imagine having the energy to move or work ever again. The notion of resuming our world travels seemed as remote as the farthest star.

After the Ten Rules were given to me, it was like learning to live again at an entirely different pace. I also discovered that it is life-giving and energizing not to waste time being unhappy about a particular day. When I experience contentment with my energy level and my capacity to do things—or not—it keeps my soul on an even keel.

Time is one of our most valuable, nonrenewable resources. A life of grace requires us to manage it mindfully. This chapter will help you to explore your own stewardship of time, to discern your own rhythm of sustainability, to find your balance. It involves a gentle shift into a lifestyle of grace that will not only sustain you spiritually and physically but will also help you to be—dare I say it?—more productive.

When you relax into the virtues of moderation, peacefulness, and contentment, you will find that you no longer digress into scattered, anxious multitasking. Thus, the energy you spend working on whatever task is before you will be far more purposeful and focused.

After I began to practice the Ten Rules for Health, my faith in the goodness of each day was gradually restored. Little by little, day by day, I was able to emerge from total exhaustion and begin to have the energy to walk, to work, to cook a meal. Now I have abundant energy, and I can trust it to be there as long as I continue to practice the rules for health—as long as I refill my cup *before* it empties.

As I recovered I found that of the Ten Rules, the one that seemed to have the greatest impact on my energy was the concept of pacing—to detect my own energy cycle, and rest proactively, as suggested in the fourth and fifth rules for health:

Rule 4: Proactive Rest

Take two rests each day. Do it as a routine. Stop *before* you get tired.

Rule 5: Pace Yourself

You have four hours a day for work, sometimes six. Choose carefully. Keep your correspondence current. Enjoy! Enjoy!

Rest. Pace yourself. Choose well. Enjoy your time. What radical ideas these were for me when I first received them. Yet of all the Ten Rules, these two simple practices have made the greatest difference in sustaining my energy and my peace every day.

Be a Good Steward

Being a good steward of the time and energy we are given is essential to sustaining a graceful life. Of all the elements required in healing an energy illness or an overwhelming lifestyle, I have come to believe that the most vital is the willingness to discern and then sustain our pace of grace. This means that rest must become as much a priority and part of our routine as meals, exercise, and other basic measures we take to sustain ourselves day to day. I often tell audiences of the three R's of energy conservation: Rest, Rest, and Rest.

Can you imagine taking guilt-free naps? At first, I was reluctant to make rest—and two rests a day at that—part of my daily routine. I had associated naps with a wimpy kind of indigence and indulgence. Now I think of them as delicious, diligent, and delightful. I have seen how rest has restored my energy a hundredfold, and also, as it happens, increased my productivity.

Energy is like water in a cup. When it is drained, it must be refilled. The pandemic practice of overdoing has put millions of people at risk of being drained so often and so much that they end up becoming ill with fatigue and stress. I be-

lieve this is a form of needless suffering. We make this choice, but there is
another way to live.

Just as we have the choice to create order and grace in our homes by
eliminating clutter, a powerful way to
reinvigorate ourselves physically and
spiritually is by learning to pace ourselves. Energy conservation is the main
ingredient in coping with the stress of

*We have to believe in free will.
We've got no choice.*
—Isaac Bashevis Singer, author

daily demands. It is the sine qua non of restoring energy when life or illness has
exhausted us. Good stewardship of our energy is also the most important step in
the *prevention* of burnout. To conserve our energy, all we have to do is regulate
the flow and eliminate excess.

If I repeat myself, it is because without this practice of pacing, all the other
energy-restoration practices will fail. Most individuals resist this simple truth
that we must undertake rest and restoration with vigilance, or no matter how
faithfully we follow the other rules for health, recovery from the FOG of Fatigue,
Overwhelm, and Guilt will be utterly impossible.

WHY WE AVOID REST

For a number of reasons I have found proactive rest to be not only the most
significant step in creating a sustainable lifestyle but also the most challenging.
First, the notion of a slower, less intense pace flies in the face of the collective
worship of consumerism—the compulsion of our age to have "more" and the
driven, multitasking lifestyle that we have somehow come to venerate. We ro-
manticize excess as a sign of success, despite the fact that it is destroying our peace,
our health, and above all our contentment with the simple joys life has to offer.
Even on our days off we face an enormous array of cultural, recreational, and
volunteer possibilities. Too often we are busy, but we are not happy.

When meeting with community leaders in a small, slow-paced island nation
in the South Pacific, I asked them to share their greatest challenges. I heard the
same answer from every one of them that I have heard from busy executives in
major cities. The deputy minister of health and director of nursing (who was
also in charge of cleaning services and food services for the hospital!) said that

lack of time was her greatest challenge. I had drawn four circles on a board representing the priorities for care that give us the greatest energy: self being the inner circle, then family, then the workplace, then the community. "I have it all inside out," she said. "My priorities are work, which serves the community, then family, and last myself. I'm always exhausted, with too much to do. So I never get to self-care. I have to admit I'm burning out."

I have also encountered resistance to regular rest in individuals with severe energy illnesses. Sachi, a former marathon runner and mother of a ten-year-old daughter, has myasthenia gravis. She is so often laid low by exhaustion, unable to do anything productive, that when she has even a faint increase in energy she pushes herself to "accomplish something." After attending a Pace of Grace workshop, Sachi enforced a routine of rest, and found that her energy supply increased exponentially.

A few years ago, radical Brazilian educator Paulo Freire was attending a conference of Midwestern political activists and heard constant remarks about how overwhelmed people felt about the duties they faced each day. Finally, he rose to his feet and, in slow, heavily accented English, declared, "We are bigger than our schedules." The audience roared with applause.

One of the blessings of these uncertain times is that many of us have been shocked out of complacency about this unbearable lifestyle. We are making the radical choice to become the architects of our own time, and to seek a sustainable balance for ourselves every day. In the aftermath of September 11, we've come to a dawning awareness of the preciousness of life. I personally know dozens of individuals and couples who decided to take that trip they had been saving for, or who sat down and said, "What do we really want out of life?" Some have changed their work hours in an effort to live more mindfully, with more moderation instead of more money, and in search of contentment rather than consumption. They possess a deeper willingness to accept what each day brings and to let go of what doesn't get done.

FIND YOUR FLOW

I discovered the joy of tennis in my thirties, after a lifetime of believing I was a sports klutz because of some early teasing and the awkwardness I felt after polio left me with scoliosis. I was an accomplished dancer before I had polio at the age of eleven, but even after a year of physiotherapy to bring me back to walking and moving normally again, I lacked the confidence to play sports of any kind. When I was in my thirties, our family moved to Hilton Head Island, South Carolina, one of America's tennis capitals, and I became an avid spectator. One afternoon, I was watching Australian player Evonne Goolagong in a match against Billy Jean King. Evonne seemed to be in a state of total bliss, as if she was doing an intricate yet flowing dance, always back to center after each fluid movement. It was irresistible. I had to learn to play. I became a dedicated and fairly adept player, joined a women's league and played in tournaments. I even practiced in a court next to Evonne from time to time. Far more confident at this stage of life, I wasn't concerned about how I would look, I just wanted to share in that bliss I had witnessed. I discovered the feeling of "flow"—the still point in the midst of chaos, the suspension of all distractions, being fully and utterly in the moment—just my breath, the ball, and the racket as an extension of my body. It was exhilarating!

Twenty years later, when polio impacted my life for the second time, I discovered a new dimension to that flow. It occurred when I had recovered sufficiently from post-polio fatigue to once again accept international speaking invitations. It is also the story of how I received the title for this book. Although I had been practicing the Ten Rules of Health for nearly a year, and was feeling much better, I had kept myself off the speakers' circuit for months. The nightmare of my last keynote talk lingered. I burned with embarrassment every time I remembered standing, shaking with fatigue, in front of several hundred managers and staff from companies such as General Motors, Kraft Foods, and USWest. For some reason, the speaker's podium and the stage lighting was on one level and the overhead projector with my slides could only be accessed by a set of detached, rickety steps down, with no railing to hold on to. The silence went on and on as I left the microphone and tottered up and down the steps over and over. My mind blanked out the talk I had prepared, and I practically fell off the stage with humiliation and exhaustion. The worst part was that my brilliant, vibrant husband was my cospeaker, yet I didn't have the presence of mind to step aside gracefully and let him carry on! I just soldiered through my half of the talk. Almost a year later, I e-mailed the organization an offer I thought they couldn't refuse, explaining I had been ill, and offering to speak at another conference gratis. Their silence was deafening.

After a year, I felt well enough to consider getting gently back on the circuit, yet I had huge concerns about whether I could speak with my old energy, much less be able to facilitate an intensive Virtues Project workshop of several days.

The first opportunity my husband and I accepted was a tour in the South Pacific for several weeks, including a five-day Virtues Project Facilitator Training in Rarotonga, Cook Islands. I knew we would be working with government leaders as well as villagers, some of them with strong English and some with little—a challenge under the best of circumstances. On the first morning, before departing for the venue, I expressed my fears in prayer. I asked, "How will I be able to sustain my energy and offer excellence to these people? You know I can hardly stand for more than a few minutes." I heard in response, "Keep a pace of grace." I felt a tingling sensation in my body as I wrote these words in my journal and contemplated them for several minutes. I spoke them aloud so I could hear them. I felt a peace come over me and knew I was ready.

This seminar turned out to be the most seamless one I had ever given. Instead of pushing the agenda along so that participants would perfect their understanding of The Virtues Project strategies, I flowed with their receptivity. Laughter and tears flowed too, as participants received deep awareness of the virtues as their inner gifts. While I took time during the lunch break to rest on the mattress I had asked the coordinators to provide, all the participants were free to rest as well. Later on the tour, in countries such as Australia, where my husband and I had presented virtues seminars many times, I received feedback from one of our facilitators, who had often seen me present before, that the quality of my speaking and teaching had deepened and become "more graceful." As Dan said to the participants, "You don't have to get it right, you just have to get it." Instead of pressuring participants to get it all and have instant facility with the Five Strategies of The Virtues Project, I understood for the first time the value of their experiencing the message of virtues at a deep level. Not only was I sustaining myself through a pace of grace—I was nurturing those I was teaching!

Whatever we are doing, there is a state of flow. Whether we are making love, making a meal, negotiating a contract, teaching a class, or doing our best to live through a day of fatigue, finding our own pace of grace allows us to enter a state of flow.

SEEK PRISTINE MOMENTUM

I once asked a young man of seventeen what it was about skateboarding that made it his passion. He closed his eyes, smiled rapturously and said, "It's the pristine momentum."

Momentum is hardly a state that one who is bogged down with fatigue would ever hope to attain again, yet for me, it emerged as a promise concealed in the fourth and fifth rules for health: "Proactive Rest" and "Pace Yourself."

Pristine momentum is our reward for discerning our own rhythm, our pace for the day. I found that I needed to focus on Rules 4 and 5 together in order to detect my cycle of energy on a particular day. To rest proactively means we don't work until we run out of energy—the typical style for most of us, if we are truthful. "Give until you drop" seems to be the common practice. How noble. What sacrifice. Yet the net result is a deterioration of our energy supply and a reduction in overall functioning. There is nothing noble about running on fumes. Does it make sense for us to end the day by giving our most irritable, exhausted, cranky hours to our own families?

Athletes know the value of pacing themselves. There are lessons to be learned from the energy-conservation practices of long-distance athletes, such as cyclists. The Tour de France is a team sport. Interestingly, it is the slower members of the team who set the pace. They ride in front of the fastest cyclists as long as possible, and when their energy is spent, the faster cyclists pull out and speed up for the final miles. The wisdom in this is that if the fastest cyclists set the pace with too much speed, there would be too high a danger of burnout before the goal is won.

Once we discern the natural rhythms of our energy as it moves and flows, recedes and returns, we will know the ideal times to rest, to restore, and to revive ourselves. Each day will be a good day. Since I began this practice of pacing and proactive rest, I have experienced so much more joy and satisfaction that it often feels as if I am in the flow of a gentle river, experiencing pristine momentum.

REST PROACTIVELY

One way to sustain our momentum is to rest *before* we get tired. Proactive rest— or as my friend Radha Sahar has renamed it, being "pro-restive"—means to be so mindful of our energy flow that we consciously stop to rest *before* the flow starts to drop off. I discovered that if I waited until I was drained to rest, it took much longer to refill my energy supply. This new pace of grace requires that we plan the pauses in our days. I found that once my energy level was healthy, this practice required true self-discipline.

For me, the four-hour cycle suggested in Rule 5 was very helpful. In the morning, four hours after I started being active for the day, I would lie down on the couch. In the afternoon, I would rest sitting up watching *Oprah* on television or reading.

We can reach a point of no return if we are in a state of fatigue and fail to rest early enough. We will be forced onto our backs far longer if our fatigue gets out of control. I found that if I went beyond my energy cycle without resting, I would have the following symptoms:

- Light-headedness
- Tiredness
- Hunger—a drop in blood sugar
- Shallow breathing
- A heavy-chested sensation
- A rise in temperature
- Mental "waftiness" and foggy brain

Whenever you notice any of these symptoms, particularly if you are becoming flushed or your temperature is rising, this is a signal to stop whatever you are doing and gently take yourself off for a rest.

I have often seen this pattern of symptoms in others, including people with chronic fatigue, posttraumatic fatigue as the result of whiplash from an accident, or a host of other energy-related illnesses. Not being a person in the habit of taking any notice of my body, much less "listening" to it or having compassion for it, the mindfulness required to detect when to lie down before the symptoms of fatigue appeared took some doing. Several months after resting on a four-hour cycle, I discovered that six hours would work just as well. I work a total of *only* six hours a day whenever possible. As an early riser, this means that when I am working at home, whether writing or doing office work, my workday ends early in the afternoon. I then have leisure time to play, walk, clean, cook, or spend quality time with people I love, and I have more time for solitude. When my husband and I are on the road speaking at conferences or giving seminars, I set boundaries around times for rest. I either return to our room, or, if the venue is separate from our accommodation, I go to a prearranged rest area our clients provide. At times it has been a supply closet with a sleeping bag. As long as I can lie down, I know I can restore my energy.

Everyone's rhythms differ. If you have been ill, or exhausted, your rhythm will be different from times when you are at your peak of energy. I recommend that you experiment. Perhaps you can begin, as I did, by creating a space in your day for two rests, one four hours after you begin your day and another four hours later. I find that for most healthy people, a rest six hours after they get up seems to be the time they need it. If you rise at 7 A.M., your rest time would be at 1 P.M., just after lunch. Try it, even if it means laying your head down on your arms at your desk for fifteen minutes. It will reinvigorate you.

Looking back on my work life with a truthful eye, I recall years of slogging through afternoon hours getting little or nothing done. Once I established a routine of resting before I got tired, I was often able to say at the end of the day, "This has been a good day."

Pursue the Perfect Nap

I have become a confirmed napper. Forced to slow down in order to survive physically, I clearly saw that unless I continued to keep a true pace of grace I would be risking my hard-won health. More importantly, I could not and *would* not go back to an overwhelming, supercharged lifestyle. I have discovered an unfamiliar joy in living more simply, pacing my days with gentleness and rest. I refuse to give it up and reenter a state of FOG, no matter how energized I become. My health has been amazingly restored by keeping moderate working hours and preplanning regular times of rest.

One day I was speaking on the phone with a friend who was battling cancer and had only months to live. Her goal was to survive until her son and daughter graduated from university that June. I mentioned to her how much better I was feeling because of my naps. She said that she was living on borrowed time and wanted to get the most out of every day, so she just soldiered through. What troubled her was that she was cranky with her husband and children. She decided to try my formula of proactive rest on the four-hour cycle. She called me a week later, full of enthusiasm for her new lifestyle. "Even though I'm still not able to get much done, I have more to give," she said. "I'm drained unless I take my proactive rest. Now I feel refreshed most of the day and I'm more like my old self." The next week, a gift from her arrived in the mail—SARK's *Change Your Life Without Getting Out of Bed: The Ultimate Nap Book*. I heartily recommend it. My friend did indeed meet her goal, and though she was frail, she lived just long enough to celebrate her children's graduation. The last months of her life held an added gentleness because of her increased self-care. She replaced her un-

> *Naps are the adult version of a child's fort. A love of privacy and a place for make-believe. Rest adds strength to our souls.*
> —SARK, *Change Your Life Without Getting Out of Bed*

derstandable greed for time with a pace of grace, and received far more quality time with her family.

Let me share my perfect nap. When I am at home, I prefer to lie on the couch rather than going back to bed. Bed is for a good night's sleep. Naps are special and for me require a special place. I have a large, comfortable couch that holds me firmly and gently. On the couch, a beautiful quilt is folded. It is just the right weight. Beneath it is a pillow of the right height to support my head, covered by a clean pillowcase in a matching color. A novel sits ready on the coffee table beside my ever-present bottle of water. When I am traveling and speaking, I typically go back to the hotel room during prearranged breaks in the day and have my novel, a bottle of spring water, and a pile of pillows waiting. I always order up extra pillows for support. I often rest for twenty minutes, then return to what I am doing refreshed and ready. I keep a small alarm clock handy in case I fall asleep.

Curl Up with a Good Book

Why the novel? Reading protects me from thinking about the work I have just left or the audience waiting for me to return an hour later. Immersing myself in an engaging story allows my mind to rest and my body to relax. It also helps me to drift off to sleep. Carol Shields, author of *Unless,* said, "Novels help us turn down the volume of our own interior 'discourse.'"

If you have a nine-to-five job and cannot have the perfect nap at work, take time on your days off to indulge rather than filling every single weekend with activities. Plan for it. Everyone needs quiet time, down time, even your kids.

⇢ *Favorite Novels to Curl Up With* ⇠

Fried Green Tomatoes and other novels by Fannie Flagg

Practical Magic and other novels by Alice Hoffman

The Underpainter and other novels by Jane Urquhart

Sea Glass and other novels by Anita Shreve

The Shell Seekers and dozens of others by Rosamunde Pilcher

The Pelican Brief and other novels by John Grisham

The Stone Diaries and other novels by Carol Shields

Pigs in Heaven and other novels by Barbara Kingsolver

What We Keep and other novels by Elizabeth Berg

Alias Grace and other novels by Margaret Atwood

Suzanne's Diary for Nicholas and other novels by James Patterson

The Power of One and dozens of historical novels by Bryce Courtney

The Hand I Fan With by Tina McElroy Ansa

True Lies by Margaret Johnson-Hodge

Bel Canto and *The Magician's Assistant* by Ann Patchett

Whispers and dozens of other novels by Dean Koontz

PROTECT YOURSELF FROM "BUSY MIND"

One of the symptoms of fatigue illnesses is interrupted sleep at night. Many things can cause it: joint or muscle pain, overstimulation during the evening, or an unexpected stress during the day. Also, many people require less sleep as they age and find that they wake up at least once during the night and cannot return to sleep easily. The worst thing about this form of insomnia is what a friend calls "busy mind"—the obsessive, swirling thoughts and worries that go round and round but we never resolve. This causes tension, stress, and further wakefulness. I have found that a good novel illumined by a small reading light (to keep my husband from being disturbed) stops the circular thinking before it gets started and allows me to return to sleep quite quickly. Homeopathic remedies such as Calm Forte are helpful too.

> When I started this journey, I had pictures of the right way to be and the right things to do . . . now this quilt, this book, this life is teaching me to trust, no matter what life turns out to be—even if it is not what I expected or what I thought I wanted.
>
> —Sue Bender

HAVE RESTORATIVE QUICKIES

There are times when a particular day's schedule simply does not permit a rest for more than a few minutes. A quick way to restore energy is to take five to ten minutes in a quiet area, such as an office with the door closed. Use one or more of the yoga exercises in chapter 3 to refresh your breathing. Think of a peaceful scene you have visited in the past and meditate that you are there now. These few minutes will restore you when longer rest is not possible.

Margaret, an active, vibrant friend of mine who has lived for many years with multiple sclerosis, has a very graceful way of resting even when she is out and about. She goes quietly to her car for her rest during a busy day of facilitating Virtues workshops, chauffeuring grandchildren, or attending meetings as a volunteer in her church community. She lays her head back on the headrest and goes to sleep for fifteen or twenty minutes. She is completely relaxed and refreshed by this practice. When at home, she says, "I curl up for twenty minutes with our two cats." Margaret has a youthful radiance about her, reflecting both the joy she creates in her life and her excellent practices of self-care, including proactive rest. She says, "My activities help me to forget about my MS. I would never just stay home doing nothing. Doing something purposeful gives me so much extra energy. Rest is the time to meditate and restore. You need that rest just like you need lunch."

CREATE A WORKPLACE OF GRACE

You might consider it impossible to keep a regular routine of proactive rest during a normal busy day at work. However, many workplaces now understand the value of rest and are providing space and time for employees to restore themselves through "power naps."

One of the most creative and beautiful rest spaces I have ever seen in a workplace was at the PBS affiliate television station KCTS in Seattle. I was there to discuss a potential television show on the virtues. The producer told me we were meeting in the "Quiet Room," which had been created as a memorial to two beloved staff members killed in a car accident. I was amazed to walk into a room with soft lighting and silence, insulated from the noise of a busy television station. One wall is covered by wallpaper containing a forest of birches with soft light pouring into the trees. A real birch tree graces the corner. Comfortable couches in muted earth colors of rust, moss, and soft gold are arranged to create smaller spaces for rest or conversation. The room has an aura of peace, even reverence. What a simple gift to give employees, letting them know, "You are valued. You have the right to rest. We nurture you here."

PEACE IS PRODUCTIVE

Some organizations have discovered that routinely providing a quiet space or time not only nurtures employees but also dramatically increases productivity. The owner of a real estate company became enamored of meditation and found it energized him so much, he decided to teach his realtors. Each day there were periods of silent meditation in the office. To his delight and astonishment, their productivity soared by 400 percent!

Schools throughout the world that are applying The Virtues Project as their character education program start the day with a virtues reflection time. The principal or a student reads a paragraph each day on the Virtue of the Week or of the Month over the public address system, while students listen in silence. Then they take a few moments to reflect on it and share in their homerooms their own thoughts on this virtue, a time they have practiced it, or how they will use it today. This practice creates a source of peace for enhanced learning and results in dramatically reduced discipline referrals as well.

Once proactive rest became part of my daily routine, I noticed that I felt unusually peaceful rather than anxious about how much I could get done. Somehow, knowing that rest was coming soon quieted me down. To my surprise, the days, and now years of my recovery, have been the most productive of my life. When one of my closest friends learned what I had accomplished in three months, she said, "Linda, I honestly can't believe this. How do you do it?" When I described the power of pacing, she was all ears.

⤙⟐ The Virtue of Moderation ⟐⤚

I call that true piety which most removes earth-aches and ills, where one is moderate in eating and in resting, and in sport; measured in wish and act; sleeping betimes, waking betimes for duty. —Bhagavad-Gita 6:17

Moderation creates balance in our lives. It is having enough—not too much or not too little. It is using self-discipline to keep from overdoing. Moderation is what keeps us from being blown about in the winds of our desires.

Signs of Success

I am practicing Moderation when I . . .

- Know what I need and get enough—no more, no less
- Take care of my health by getting enough of what I need
- Use self-discipline to stop myself from overdoing
- Balance work and play in my life
- Set boundaries for myself
- Am content with enough

Affirmation

I am moderate. I am thankful and content to get what I need. Work, rest, and play are balanced in my life. I don't overdo or underdo, but find what's just right for me.

Don't Work Harder, Work Smarter

When we are kind to ourselves by setting a pace of grace, it naturally follows that anxiety about "getting it all done" will no longer distract us from giving our best attention in the time we allot ourselves. Sometimes the most innovative ideas come when we step away from our work. Providing a space for grace is also about giving room for creativity to supply fresh ideas. If you are struggling with a knotty problem, don't bite and claw your way into it. Stop and rest your mind. Invite inspiration. The knot may unravel in some simple, unexpected way.

Some jobs give us no choice. Our hours are set. However, we have the freedom to choose how to spend the rest of our time, creating quality moments in ways that really matter or drifting into mindless hyper-scheduling.

A peaceful mind is simply a more productive mind. We are able to approach our work in a more focused, orderly way, especially if we are applying the principles of order and beauty in our work space. With the power of relaxed concentration, the work we are doing becomes an engaging delight rather than a chore.

Put People First

What's the purpose of our time? Isn't it to spend it on what is most important? The Maori of New Zealand have a saying that reflects a long-cherished value: "What is important? It is the people. It is the people. It is the people."

In my work as a hospice spiritual care director, I found that only two things matter at the end of our time on this earth—love and service. As they are dying, folks seem to care the most about their relationships, and also about what difference they have made. No one ever seems to say, "I wish I'd spent more time at the office." Yet, in our drivenness, we too often sacrifice relationships for work, which we deem to be so all-important.

Take Your Time

One of the symptoms of the unsustainable task-focused, graceless life to which we have succumbed is that we—and our children—are chronically rushed. Because we are exhausted and sleep deprived, bringing files and briefs to bed,

working too many hours, overwhelmed by too many phone calls, we are not enjoying our time, much less feeling in control of it. So, we rush.

We rush in the morning to get ready for school and work. We rush to pick
up our children. We rush to meetings after dinner. We rush bedtime. Our children rush from school to sports practice or dance lessons.

The price for all this rushing is that we do not experience the peace of being
with one another, connecting with one another lovingly, graciously, kindly, or patiently. A pace of grace with our children doesn't mean to give up all our activities,
although being selective and moderate would do us all a world of good. Slowing
down to the speed of gentleness, remaining aware of the value of being together
rather than just focusing on what needs to "get done" can lead us all to grace.

One busy mother of four who also works as an organizational executive told
me she had been shouting orders at her kids for years, simply because there didn't
seem to be time for any other way. After attending a Virtues Project workshop, she
began speaking the Virtues Language and practicing peacefulness and gentleness
with her children. She said they had been having lots more hugs and giggles together and that life, especially each morning, was far more peaceful and orderly.

One day she did an experiment to assess the effect of this change. She went
back to her habitual yelling and ordering. By the time the kids were in the car
ready to leave for school, they were all in tears. "Mummy, what's wrong? What
happened to your virtues?" her seven-year-old son asked. "I'm sorry, darling.
Please forgive me for forgetting my patience today. I promise not to turn back
into 'General Mom.' I'll be gentle Mom again." From that moment, she has maintained a more gracious attitude, connecting more lovingly with her children and
her husband. They continue to have a very full life, yet through some simple
shifts, life in their family has maintained a pace of grace:

- Using gracious language—the Language of Virtues
- Enjoying some personal time with each child before bed whenever possible
- Planning ahead—preparing clothes, homework, and lunches the night
  before

Do One Thing at a Time

In pacing ourselves, we rarely need to rush. We don't have to make other people's
emergencies our own. Being responsible is the ability to respond ably. Of course,

we want to be trustworthy and considerate in our dealings with people. However, the pandemic of urgency about everything shouldn't dictate our way of being.

Have you ever had the promise of a deadline by a housing contractor, only to find that the project goes months beyond it? Have you ever waited in a doctor's office or a clinic for hours? Doctors work on too many patients at a time. Builders habitually overextend themselves working on too many houses. If they were more gracious and trustworthy, more focused on completing fewer projects with more timeliness, I believe their reputations would precede them. They would be very sought after indeed.

One of the boundaries I developed while practicing the Ten Rules of Health was to do only one thing at a time. Because I began to tune in more mindfully to my body, I found that if I was cooking and I answered the phone, I couldn't concentrate on either one very well. I found it draining. If I'm having a massage, conversation distracts me and I can't feel the massage fully. If I'm writing, I write. If I'm resting, I rest. I have seen people in cities rushing across a busy street, dodging traffic, with a sandwich in one hand and a cell phone to their ear. They are hunched over, looking anxious and distracted. They remind me of small animals with rapidly beating hearts. Is this what is meant by a "mover and shaker"? That's no way to live.

If we are to savor the moments of our lives, we must resist interruptions. The first time I was invited to be on the *Oprah* television show, I was in the desert of Alice Springs, Australia, working with aboriginal teachers. I couldn't make it back in time. Two years later I received a second invitation to speak about raising children to "Do the Right Thing"—the theme of the show. There were several other guests, chosen for the dramatic stories of how they braved the odds or withstood public opinion or even risked their lives to do the right thing. The green room was very crowded. My segment was the longest one and was to close the show, focusing on the Five Virtues Strategies for raising children with integrity and courage. Everyone was chatting and sharing something about their stories. When one woman asked me what my story was, I told her I was going to talk about my book, *The Family Virtues Guide,* and how to raise children with the virtues of generosity, service, integrity, and so on. All conversation stopped and I was bombarded by questions. After answering a few, I was about to stop and tell them I needed to save my voice for Oprah, and was relieved when the makeup

*Do you want to be driven or
do you want to be led?*
—Robert Greenway

woman came for me. She took me into an adjoining room. For me, this was an exciting part of the experience. One of the guests followed me into the makeup room and kept asking questions. I said to him, "I'd be glad to talk to you when I finish in here." He ignored me and kept talking. More assertively, I said, "I appreciate your enthusiasm for my project and I'll be glad to talk to you after the show. I have a personal rule to do one thing at a time. Right now I'm enjoying having my makeup done." He got it that time.

ACCEPT WHAT YOU ARE GIVEN TODAY

Realistically, how can we be content with what we have achieved or experienced on a given day? There always seems to be so much more we have failed to accomplish that it is rare to end the day with a sense of contentment and pleasure. This comes, I believe, from an imbalance that has crept up on us, and the fact that we have come to value tasks more than experience or people or joy.

We use the expression "God willing" to mean that we can only do what we are meant to do at a given time. Creating a pace of grace is wholeheartedly accepting the rhythm each day brings and surrendering to what is realistic and possible on a particular day. It is a powerful practice of the virtue of contentment. At the deepest level it is an act of surrender, transformed into gratitude.

Surrender is not giving up. It is accepting things as they are. It is discerning what is possible and trusting what is provided. It is relaxing into the pace of the day, whatever that day brings. I have often heard the message in prayer, "Take your time, and follow My lead." It has come to mean doing what I can with whatever I am given that day—time, energy, opportunity—and being content with it, rather than stressing out and resisting things as they are. It is also following the leads that our inner wisdom detects as important. Unless we have a quiet mind and a spacious sense of time, these quiet breezes of guidance will simply pass us by. Some of the most meaningful moments in my life have come as a result of listening to that quiet inner voice of discernment.

Take Time Off
and Time Out

The radical shift to acceptance makes life so much easier. We cannot squeeze blood from a stone, nor can we squeeze a drop more energy from ourselves than we have. It is far more efficient both spiritually and materially to open ourselves with gratitude to whatever

> *Be content with what you have;*
> *rejoice in the way things are.*
> *When you realize there is*
> *nothing lacking,*
> *the whole world belongs to you.*
> —Lao-tzu, Chinese mystic, founder of Taoism, 604–531 BCE

energy we are given today and to accept the times when nothing seems to go right or we just can't muster our energy for anything other than a "mental health" day. I recommend this for adults and children. When you know you just don't have the energy for another day of school or work, go on a picnic. Take a drive. Take the day off. You will return to the tasks of the next day with renewed vigor.

One day when nothing seemed to go right and my efforts to get things done were frustrated or blocked at every turn, my husband reminded me, "Some days it goes easy and some days it goes hard." The notion that it isn't our fault and that actually we have little control over what is happening is a relief in itself. Some people believe that there are certain times when the forces of the world block everything from turning out right, such as when the planet Mercury goes retrograde. I must say I have noticed more mechanical things breaking down, as well as communication, at such times. I used to drain myself of precious energy by fighting these rifts in the flow of time. Now I think, "Maybe it's time for a walk on the beach or lunch with a friend or a day on the couch with a good book."

Have a Good Day

I have come to realize that work will always expand to fill whatever time we allow for it. Whether it is housework or service projects, office work, or whatever job we go to each day, we will always have more than we can finish. We will never experience closure of the sort we seem to pursue so relentlessly.

To have a good day is to find our pristine momentum while cherishing and balancing each of the elements of our lives. By balancing purposefulness with moderation, people with tasks, and discerning our pace of grace we will achieve this not-so-modest goal. A good day is a gentle weaving of reflection, exercise, work, rest, and play, with simple gestures of generosity and kindness. If our spiritual task of the day involves reaching out in compassion to a friend who needs us, it will be a good day if we put our other priorities aside. Most days, it only takes small acts of consideration and love to make a world of difference—a love note slipped into a child's lunch box or our partner's pocket, the planning of a favorite meal for dinner, a flower on a pillow, an extra errand run when someone doesn't have time, a dish of food for a family having troubles. These simple acts of kindness rarely take much time. They easily flow from a mindset of grace. They sweeten our lives, allowing us to be a source of grace to others.

As you discern the cycles of your own natural rhythm, you will find your pace of grace within the possibilities each day brings. May every day be a good day.

Naps fluff us up and make us more kind . . . As adults we still need tender places in which to repair our souls and put special glue on the broken places.
—SARK, *Change Your Life Without Getting Out of Bed*

⤙▨ EXERCISE GRACE ▨⤚
Plan Proactive Rests

This exercise will help you to discern your own natural pace of grace and to discover the best way to restore your energy with proactive rest.

Begin by keeping an energy journal for a few days. Notice your peaks and valleys, the times you wish you were lying on a couch under a comforter. With this rhythm in mind, plan your rest times before you typically reach a low energy point.

Gather the materials you need to take a rest. Plan your rest no more than six hours after you begin spending your energy in the morning. If you are in a state of severe fatigue, make it four hours, or less. For some, this time period comes at late morning. For others, it is right after lunch.

Materials for your Rest Kit may include:
- an engaging novel
- a comforter or large cotton cloth and pillows
- a rolled-up towel to place under your knees or neck
- a Yoga mat if you plan to rest on the floor
- a drink of fresh water

Take your second rest just before dinner preparations begin, relaxing in a chair, watching television, playing quietly with your children, lying down together, or reading quietly. Have easy nutritious snacks ready to nurture everyone at this time of lowered blood sugar. This prevents you from the mad scramble to prepare dinner when everyone is ravenous and often irritable with low blood sugar.

When you set a clear boundary for rest and reentry time, your entire family will adapt to this rhythm, and the atmosphere will become peaceful and loving. The need for quiet, close contact can be met while also allowing everyone a restful transition from the busyness of the day. If you are living alone, create your own nurturing ritual for this transition time of the day.

SUMMARY OF CHAPTER 8: CREATE A PACE OF GRACE

- Manage your time and energy mindfully. It is the only sustainable way to live.
- Regulate your energy each day by finding your natural flow and seeking your pristine momentum. And don't rush.
- Rest proactively—*before* you get tired. Plan your rest periods and be disciplined in keeping to your routine. If you are in good health, this is likely to be six hours after you start your day.
- Indulge in perfect naps whenever you can. If you work a five-day week outside the home, plan naps on weekends. They will restore you.
- Suggest a rest and restoration area at your workplace.
- Don't work harder. Work smarter. Rests and breaks open up a space of grace for fresh ideas and creative solutions.
- Put people first. They are more important than the tasks you get done. Speak with kindness, spend quiet time each day, lay things out the night before to keep mornings peaceful.
- Take time off. Nothing else restores your body and soul like time for just being.
- Let every day be a good day. Small acts of grace make a true difference.

As you pace yourself more gracefully, you will develop a more loving connection to your body, mind, and spirit. We'll look at other ways to nurture ourselves in the next chapter.

ᘒ⇒ *NINE* ⇐ᘒ

Support Yourself

*We do not possess our homes, our children, or even our own body. They are given
to us for a short while to treat with care and respect.*
—Jack Kornfield, American Buddhist, author of *A Path with Heart*

Of the many gifts I received when I was forced to slow down to the
speed of grace, one that surprised me was being reintroduced to my body. I can
say honestly that my illness gave me an intimacy with my body I had not known
since childhood. I have always loved to watch babies and toddlers. They are so at
home in their bodies, so at one with their parts. They suck their toes, gaze in
wonder at their own fingers. They frown if the slightest gastric discomfort ap-
pears, and smile a moment later as it passes. A baby's expressions are like clouds
moving across the sun. We adults have learned to be so task-focused that we
hardly notice our thirst, our discomfort, our fatigue, or our tension until we
nearly reach a point of no return.

I don't know how I ended up living in the cramped attic of my mind, but when
post-polio pried me from it, I came to know the realm of my body as new territory.
I started really paying attention, like a new nanny who enjoys her charge. I have
learned to stop if I am feeling irritable, or flat, or uncomfortable, to ask, "What do
you need, sweetheart?" My day is far more graceful when I listen to my body.

At first, by necessity, this new self-centeredness restricted the attention I
could give to others, but as I became a more mindful and trustworthy steward, I
had far more to give. I was sharing from a fuller cup.

Paying attention to the cues my body was sending gave me some of my most
creative healing strategies. Although they are particularly helpful for people with
energy challenges or chronic pain, I believe anyone can benefit from supporting
and restoring themselves on a regular basis. It greatly expands our sense of harmony and makes us more at home in our bodies.

Three healing strategies that have been of immense help in my own recovery are:

1. Massage
2. Physiotherapy
3. Physical aids such as "pillow props"

THE HEALING POWER OF MASSAGE

Massage and other forms of bodywork are invaluable in purifying the body of toxins, thereby releasing the body's natural, self-healing energy. Bodywork also assists greatly in the relief of muscle and joint pain.

Body treatments such as massage, body wraps, facials, manicures, and pedicures are very healing. One of my favorites is a treatment I always get when we travel to Australia—Vichy water massage. This treatment consists of strong jets of water from an overhanging spray moving along your body. Always drink plenty of water afterward to help flush out the toxins being released.

Body treatments are a very soothing way to decrease pain and fatigue and to purify the body of stress. Scheduling massage on a regular basis is a routine part of self-care. I'm happy to learn that about 40 percent of the people going for regular massage are men. Taking time to replenish and pamper ourselves revives our bodies and our minds. For me, it is a critical part of my pace of grace, and no matter how much I have going on, I schedule massage. I have sampled massage in many countries on the days off I schedule between each presentation. I find it fascinating that every single masseur or masseuse has his or her own technique, from vigorous and stimulating, as I found in Europe, to the languid, graceful, and spiritual style of Lomi Lomi massage in Hawaii.

I have also found that I am very affected by the spirit of the individual giving massage. When I am with someone peaceful, I often have visions while they are massaging my head. Massage can be merely soothing or profoundly restorative depending on the spiritual connection we make.

RECEIVE PHYSIOTHERAPY

Many physicians recommend physiotherapy as a treatment for post-polio and other energy illnesses. The simple, strengthening exercises these specialists teach are excellent. They also offer cold and heat wraps, and electrical stimulation of the muscles by TENS (Transcutaneous Electrical Nerve Stimulation). These methods are very helpful in pain reduction and building muscle strength, and you will go home with some easy exercises you can repeat on your own.

One of my favorite exercises a physiotherapist taught me is a very simple one. It is the repeated exercise throughout the day of pulling the stomach muscles in as one exhales, and releasing the abdomen as one inhales. Breathing from the abdomen rather than the chest deepens our breath and disrupts the habit of shallow breathing. This is a simple exercise that can be done anywhere and takes little time. It is excellent for flattening stomach muscles as well! We need strong stomach muscles in order to walk erectly and support our back muscles.

Other types of body work that people report to be deeply healing are acupressure, acupuncture, healing touch, and Reiki.

Pillow Yourself

As mentioned earlier, when I contracted bulbar polio at the age of eleven, it attacked the muscles of my throat, affecting breathing, swallowing, eating, and speaking. I was unable to speak at all, and could be fed only intravenously. When post-polio syndrome struck about forty years later, I began to lose my ability to swallow. Because my neck and throat muscles are my weakest area, talking for any length of time, especially on the phone, became utterly exhausting. On the rare occasions we would be visiting with people in those days, or having dinner out with someone, when Dan noticed that suddenly I had both elbows on the table and hands propping up my chin, he'd say, "Time to go."

One day, when I noticed how difficult it was to hold up my head, I recalled the inflatable neck pillow I used when traveling on planes. I dug it out and began to use it when I sat at my desk, or talked on the phone, or drove the car. My energy immediately increased. It is now my trademark "prop," and when I am resting during conferences or speaking engagements, I place a chair against a wall and lean against my neck pillow. I recommend it to anyone as a simple preventative to fatigue, or a way to rest when you feel tired, since the head is the heaviest part of our bodies. When I am at home I have a La-Z-Boy chair to rest in that provides full neck support. I also slip a flax-filled pillow under my neck. My office chair is also high-backed. As I write this, I am leaning against my inflated neck pillow in my high-backed chair. It gives me hours more energy each day.

One of the best ways to prevent lower back pain, a common problem as we get older, is to use pillows for support. Sleeping with a pillow between your knees or supporting a raised leg will take the strain off your lower back. Some people find that another pillow beneath your arm takes the strain off shoulder joints. Any chiropractor will tell you that it is important to have just the right support for your neck, using pillows that lift and cradle your neck muscles. These simple, inexpensive supports will keep you as pain-free as possible during the night. A massage therapist calls this the "Queen of Sheba Syndrome." Why not? For men, perhaps it can be thought of as the "Roman Emperor Syndrome."

WHAT YOU RESIST WILL PERSIST

We often exhibit great resistance to using medical aids and devices. I know a woman in her eighties, with excruciating knee pain from arthritis, who doggedly refuses to use even a cane. So she hobbles painfully and her knees continue to deteriorate. This is truly foolish pride, a choice to get worse instead of better. A physician told a friend of mine in her forties with fibromyalgia that if she used a walker with a seat when shopping for any length of time, it would greatly decrease her fatigue. She refused, "Because I don't want people to know how sick I am."

Many of us resist the use of canes and other aids because we don't want to "give in" or admit to aging or illness, but this merely stresses the body further and increases our distress. In this age of makeovers, when reconstructive surgery is a booming business, we have greatly overinflated the value of appearance. Our society stigmatizes illness, and we seem to be phobic about the loss of youth and health. There is pressure to "fight" it. We experience a subtle form of shame about using a medical device, which is a visible admission that we have a medical problem or that we are aging, and that we are somehow giving in and giving up. Yet avoiding the support we need when we need it is not merely a form of vanity, it robs us of the opportunity to get better!

Spiritually, keeping up appearances in service of the ego rather than living the truth and accepting what is drains us deeply. In a sense, it is a form of pride before God, a refusal to accept what we are given. When we attempt to cover up infirmity or aging, we are saying that we *are* our bodies. We devalue ourselves by resisting the truth. We ignore our needs, and even our pain, to try to impress others. Failing to live the truth exacerbates our fatigue, steeping us in a sense of anxious pretense. It also prolongs our pain and may, in fact, keep us from healing. Actually, it ages us needlessly! As in any challenge life brings, we ought to do everything possible to get better. We must hold on to hope.

⤖ The Virtue of Acceptance ⥢

Love came up to me, showing that a contented mind is best for growth.
—Yasna 43 (Zoroastrian teachings)

Acceptance allows us to be open to the gifts and lessons in every situation life offers. With it, we have the courage to accept the things we cannot change with good grace. We can surrender to the truth of what is and make the best of it. When we are accepting, we affirm others and ourselves for the qualities we do have, and avoid criticism for what we don't have. Acceptance leads to peace.

Signs of Success

I am practicing Acceptance when I . . .
- Accept my challenges with humor and grace
- Accept others and myself as we are
- Accept the things I cannot change
- Show tolerance of things that I wish were different
- Am content with what I am given
- Am open to finding the gifts in everything that happens

Affirmation

I accept what life brings me with contentment and grace. I accept others and myself with tolerance. I discern the gifts in all that happens.

A friend with chronic fatigue syndrome was given a helpful analogy by a medical assessor: "You have one hundred pebbles of energy a day to spend. If using aids saves you some of those pebbles, it leaves you more for doing the things you love, and it will help you recover."

Excellent aids are available in medical supply stores that we must not avoid out of fear or denial. When we need them, we need them! They can really help to support painful muscles and joints. Pardon the graphic example I am about to give. For a while I could not lift myself unaided from the toilet because of the pain in my knees. A portable raised toilet seat (which of course I called my "potty chair") was extremely helpful during the first years I was battling post-polio. And yes, I was really happy when I could do without it again. If you need help in this way, have hope. You may eventually be free of the need if you are actively practicing a good health regimen.

When we have the courage and determination to obtain all the help and support we need, we've achieved a spiritual victory. We are deepening our virtues of honesty and acceptance. We are meeting ourselves fully.

Be a friend to your body. Have compassion for yourself. Be the caregiver to yourself that in your heart of hearts you know you need. Surrender to what you need while having the courage to sustain your hope. Aim for the highest level of health. The balance between acceptance and hope is your holy ground.

God grant me the serenity
to accept the things I cannot change,
the courage to change the things
I can, and the wisdom to
know the difference.
—Reinhold Niebuhr, American religious philosopher

⇢≈◌ EXERCISE GRACE ◌≈⇠
Deepen Your Self-Care

In the next two weeks, do three things to better support yourself.

1. Purchase a neck pillow, either flax-filled or the "airplane" variety. Rest by leaning several times a day.
2. Make an appointment for some kind of bodywork, such as Reiki, massage, or acupuncture.

3. Pamper yourself with a salon manicure, pedicure, or facial. Give yourself a manicure if you know how. It is a contemplative exercise.

SUMMARY OF CHAPTER 9: SUPPORT YOURSELF

- Tune in to your body. Stop and ask yourself what you need.
- Go to a physiotherapist, acupuncturist, or other body treatment specialist when you need relief from muscle weakness, pain, or discomfort.
- Take the time to pamper yourself on a regular basis, with a massage, manicure, or other body treatment.
- Pillow yourself when you sleep. Rest your upper body several times a day by leaning with a neck pillow for support.
- With the power of the virtue of acceptance, meet yourself fully. Only then can you hope for healing.
- Have the humility to obtain the help of medical aids when you need to. It will help to regenerate you!
- The balancing virtues of acceptance of what is and hope for what can be is holy ground.

We can only create and sustain a pace of grace when we know our own limits and set clear boundaries for the way we choose to live.

TEN

Set Clear Boundaries

If you don't stand for something, you'll fall for anything.
—(attributed to many sources, including Abraham Lincoln)

Too often, an illness, a life catastrophe, or a world event becomes the catalyst for creating clear personal boundaries around our time and energy. Treating our life as a gift requires that we recognize not only that life itself is precious but that each of us is worthy to live it. We have the right to keep ourselves safe from what steals our energy away. It is not only a right, but an obligation, if we want to live as fully and purposefully as we are meant to live. I think it's time for a conspiracy of gentleness.

World events have brought us to a deeper consciousness of how fragile and precious life is, inspiring us to protect and nurture our quality of life. This awareness is also one of the gifts an energy illness brings. Energy becomes as precious as water in the desert. We cannot afford to waste a single drop. A fierce protectiveness arises as we are forced to recognize the things that drain our energy. I'm sad that it took an illness for me to have an "excuse" to slow down into mindfulness. Please recognize that you don't need to be sick to get better. You don't need an excuse to become the architect of your own life—only the awareness that your life is your own and that you deserve to live well.

Yes, I am full of the righteousness of a new convert to self-care. I just feel so incredibly better when I keep my pace of grace. I am continually humbled by the nascent self-discipline that protects me like a highly paid bodyguard, whose warnings I dare not ignore. Whenever I rationalize that "I'm feeling so much better; can't I just . . . ?" and spend a day overdoing, or have one too many "quickies" instead of the full forty-five minutes my body needs for rest, or wait until I get tired to rest, the cost is more than I am willing to pay. I scuttle back inside the safety of my guardian's arms. Because I have been consistently living for six years within the boundaries of the Ten Rules for Health, my body now amazes me with its resilience. I can have a day without an actual nap and get back on track the next day, only to find that my cup of energy refills quickly once I reestablish my regular routine.

Setting Clear Boundaries is the Third Strategy of The Virtues Project. It is about protecting our children, our health, our time, and our dignity. The fifth rule for health presented earlier suggested a number of different boundaries.

Rule 5: Pace Yourself

You have four hours a day for work, sometimes six. Choose carefully. Keep your correspondence current. Enjoy! Enjoy!

When I unwrapped this rule, I saw that it contained five distinct ways to practice the virtue of Moderation:

1. *Establish a gentle pace*

Set your own pace for the day. Do not allow others to determine how you will spend your energy.

2. *Determine how many hours you can be productive*

Set boundaries around the time of your day that you can control. You will discover an abundance of free time you didn't know you had.

3. *Choose your activities for the day carefully*

Remember that you are responsible for the things to which you say "Yes."

4. *Keep up with correspondence*

Stay on top of e-mails, mail, and bills. More on this in the last chapter, "Plan for Grace."

5. *Enjoy yourself*

Set boundaries around your time and energy so that you are basically doing what you find life-giving and enjoyable.

I realized that only by setting firm boundaries could I make it possible for this revolutionary shift to occur in my life. This meant I would need to hone my virtue of assertiveness.

SET A SUSTAINABLE PACE

Over the years, as a psychotherapist and organizational consultant, I have companioned hundreds of people and found that most of them—even the most powerful and highly respected—don't feel deserving of boundaries. The virtue of assertiveness does not come easy. Yet the price we pay for living without sustainable boundaries is simply too high. In Japan, there is an extreme example of this in the growing phenomenon of men dropping dead in their tracks. It is called "Salary Man Disease." These are individuals in their forties and fifties who work such long hours for so long that their bodies literally wear out and their hearts break. The work ethic in Japan is inhuman. Younger people are now starting highly successful businesses there and keeping more moderate hours, demonstrating that it is indeed time for a pace of grace.

Other dangers lurk in living without conscious boundaries. If we give too much of our time to work, we lose the quality of our relationships, and often we lose them altogether. If we overspend our energy, we lose our health. If we scatter our energies responding to people's demands, we may well lose the God-given opportunity waiting patiently for us to notice it.

Discover Your Natural Boundaries

Learning to pace myself and set clear boundaries meant first of all observing what activities drained me. In the early days of the heavy fatigue that post-polio brought, I discovered that there was one activity that drained me more than any other. To my surprise, it was talking on the phone. One long phone call would literally cost me a full day. Overcome by fatigue after the call, I would have to cancel my plans for the rest of the day and could do nothing but lie on the couch, read, and doze. I had absolutely no choice. This was terribly depressing and disconcerting, especially when I had a deadline to complete an article or an outing scheduled with my husband.

I decided to set phone hours to protect my rest periods. I used my home answering machine more often, and my assistant at the time screened all my business calls. She would e-mail me a daily list of calls, including how she had responded or noting which I should respond to personally. I would do so within the hour per day I allotted for calls. I encouraged clients and friends to e-mail rather than call as well, allowing me the freedom to answer as I had the time and energy to do so. Even my sons learned to schedule calls with me when I was free to talk and could give them my full attention.

Cultivating your assertiveness to set clear boundaries places you at the helm of your life rather than tossing you about in the sea of "whatever happens." It allows you to manage your time, protect your health, make your family life more harmonious, and live by your true calling. Boundaries safeguard your joy.

⇢⟡ The Virtue of Assertiveness ⟡⇠

Are not two sparrows sold for a farthing? And not one of them shall fall on
the ground without God's notice. Even the hairs of your head have all
been counted. Do not worry. You are worth more than many sparrows.
—Matthew 10: 29–30

Being assertive means being positive and confident. Assertiveness begins
by being aware that we are worthy people. We have our very own special
gifts. When we are assertive, we think for ourselves and express our own
ideas, opinions, and talents. We make a difference in the world in our own
unique ways. We know what we stand for and what we will not stand for.
We refuse to be passive and have no need to be aggressive. We set clear
boundaries in our lives.

Signs of Success
I am practicing Assertiveness when I . . .
• Think for myself and stand up for what I believe
• Share my own ideas and feelings with others
• Have no need to be either passive or aggressive
• Choose not to allow others to lead me into trouble
• Expect respect at all times
• Ask for what I want
• Have clear limits that protect my energy, my health, and my choices

Affirmation
I am assertive. I think for myself and do what I feel is right. I have clear
boundaries. I tell the truth about what is just. I am my own leader.

Resist Telephone Tyranny

You don't have to have an energy disease for the telephone to exhaust you. Without assertive time management, the telephone is one of the most time-consuming, draining, and wasteful implements in the world. If we keep going the way we are, future generations will be born with an electronic ear implant. With the advent of the cell phone, which we carry everywhere, we are never out of reach of the demands others make on our time. Isn't it time for us to reclaim our right to silence, giving us time to concentrate on a project that requires our full attention? In an office where I once worked the phone rang so incessantly, we had the expression "workus interruptus." We were terribly unproductive because the telephone always took precedence. Allowing that to happen is a very inefficient choice.

It has now come to the point where our privacy is severely threatened. A young woman in her teens complained to me once that she was being harassed by her boyfriend, who called her cell phone dozens of times a day to check on her whereabouts when she wasn't with him. We had a talk about personal boundaries. Because she still wanted to be in the relationship at this point, she decided to tell him, "If you want to be in my life, you must respect my privacy. It's your choice." Of course, she had to be willing to let him go for this boundary to mean anything. When you set a boundary, it is only real if you say what you mean and mean what you say.

I recall a petite woman in her forties who confessed at a Virtues Project workshop in Arizona that she was tyrannized by the telephone and was very challenged by the third Virtues Strategy to set clear boundaries. She admitted to the group that she felt incapable of saying "No," and that the biggest burden in her life was the time she spent listening to friends complain on the phone—literally hours each day.

"I just can't reject them," she said tearfully, "but they're driving me crazy." We companioned her to help her get to the heart of the matter—which was the fear of losing friends, and of incurring their resentment, as well as a fear of being selfish—until she discerned that her own freedom and peace of mind were actually more important to her. She was then able to come up with a boundary that felt comfortable for her and assertive words she could use when one of these friends called. She committed to setting a boundary of talking no more than ten minutes at a time on the phone, and her assertive statement was "Alicia, before you tell me what this call is about, I need to let you know I have a new personal rule that I will only spend ten minutes on any phone conversation. I'm getting lots more done these days. Now, what were you calling me about?" She set a timer for ten minutes, and when it rang, she said, "I need to go now, Alicia." She would then give her friend a Virtues acknowledgment such as "I admire your patience in dealing with your son." Then she would simply say, "Thanks for calling," and hang up.

I saw her a few weeks later at a conference. She was radiant and seemed taller, somehow. She waved wildly from across the room, and we made our way toward each other. "Linda! I am so happy! My life is just fantastic since I started setting boundaries. I don't let anyone disrespect my time anymore. I'm free! My friends think it's a great idea, and they're starting to set boundaries too."

Having said this, I want to acknowledge the fact that for many women, isolated at home with children, the phone is their lifeline of sanity and support. It is almost a certainty that the minute the phone rings, a baby will start to whimper, a toddler will desperately need a drink *"Now!"* or a teenager will have a dire emergency. This is a sign that the phone is being used excessively. If there is a routine to a parent's calls, children are far better able to adapt to it. You can leave a message on an answering machine about "best times to reach me" or answer briefly and call the person back. Life will work far better if you decide when to answer and when to give total, focused attention to your children.

ARE YOU AN E-TYPE PERSONALITY?

Earlier I mentioned the E-Type personality—someone who tries to be everything to everyone. If you fit this category, you must take steps to detach from the need to please. One way to do this is to realize that you are worthy of setting limits. I think one of the biggest challenges for us E-Types is that from the time we were young we didn't want to miss anything. We must heal the fear of losing our place if we refuse an opportunity. We must become more discerning about what we choose to do or not do. The cost of failing to do so is high. We will lose our health and spend our precious life doing things we wonder how we got into in the first place.

In my world travels, I have met many people of capacity who are like a magnet for responsibility in their workplaces and communities. Because they do things with excellence and are outstanding at completing responsibilities, everyone thinks of them first when a job needs doing or a committee is formed. Often these natural leaders become overburdened. When I companion them about their stress level and ask them what they are doing for self-care, they say things like, "I finally took a holiday . . . but I got sick." I believe that this is one of the symptoms of the E-Type personality and comes from an addiction to approval and a compulsion to be important. They appear to be selfless, but I believe that this is a cover-up for a kind of selfishness—a hogging of responsibility, based on the fear of losing one's special place as "the one who can do it all." It is self-indulgent and self-destructive. No one is that important. I speak from experience.

Choose Quality of Life

Chad, a gifted teacher I met at a Virtues Project educator's conference in Western Australia, shared his story with me about a boundary he had set to increase his quality of life. He made a choice at thirty-five to leave business and go into teaching. He loved it. As he became known for his leadership skills and trustworthiness, he began to be overwhelmed by extracurricular activities. "Once they know you're good at something," he said, "they pile everything onto you."

Chad finally decided he had to leave his beloved profession or he would collapse. "It got so bad, I left and went back to business. That stressed me out so much, I decided to take up Yoga." His Yoga practice allowed him to center and calm himself. He realized he was miserable being away from teaching, so he went back. However, this time he was unwilling to go back to an unsustainable schedule. He summoned his courage and set some boundaries. He now has a vital teaching career and two extracurricular activities at any given time. "Now I'm clear. I go home at five fifteen no matter what. I don't take on the world anymore." He puts all his responsibilities aside before he leaves school and is able to be truly present to his family. Chad is a very happy man, with a balanced life.

Have faith in the fact that you are valued and worthy—deserving of a pace of grace in your life. Once that shift in awareness occurs, you are free to observe and discern where your limits need to be, and to have the determination to set clear boundaries around your time and energy—in your work, and with your family and friends.

What Is Your Yes?

Do you realize that if you say yes to everything, you may be saying no to God—to your true calling? At each stage in life, we have a sacred task. It may not be what we expected or even wanted, but it is ours. It may have to do with seeking our life partner, nurturing a marriage, raising a child, discovering our life service, or establishing a new standard of excellence in our profession. It may be breaking a cycle of addiction or abuse in our family. In his groundbreaking work *Soulcraft,* Bill Plotkin presents a model of the life of the soul that delineates each phase of life from birth to elderhood and the soul tasks that accompany each stage. We need to cultivate specific virtues at each stage. At times we need the virtues of purposefulness and determination, at others gentleness and detachment. Each of us is here for a purpose and it is our sacred obligation to become mindful enough to discern it.

An elderly friend of mine suffering with severe rheumatoid arthritis gave me one of the most valuable lessons in my life. When I asked her, "How are you doing these days, Marguerite?" her face lit up in a radiant smile and she said, "I'm learning what to say 'Yes' to." She went on to say she was choosing carefully how she was willing to spend her life, with prayerful discernment about how she was called to balance prayer, work, and play. She had taken up painting and was gently working away at a self-portrait. I saw this as an act of true courage in Marguerite, who is a member of a religious order that highly values diligent work and selfless service. What a model she is for me of the virtues of detachment, acceptance, joyfulness, and yes, assertiveness.

Patricia is another woman I greatly admire, who was in her late seventies when she first attended a Virtues Project workshop. She promoted the project for years in her own international work on peace building with children and youth. She is one of the most gracious, elegant, and beautiful women I have ever known. Dan calls her "a woman of class." During one of our visits, she told me she was preparing for her next stage of life, knowing that at the age of eighty-three it would likely be her last. She was mustering the courage to give up the many services she had done for years for her local community in order to focus her attention on composing peace music as well as working with youth for peace at an international level. As she spoke of music, her face lit up. As she spoke of her many duties she was struggling to pry herself away from and the fact that people still called her "for everything," her brow was furrowed. I pointed this out to her and she laughed.

We talked about the fact that if she continued to say yes to the many requests she received to "help," she would be saying no to her heart's true work—to leave her music as a legacy. Composition requires contemplative time, free time unencumbered by interruptions. I urged her to come up with a simple phrase she could use to tactfully turn down the constant requests people made on her time. It took her a few days to come up with it: "You know I would love to support you in this, but I'm quite involved at the moment." No need to explain or justify—just a simple statement. She was delighted by this life-changing decision to assert her boundaries.

> *If it be Thy pleasure*
> *make me to grow as a tender herb*
> *in the meadows of Thy grace,*
> *that the gentle winds of Thy will*
> *may stir me up and bend me into*
> *conformity with Thy pleasure*
> *in such wise that my movement*
> *and my stillness may be wholly*
> *directed by Thee.*
> —Bahá'u'lláh (prophet-founder of the Baha'i Faith),
> *Prayers and Meditations*

Don't Miss Your Divine Opportunities

There are many good books on time management. I believe we can take any method and make it work, but first we must take ownership of our time, for it is ours. Or perhaps it is God's—in light of our being here for a purpose. Our Creator knows our unique gifts and has created us to serve in special ways in this brief span of time.

While traveling in Iran, I heard a story of a man who went to a prophet and offered him his life. The prophet said to him, "Go to this city and open a shop." The man immediately traveled there with great anticipation that he would be able to render a service to his Lord. He became a rug merchant. For years, he simply sold rugs, made a decent living, and of course began to wonder what it was all for. Ten years after he had opened his shop, a man was being chased through the streets by guards, shouting at him to surrender. He tossed a document rolled into a scroll into the rug shop and raced down the alley. The shopkeeper immediately hid the scroll and later opened it. It was an illumined tablet written in the hand of the prophet containing precious guidance for his followers. The rug merchant was full of joy that he had the privilege of guarding this tablet until a messenger came for it.

I never want to miss my true assignment because I'm too busy doing other things. I have a deep desire to be pleasing to God and to play the part that I am meant to play on this earth. Even as a child, I never wanted to miss anything.

I once heard Ruhiyyih Rabbani, a leader in the Baha'i Faith, speak at a conference in St. Louis on this theme. To paraphrase what she said, "I'm not worried about getting to heaven. I've lived a fairly decent life. I'm not worried about my sins of commission. God is kind and forgiving. It is my sins of omission that worry me. What opportunities has God placed in my path that I have missed?"

I once spent an entire day in prayer to discern what to do about my work situation. I was feeling pulled apart by my work at the hospice with the dying and their families, which I loved, and the emerging work of The Virtues Project, which served communities. As I meditated in the meadow around our home, I heard, "You will be offered a new job. You are not to take it. I have other things for you to do." I was puzzled, because my problem involved the two jobs I already had. The next day the chairman of the hospice board asked me to lunch and offered me the post of executive director. Before I could catch myself, I blurted out, "No!" He was naturally shocked. "Linda! You haven't even heard our offer." I replied, "I feel really honored that you are offering this job to me. Thank you, but I can't accept. I have other things to do." "What could you possibly do that would make more of a difference?" he said. "The Virtues Project." "Oh," he said, "that will never fly." Since then the Project has flown me around the world, and he has offered to eat his words.

CULTIVATE THE GIFT OF YOUR ASSERTIVENESS

To protect our time and energy with clear boundaries requires the virtue of assertiveness. It is one of the most challenging virtues to practice because we have been trained to avoid confrontation, and many of us have what twelve-step programs such as Alcoholics Anonymous call "the disease to please."

Assertiveness is the virtue that helps us establish what we will stand for and what we will not stand for. It is an attitude expressing truthfulness and justice. It allows us to clear draining activities from our lives, and to detach from people who are our energy vampires. Sometimes this person may be a close relative. It may be our own child, if the child has special needs or is very demanding. It may be a needy friend who leans too heavily, or an unreasonable boss. It may be your mother. I recall the story of a guilt-addicted mother who gave her son a gift of two shirts. "You don't like the shirts? Aren't you going to try them on?" she asked as soon as he had opened them. "Uh, sure, Mom." He put on the first shirt. She said, "You didn't like the other one?"

If you feel caught, helpless, or overwhelmed by an energy-draining relationship, you may not realize it, but you have ample choices about how to respond. We can't always and may not wish to divorce ourselves from close friends or family who drain us, but we can set boundaries about how and when we spend time with them.

The first step in deciding what your boundaries need to be is to detach, to step back and take the time to think about what you need to protect your energy and keep the relationship harmonious.

Being assertive helps us avoid both aggression and passivity. It doesn't mean being selfish and pushy. It is having the self-confidence to tell the truth about what is just, to say what we think and ask for what we need. The key to effectively practicing assertiveness is to balance it with tact. Once we step back and discern the basic line we intend to draw, we then need to find tactful yet truthful words to say. With some people, words just get us more enmeshed in problems, and simple action is what is needed. You cannot control what others do but you can control what you do.

Here are a few assertive statements you may find useful:

"I'm quite involved right now. Thanks for asking."

"My schedule is full at the moment. Please ask me again." (Only if you want them to!)

"I'd love to talk but I only have a few minutes. How can I help?"

"It would be great to see you, but I'm sticking close to home these days, needing a lot of quiet time. I appreciate your asking."

"I've already contributed my quotient to charities this year. Good luck with your campaign."

"Mom, my life is really full right now, so I can't spend as much time with you as I have been. I'll be visiting once a month and I'll call you every week."

"I'd be happy to help you with this new project. Which of my other jobs would you like me to put on the back burner?"

"Let me give it some thought."

"I'll think it over and let you know."

"I'll give it careful consideration."

The last three phrases are particularly helpful in responding to children's many requests and demands. Assertiveness is essential in parenting. When we appease our children by complying with their demands in the moment, promising something we later cannot fulfill, we destroy their trust and model dishonesty. We are teaching them to lie to avoid confrontation. Peace at any price is very expensive. It costs us our integrity and robs our children of trust. Be sure to be trustworthy—as well as assertive—and after you have thought it over, let them know what you have decided.

MAKE FAMILY LIFE HARMONIOUS

Boundaries are essential to prevent conflict and create a harmonious atmosphere in family life. Using the tactful, loving, assertive Language of Virtues to appreciate each other often and firmly calling for the virtues that are needed when a correction is necessary gives everyone a sense of safety. A family without boundaries is like a leaderless group—chaotic and confusing. Children feel safe when the boundaries are clear. Without them, they get into constant wrangling and fighting. In the area of discipline, many parents are what I call "sliders." They slide from being too permissive most of the time to blowing up and losing their temper when a child goes "too far."

Developing four or five ground rules that everyone agrees to abide by can transform family life into a relative haven of peace. One of my ground rules when my three grandchildren and I are together is that they only use peaceful language, even when they are angry or frustrated. We encourage the honest expression of feelings in our family. English is a rich language and we can choose many ways to express feelings that don't include curses. The first time I recognized the need for this boundary was when I was supervising them in a swimming race across a resort pool where we were vacationing. They had chosen floats and were kicking their way across the pool. One of my granddaughters had chosen small floats that kept sinking, and she was lagging behind. Suddenly, out of her mouth came a string of expletives fit for the proverbial sailor. I immediately ordered her out of the pool, wrapped her in a towel and said, "Darling, God gave you your tongue for beauty, not to say ugly words. I want you to think about that for a few minutes." She began to pout. I added, "When those few minutes are up, you will tell me three ways you could have expressed exactly what you were feeling using clean words." She perked right up, tapped her chin with her finger and began thinking. "I could have said, 'I feel mad inside.' That's one. 'I don't like this float. It's not working.' And 'This isn't fair. Can we start over?'" "Excellent!" I said. "Those are all respectful ways to use language when you feel frustrated." The race was restarted with equal support for each child.

This is an example of restorative justice, where a consequence is given that restores respect, or justice, or unity. Just punishing a child builds up resentment. The goal of this approach is to restore the virtue that was missing and to restore the offender back to the family or the classroom or the community.

Later, we were playing golf in a grassy area full of tufts, using miniature plastic clubs belonging to my grandson. The children laughed hysterically as I hit the ball about half an inch. "Stupid grass," I said, hoping for more laughs. Instead, my granddaughter pulled me by the arm and said, "Grandma, sit over here, please. Use your tongue beautifully. Three other things to say, please."

Whether you are single and sharing a place with roommates, or married with children, you are in a community. If you want life there to be harmonious, sit down and decide on a few ground rules together that will make life run smoothly. Using positive language (what you *do* want rather than what you don't want), and adding virtues, especially when children are involved, works well. For example: "This house is a peace zone. We speak, act, and treat each other's things with respect."

Here are some guidelines for effective family ground rules:
- Short and sweet—brief and positively worded
- Moderate: just three to five rules
- Virtues-based: include virtues words
- Include ways to make amends
- Are agreed on and clearly communicated

Protect Your Family Time

We live in an increasingly stressful work culture in which the workload keeps expanding while the workforce keeps shrinking. As companies downsize to cut costs, competition for jobs has us racing to keep up. In the midst of survival pressure, how can we protect our personal time? How do we meet our spiritual craving for solitude and also have better quality time with our children, our friends, and our intimates?

Virginia Satir, an esteemed Canadian family therapy specialist, was one of my models. Her book *Peoplemaking* had a profound influence on my thinking, my approach as a therapist, and my own family life. She wrote of a concept called "family engineering" in which each person in the family schedules time alone with each other person in the family, along with the entire family as well. Think of the intimacy that you have experienced when you have spent special, focused time with your mate, or with one of your children. If we are too busy to consider engineering our time in this way, then we are too busy. Loving moments sitting on the side of a child's bed, sitting in front of the fire with your partner, going out for an intimate dinner, going fishing with a child—these are the memories that matter. This is what builds sustainable intimacy. It is one of the most important uses of boundaries. These moments won't happen unless we make time and space for them to happen.

On a flight from Singapore to Kuala Lumpur, I learned more about protecting our pace of grace from my seat mate, Nizar, a salesman from India. We struck up a conversation, and he enthusiastically shared stories of his wheeling and dealing with clients. I found his confident manner and success rate in landing new distribution deals intriguing. At one point, I asked him how the constant travel affected his young family. His expression softened as he spoke tenderly of his wife and children. He had two ways of practicing assertiveness that allowed him to be very successful and at the same time balance his career with a pace of grace in his family life.

First, he used his travel time extremely efficiently and assertively. When scouting out new clients, he would first use the phone to cold-call the president or CEO of a company, telling the secretary or gatekeeper he only needed ten minutes of the CEO's time. He told them he had flown from India to open new distribution channels, had three days for all meetings, and said, "I can meet with you Monday." If they hesitated or said, "My calendar is fully booked Monday. That won't work for me," he would say, "That's up to you. I can give the opportunity to ABC Company instead." Almost invariably, he would get his appointment. One CEO chose to open her office on a Sunday, spent three hours with him and signed a contract before he left. His confidence that he had something of value to offer and his assertiveness about the value of his time generated great success.

A second practice of assertive boundaries is that his family time is sacrosanct. He never works after 5 P.M.—"I leave the office at the office." He also turns off his cell phone. "I never answer my cell phone when I am with my family. My staff knows that if something is urgent, they can leave a message on our home answering machine and I will deal with it if and when I choose." His weekends and family holiday time are protected as well. "No one will die if they don't hear from me while I am having fun with my family. That is far more important. My children and my wife know they can count on that time."

BALANCING THE VIRTUES

While it is essential to protect the time and energy you spend with your family, it is also essential that you protect yourself *within* your intimate relationships. A balanced life also requires solitude, time to replenish yourself away from your loved ones, time with friends who support you and see you. In our closest relationships, we must balance togetherness with separateness, care for others with self-care. Our relationships with our intimates can be the most challenging arenas in which to set boundaries that keep them resilient, abiding, and above all, safe. Our intimates can be our most loving mentors, or our worst tormentors, depending on the way we use power and control with each other, and basically the extent to which we respect each other's ways of being.

Sacrifice is often called for, but it must never include the sacrifice of our sense of self. One of my dear friends, a craggy, charming Scotswoman with whom I have gone on retreat for many years, describes a deeply private sense of herself that she has never allowed marriage, or six children, or a challenging life working in the family business to steal from her—"It is my innermost self. A tender green shoot in the center of my being." The Maori have a word for personal power, which also means the spirit of a person or a people. It is "mana." I remember a Maori friend telling a woman who was continually having problems at work and in any group she joined, "Set your boundaries. Don't give away your mana."

I have discovered over the years that the spiritual practices of the virtues almost always need to be in balance, that to stand on our holy ground requires us to put one foot in one virtue and one foot in another. For example, forgiveness and justice are balancing virtues. If you go on forgiving someone and allowing them to continue hurting you, that is not just and it does not serve either of you. Tact and truthfulness go together, as do determination and discernment, helpfulness to others and assertiveness to seek help when we need it. Setting boundaries in our most intimate relationships is having one foot in assertiveness and the other in acceptance. Without acceptance of the things we cannot change about one another, assertiveness becomes rigidity. Without assertiveness, acceptance gives us no stopping place, no solid sense of what is acceptable and what is not. Spiritual and emotional abuse, as well as physical abuse, exist in many relationships in which these two virtues are out of balance.

Stop in the Name of Love

Genuine boundaries require a shift in our spirit, a resolve that "this has to stop." A decision that a relationship must change or go out of our lives is a huge one. In the category of "if only I knew then what I know now," I count my awareness that I can discern what is just and have the right to require it. When we are at the end of our rope with a relationship, we might cry, rage, or in some way try to impress on our partner how deeply we are hurt. This is meant to motivate them to change, and we are shocked when they just dig in deeper or rage back. The truth is that we are throwing ourselves on their mercy rather than having mercy and justice ourselves. We spend all our energy trying to get *them* to change, when the one and only person we have the power to change is ourselves. We decide what *we* are going to do to change things and what we require in order to stay. Only you can discern things that need to change and take action to make that happen.

A woman attending one of my retreats said that the gift she received from the weekend was a brand-new awareness that she had the power to set boundaries in her relationship with her husband. She could balance love and assertiveness. She had taken some reflection time to walk and write in her journal the three things that needed to change if she was going to stay in her marriage. She saw the ways that she was colluding with her husband's overspending, abusive language, and refusal to clean up after himself. She realized that by practicing love and assertiveness, she could stop feeling helpless—begging, nagging, and crying to get him to change.

She decided to take three actions: First, she would open her own checking account and deposit her paycheck into it, deciding what she would place in the family account and contributing to a savings account each month, rather than dumping all she earned in the family account for her husband to spend with abandon. Second, she would ask her husband to speak to her respectfully and immediately walk away if he chose not to. Third, she would wash only what he put in the hamper, piling anything he left lying around in a plastic bag in their closet. She later told me that the combination of focusing on her husband's positive virtues and her new boundaries had utterly transformed their relationship.

Assertiveness allows us to stand strong without overpowering someone or allowing them to disempower us. It is asserting in a positive way what we need: "If I am going to stay in this marriage, these are the things that must change. This is what I'm going to do differently. What else do you need from me to help this happen?" This is very different from the manipulative attitude of, "If you don't change, I'm leaving." It is taking a stand that you need to treat each other respectfully and fairly. When you do this, you are raising the context to the level of principle—of virtue—rather than condemning the character of your partner.

One time when I was struggling in my marriage, I decided to give a workshop on codependence—the syndrome of living through and for another, enmeshing yourself in that person's life, putting up with and covering up addiction and dysfunction. I opened the workshop by saying, "This is my first workshop on codependence, but don't worry. I'm an expert on codependence, because I'm an expert codependent. I'm giving this workshop because I need to take it."

I have learned through years of struggle to distinguish my spiritual work from my husband's work, to distinguish between responsibility and control. Whose power do you carry? Whose issues do you focus on? We must not carry what is not ours to carry, because while we are busy trying to control or protect or change someone else, our own spiritual work will languish.

Having the courage and assertiveness to set clear boundaries with our time, energy, and relationships is a powerful way to sustain a pace of grace and lead our lives as we choose.

Your time . . . is property that belongs to the Lord . . . and if [you]
do not make good use of it [you] shall be held accountable.
—Brigham Young,
Church of Jesus Christ of Latter-day Saints

⊷≋ EXERCISE GRACE ≋↢
Set Three Boundaries

Take a look at your first Exercise of Grace in chapter 1. What stresses you and what blesses you? This is key to discovering the boundaries you need to create in your life. Observe the activities that, if you set limits on them, would really help you conserve your energy and enjoy your life more.

During your quiet time, reflect and journal about how effective your boundaries are in the three areas of time, energy, and money. Think about where you feel the greatest energy drain and begin there. Is it overspending? Is it too much wasted time on the phone? Is it allowing constant interruptions in your work? Do you need to schedule personal time? Do you need to be a more assertive disciplinarian with your children?

Make a start by setting three clear boundaries:

- Word them positively.
- Word them in the present tense ("I am," not "I will").
- Include a virtue, the language of your personal power.

For example:

1. Respect: I am willing to continue conversations only when they remain respectful.
2. Moderation: I screen my calls and keep each call to ten minutes.
3. Joy: One hour a day is mine to do whatever I want, as long as it brings me joy.

SUMMARY OF CHAPTER 10:
SET CLEAR BOUNDARIES

- Be the architect of your own time. Commit to a gentle pace. You deserve it.
- Discover your natural boundaries and lead your life accordingly.
- Reduce the time you spend with people and activities that drain you. Choose what sustains you.
- Avoid telephone tyranny. Decide when *you* want to be available.
- Realize that trying to be everything to everyone—the E-Type personality—may cost you your health and your life.
- Put people first and protect your family time.
- Create clear ground rules to make family life run smoothly.
- Create boundaries for yourself within your intimate relationships.
- Never give your power away.
- Establish your balancing virtues. They are your holy ground.

As you explore the boundaries you want to set in your life, there is another essential element to consider—time for play. The next chapter focuses on play as the balancing element that keeps our hearts beating gently, nurtures our relationships, and feeds our spirits.

$\mathcal{P}$lay!

One ought every day at least, to hear a little song, read a good poem, see a fine
picture, and if it were possible, to speak a few reasonable words.
—Johann Wolfgang von Goethe

What are the happiest memories of your life? I imagine that for most of us they include lazy summer afternoons, playing with our children, an adventure trek in a place of beauty, a moment of laughter with friends. Yet we get so caught up in the daily flurry of work and duty that we give little time or thought to doing something fun, something purely enjoyable to loosen our tight grip on ourselves, to invite surprises.

When we are in survival mode, just trying to get through the day at a time of illness, the notion of play may seem absurd, even frivolous. Yet two of the Ten Rules for health focused on the value of play and the pursuit of joy:

Rule 7: Pursue Peaceful Activity
Cut television down. It depresses you. Read what comes to you. Listen to music, clear and clean in small ways, watch the fire, write letters to your friends.

Rule 8: Play!
Spend time in ways that give you joy and make you laugh.

I spent much of my life as a workaholic who felt I could never "afford" free time, so I felt guilty spending it. The morning the Ten Rules were given to me, I was very ill, unable to walk. I felt I could hardly breathe from the dense weight of fatigue and was puzzled as I looked at these two rules. I realized I had absolutely no idea what play meant in my situation. Then, a memory dawned of being mystified by the word "play" years before.

I blushed with embarrassment as I recalled my interview for the job of Hospice Spiritual Care Director. Because it was the first time they had created this role they felt it essential that all department heads as well as the executive director and medical director choose the individual. They were all crammed into a small room to interview the candidates. When I was escorted into the room, my first words were, "Oh, not too intimidating." They laughed, and someone tossed me a teddy bear. They peppered me with probing questions, including the approaches I would take to offer spiritual care in several challenging case histories they had sent ahead of time. Never at a loss for opinions, I enjoyed the rigor of the interview and seemed to be sailing through the questions—until I was floored by a question asked by the head counsellor: "How do you play?" I literally misunderstood the question, thinking she meant "the rules of the game" or something. I nattered on about volunteer structures I might put in place for spiritual care, then wound down and said, "What was the question?" She repeated it and I admitted, "I'm not sure what you mean." I believe she had her answer, although I did get the job anyway.

Over the months, as I did my best to follow the Ten Rules, I came to understand that I can't afford *not* to play or pursue peaceful activities. Not only do they bring grace into my day; they also revive and refuel my energy for the more focused and purposeful activities. Not that you do them for that reason! You just do them because they bring you joy. Being the task-focused woman I am, I admit it took me a while to figure out what play is for me, but now that it has become part of the flow of my life, I am utterly enamored of it.

HAVE A GOOD TIME

Just because I didn't grasp the notion of play easily, please don't think I was humorless. Far from it. One of the ways I did play was to laugh with Dan every day. Before post-polio hit, I regularly took walks with friends. Then, with limited activity possible, I had to be more creative about it. So I became a guilt-free "lunchist," arranging for lunches with my friends when energy permitted. As I began to regain my strength and get back on the road, whether traveling alone or with my husband, I made sure to insert time off in my schedule. I arrived one or more days early before a workshop, retreat, or conference to get the lay of the land and do something fun. I would pack my spa things so I could give myself a personal spa treatment. If I was involved in a longer community-development project, I would get the name of a massage therapist in the area and schedule a massage on

⇒ *The Virtue of Creativity* ⇐

Let us use the different gifts allotted to each of us by God's grace.
—Romans 12:6

Creativity powers the imagination. Creativity is discovering your own special talents. Dare to see things in original ways and find different ways to
solve problems. With our creativity, we can bring something new into the
world. Spending time recreating ourselves brings joy to our lives.

Signs of Success

I am practicing Creativity when I . . .
- Discover and develop my gifts
- Think of new ways to make things work better
- Use my imagination to bring something new into the world
- Take time for dreaming
- Use the originality of my soul
- Enjoy my recreation

Affirmation

*I am creative. I have special gifts and use discipline to develop them. I am
open to inspiration. I am happy to be myself.*

a day off. When scheduling a trip together, Dan and I plan extra time on either side of the presentations for touring or lying on a beach. I adore snorkeling and make time for it on every trip to the South Pacific.

This is a far cry from my days as a management consultant, when I would fly into cities like Washington, D.C., Portland, or Dallas and leave no time for anything but meetings with clients. What absurd deprivation I created by taking myself, and my work, far too seriously.

I once asked the owner-manager of a small resort hotel in the Solomon Islands how it felt to have one of the world's best snorkeling spots in his own backyard. Within a few feet of the small beach behind the hotel was a deep canyon with brilliant schools of fish and pristine coral in pastel shades of pink, blue, ochre, and green. After our daily seminar ended, I would rush to our room, slip on my bathing suit and snorkel and run to the beach to plunge into the warm tropical waters. I immersed myself in this undersea world. The manager said to me, "Oh, I haven't done that in years. Too busy."

HAVE FAMILY FUN

One of the ways family life can be more fun is to regularly play with our children. Hugs and giggles, spontaneous surprises, sudden adventures can be short and very sweet. Play is a bonding agent. It is the glue that holds a family together in joy and makes life smoother.

One of the happiest memories my two brothers and I share of our mother is her habit of sudden surprises. She'd say, "Let's have an adventure!" and we'd all jump in the car. As she revved up her '57 Chevy, she'd gaily shout, "Off we go in a cloud of smoke!" Then, we had the exciting job of guiding the car: "Turn at the next corner, Mom," we'd say. "Go around in a circle in this parking lot," and she would. We would end up somewhere in our town we had perhaps never been. It was exhilarating to be in her laughing presence. These moments of the pure joy of just being together made happy memories.

TRANSFORM FUN FROM VIOLENCE TO VIRTUES

I am very concerned about the things children associate with fun today. The entertainment generation is hooked on overstimulating simulations through sophisticated computer games. Children become inured to violence, watching tens of thousands of violent acts each year on television or in video games. In this world, violence is typically merged with heroism. No wonder murder is one of the leading causes of death for youth from fifteen to twenty-four. They cut their teeth on it.

I believe children need to be protected from excessive electronic and visual stimulation. As they get older, "going drinking" is supposed to be fun. All these things are dangerous for them, not only physically, but spiritually. They need time to stare at clouds, to canoe down green rivers, to flow with their imaginations. They need time for dreaming.

More and more youth programs are springing up that are based on adventure. The National Youth Mentoring Network in the United States uses mountaineering and ropes courses to inspire courage and self-reliance in students. Alternative Youth Adventures takes incarcerated youth out of jail into the wilderness for months, where they find healing, respect, unity, and a fresh sense of who they are.

We had the opportunity to meet remarkable students and a special teacher at Stelly's Secondary School in Victoria, British Columbia, when filming a television series on youth and violence prevention. Four times a year, Peter Mason, a local high school teacher, takes a group of his students mountain climbing. "Kids are basically good," he says. "They just need a healthy dose of adventure." One year, high school student Ryan Human, who is quadraplegic and wheelchair-bound, shared his secret wish with this teacher that he too could climb a mountain. Mr. Mason recruited students willing to practice self-sacrifice, knowing they might not make it to the summit but willing to try what seemed an impossible task. On this difficult trek up steep, snowy, and often thickly forested areas, they used every bit of their ingenuity and stamina. One time, they devised pulleys to get Ryan's sled up a particularly steep incline. At last the summit was in sight. When Ryan has support on either side of him, he can walk a short distance. With Mr. Mason and another teacher holding him on either side, Ryan made it to the top of that mountain. Can you imagine the joy those young people felt to have fulfilled Ryan's dream? "It was just indescribable helping someone to do that," said one of the students. This was fun they will never forget. This was sacred.

Know When to Retreat

We have a deep need for spaciousness in our experience of time. Our souls require noncompulsory time on a regular basis—time in which nothing is asked of us, nothing is required. Our relationships thrive in an atmosphere of simply being together, spending time doing nothing in particular in a place we enjoy.

A dear friend of mine works as a music therapist and has four children. Ron regularly takes himself off for free time—noncompulsory time—to a beach house owned by a friend. He thirsts for solitude, for strumming time, for gazing at blue water. When he begins to feel empty, and notices his short temper or irritability with his wife, he knows it's time for a retreat. He returns full, ready to resume loving and serving.

In my abundant life, which is as full as I allow it to be, what sustains me throughout the year is the promise that I will have retreat time in three ways: a retreat alone, a retreat with my husband, and at least one retreat in the company of women. Each of these is in a place of great natural beauty and quiet. For my private retreat, I go to a convent only a couple of hours from my home, where my room is simply furnished with a single bed, a comfortable chair by the window, and a small vase of fresh flowers on a shelf. I love the cool sheets smoothed by hundreds of washings. The meals are simple, delicious, and nourishing. I meditate while I swim in the heated pool and walk the labyrinth, and take walks to a nearby beach, where I sit and watch eagles and seals. In this place, I have a sense of being wrapped in loving silence. Dan and I often take our retreat time on a beach in some exotic country after a presentation, or we go to the pristine wilderness of a lake in northern Canada and float for a week in a houseboat.

Every year for the past ten years I have gathered with a group of women at a riverside lodge in the forest. We are more sisters than friends. We float, sing, dance, swim, and do crafts on the deck in the sun. We paint each other's toenails in outrageous colors. We play. Every year, we say we need more time. At first it was a weekend. This year we will be playing together for a full week.

HAVE A PLAY SPACE AT HOME

One of the ways men obtain their grace time is to have a place for their tools and their projects, a place to dream and while away the time—to putter. It is a wonderful, restorative form of meditation whether or not they produce anything recognizable or useful. It is a way for them to play. Men's dens and workshops are their sanctuaries. I read a marvelous book by Mark Thomson during our travels in Australia, *Blokes and Sheds*. It features wonderful photos of guys leaning lovingly against dilapidated and overstuffed lean-tos, while others proudly display their neat arrays of tools. They have an almost smug look of pride and fierce contentment in their eyes, as if to say, "Yeah, mate. This is my place."

I think we all need our corner of creativity—for crafts, projects, and above all spending nonobligatory time just being. Whenever my husband and I have looked for a home, the existence of a refuge room for each of us has been a leading criterion. In our home of fifteen years, Dan has an entire outbuilding to himself and I have a smaller room within our home that serves as my play and work room. I need nesting. He needs space for his huge array of projects and massive book and music collection. It works well for us. Even a small corner in one room can be your special place of creativity. Make a place for it. It will bring you joy.

CHANGE IS THE SPICE OF LIFE

Refreshing ourselves requires variety—fresh experiences that lift us out of our ordinary lives. Because my normal life involves a good deal of travel to exotic destinations, I find it luxurious to stand in my kitchen cutting up fresh vegetables for homemade soup, wandering out in the early morning to pick flowers from our deck garden and slowly arranging them in a lovely bowl—doing everyday chores slowly, folding laundry contemplatively. Time off at home refreshes me. Others need a trip away to step out of their normal world.

Jennifer, a young business executive, has to get completely away for her noncompulsory time. She says, "I like to get completely out of my realm. I can live out of a backpack for ten days." She and her husband plan well in advance each year for wilderness treks, such as biking and hiking the West Coast Trail in British Columbia or canoeing the Green River in Utah. They ship bikes, clothes, and basic supplies ahead to their destination. "It is really grounding for me. It reminds me how simply we can live, how fragile the balance of nature is."

Many people in midlife have discovered a thirst for this sort of adventure and are following in the footsteps of their twenty-something children. They have no interest in packaged tours and predetermined holidays. They take off for months at a time across Europe or Asia or Australia with nothing but backpacks and a general sense of where they want to go. They stay in youth hostels and teahouses. One travel article said some baby boomers are discovering that "after a lifetime of accumulating wealth and possessions, sometimes the best plan is no plan at all." They crave adventure, simplicity, awakening of their senses and a deepening of experience—time to be.

PLAY EVERY DAY

Actually, we need time just to *be* every day. This is a stretch for most busy people. However, it is essential to our quality of life. Busy parents may wonder how this is possible. Professionals whose workdays are long may wonder how realistic this is. Even someone homebound by illness may be challenged by this notion. Again it comes back to the issue of valuing ourselves

> *A good traveler has no fixed plans, and is not intent on arriving.*
> —Lao-tzu

enough to become the architects of our time rather than at the mercy of the demands that always come to fill the time. The key is to plan our days and to include interludes to enjoy ourselves and make ourselves peaceful.

Make a list of things you enjoy, for example:

- Lunch with a friend
- A night out with the guys
- Sorting jewelry
- Dancing
- Singing
- Playing an instrument
- Listening to good music

- Staring at clouds
- Reading a good book
- Building a model
- Gardening
- Making bread
- Quilting
- Going fishing
- Drawing
- Crafts

- Making innovative gifts
- Playing with your children
- Taking a walk in a new place
- Playing a sport
- Doing a crossword

Or don't make a list. Just wake up your imagination. Do something spontaneous. Have a picnic in the park. Spread newspapers on the floor and make bread with your three-year-old. Almost all of these things are activities that take little time, and most of them can easily happen on a daily basis. We just have to make time for them.

> *When you discard arrogance, complexity, and a few other things that get in the way, sooner or later you will discover that simple, childlike and mysterious secret . . . Life is Fun.*
> —Benjamin Hoff, author,
> *The Tao of Pooh*

RE-CREATE YOURSELF

Many of us flop down in front of the television as our only way of taking time off. Yet it does not re-create us, especially if it is excessive. It depresses our breathing and our minds. If we replace this habit with at least a half hour of doing something fun either alone or with friends or family members, it will give us a great energy boost, especially if it gives us a chance to laugh. Laughter releases endorphins into our system, which are natural antidotes to stress.

One of the things that delights me is making something creative with my hands—a Collage of Dreams, representing my personal vision; decorating storage boxes for my office supplies with decoupage; or constructing something out of papier-mâché. I find it utterly engaging and one of the few activities that frees me from thinking. I can just be. When I am on retreat with my women friends, we luxuriate in leisurely hours making crafts.

One of the happiest childhood memories for my son, Craig, who is now a full-grown engineer and software developer, is the elaborate thingamabobs and whatchamacallits he would construct with the recycled materials I saved in a craft basket: toilet paper and paper towel rolls, macaroni boxes, coffee tins, and anything else that seemed reusable. The family would gather around for the big moment when he sent a golf ball careening through loops and tunnels, or a coin coursed through a three-dimensional maze to finally plunk into a waiting "bank" of some exotic shape.

Having fun on a regular basis needn't be expensive. It is expensive not to. Fun is doing, and it is also being. It is an attitude of enthusiasm for whatever we are doing.

HAVE FUN AT WORK

Small acts of kindness and creativity can light up the day for people in the workplace. My brother, John Kavelin, is now an executive with the Walt Disney Company. He has a practice of carrying a basket of sweets around to his staff at the time of day when energy is low. He also sweetens their day with virtues acknowledgments and words of encouragement and humor. The CEO of a consulting firm I worked for used to leave appreciation notes and bits of glitter ("fairy dust from the Excellence Fairy") on employees' chairs or desks if she was pleased with something we did. My son worked for a software company in Seattle for several years. He was deeply impressed during his first week on the job when his supervisor took all the employees off to see the latest *Star Wars* movie. These are small things, yet they mean a lot. They brighten the day.

Don't Worry, Be Happy

My friend Judi Morin, a Sister of St. Ann, describes six things people who lead happy lives have in common. Very happy people:

1. Expect to enjoy the day
2. Spend energy on fixing, not complaining
3. Spend at least ten minutes each day doing what they thoroughly enjoy
4. Do kind acts for others
5. Go on adventures
6. Find the gift in every experience

Happy people center their days on joyfulness, live with a sense of purpose, accept what can't be changed and fix what can, show kindness on a regular basis and live with enthusiasm and gratitude for the gifts in everything. These uplifting virtues are the real gifts of a graceful life.

What gives you joy? In our workshops, we have an activity called a "Joy Mixer" in which each person walks around the room, stops and stands facing another person, asking this question of one another. Each time people answer the question, they have to come up with a new answer about what gives them joy. I notice when people take their seats again, their faces are beaming with smiles. When we weave more play into our everyday lives, it gives us a way to sustain our joy. It lightens our lives.

May you be filled with loving kindness.
May you be well.
May you be peaceful and at ease.
May you be happy.
—ancient Tibetan Buddhist blessing

⤙⟾ EXERCISE GRACE ⟻⤚
Plan a Personal Retreat

Decide what you need most: a retreat for solitude, or one for creating intimacy with your partner, a friend, or your children. Do some research to find a place that is easy to get to and affordable, and schedule the retreat. Take your time deciding what you need to take with you and keep a list. Keep it simple. Examples are:

- a journal and pen
- good walking shoes
- a camera
- at least one novel
- bathing suit
- massage oil

If you have children, you may want to offer to trade weekend child care with a friend so that you can have some time alone. Decide the length of time you need or feel you can take, guilt-free. For some it will be two weeks, for others it will be a mini-retreat of two days. Enjoy!

SUMMARY OF CHAPTER 11: PLAY!

- Spend time in ways that give you joy and make you laugh. It's essential.
- Find simple, spontaneous ways to have family fun by using your creativity.
- Give children alternatives to electronic and entertainment violence. Nature provides the best adventures.
- Have a place in your home for creativity and play.
- Change your normal routine. Step out of your normal world. Design personal getaways with enjoyment in mind.

- Dare to just go, without definite plans. Let the road take you.
- Play every day in some small way.
- Engage in activities that re-create you. Don't settle for boredom.
- Have fun at work. Do something creative and fun.
- Find the gifts in your grace-filled life.

In Part Three, "Practice the Presence," we will explore the experience of grace more deeply, with ways to invite the grace of God into our lives and to be God's grace in the lives of others.

PRACTICE THE PRESENCE

*We may desire to bring to God
a perfect work.
We would like to point, when
our work is done,
to the beautiful ripened grain,
and bound up sheaves,
and yet the Lord frustrates our
plans,
shatters our purposes,
lets us see the wreck of all our
hopes,
breaks the beautiful structure
we thought we were building
and catches us up in His arms
and whispers to us,
"It's not your work I wanted,
but you."*

—Quiet Moments: A Collection
of Prayers and Meditations,
Lyn Whittall and Judy Hager,
editors

⤳⟺ *TWELVE* ⟺⤳

$\mathcal{P}$ray

One of the most fruitful ways of drawing grace into one's life is a heartfelt prayer.
—Swami Chidvilasananda, Yogi of Siddha Yoga, also known as Guru Mayi

Have you ever been in a state of grace? A few times in my life, I have been fortunate to experience a blissful, mysterious condition that I can only describe in those terms. I experienced bright awareness, a luminous clarity in the air, when all my senses were attuned and alive, and all felt right with the world. I felt utterly at home in the presence of something equally intimate and mysterious.

Small children have a natural sense of awe and wonder. As adults, we easily forget how awesome life is. When we get up in the morning and rush into busyness, we cannot easily connect to our own feelings or thoughts—much less tap into our virtues of reverence, gratitude, or awe—as our "setting" for the day. When we practice a pace of grace—by purifying our bodies, our thoughts, and our language, resting and playing daily, and seeing every day as a good day—we may find that a state of grace is not necessarily a singular, dramatic event. It is a regular attitude of receptivity—an openness to grace. Life is, more often than not, a prayer.

The sixth of the Rules for Health involved prayer. At the time I first received it, I failed to understand it as an invitation rather than an obligation. It puzzled me.

Rule 6: Pray Every Hour

To be honest, as those words came to me in meditation, my first thought was, "Isn't that a bit much?" I was already spending a half hour to an hour every morning trying to pray despite my brain fog. As if reading my private doubts, the message continued:

Let your movement be a prayer, your work, your daily food.

At the time I was too fatigued to recognize the meaning of these words and the invitation they held. As the months went by, I found it difficult to remain

mindful with such regularity. I made feeble attempts to remember to stop and
pray during the day but just couldn't stick with it. I was quite faithful to the other
rules, and little by little my energy began to be restored. For a time, I funneled it
greedily into the task of the moment—glad to be able to think and do again.
Eventually I was overtaken once again by a task focus rather than being equally
aware of the people around me. My husband pointed out that he could be standing right beside me talking to me and if I was hammering away at e-mails, I
couldn't hear him, much less remember what he said.

Over time, it dawned on me that hourly prayer was not meant to be some
rigid ritual to steal me away from my "important work," but rather a way to sustain my connection to grace *as* I worked, read, gardened, or engaged with my
husband. By practicing the presence of Spirit, I began to act, to move, to work,
and even to eat mindfully. I tasted my food instead of mentally wandering away
to forage for ideas. I was more connected to my body.

Being sufficiently mindful to recall Spirit each hour is a simple and profound antidote to the experience of being completely sucked into the task of the
moment. It allows us to hold a task lightly, with single-pointed intention and
concentration, yet without losing an awareness of our bodies.

As a child, I took Divine grace for granted. I prayed with the absolute con-
viction that I had God's ear, and that the Creator was abidingly interested in my
thoughts and needs. I remember a moment of grace when I was a girl of five,
pacing the perimeter of our yard, and chatting to God. A powerful thought
formed in my mind—more than a thought, a calling. "When I grow up, please let
me help people." I had a sense of a connection to the whole earth and to many,
many people. I felt God's smiling consent. Perhaps the prayer started on God's
end. That happens when prayer is an ongoing conversation. As Brother Lawrence,
a seventeenth-century monk said, "There is not in the world a kind of life more
sweet and delightful than that of a continual conversation with God."

As I grew older, notions of authority and guilt tainted that pure presence for
me. I became dutiful in my devotions, more abstract and distant. A crisis of faith
in my thirties catapulted me out of this flat, impersonal practice. While going
through the pain of my divorce, I went right off the mark—the simple definition
of sin. At my lowest ebb, I realized I had cut myself off from God and wanted
back in. One night when I was alone in the house, I paced the bedroom, screaming a childish prayer of rage and longing to a God I assumed would reject me for
my betrayal. Suddenly, the air around me became charged. I became very still

and felt I was being enfolded in pure tenderness. I melted in this embrace of for-giveness and reunion. This experience was a turning point leading me to a more meaningful practice of my faith and into a renewed and richer prayer life, far more intimate and honest than before.

Prayer as Relationship

One of the Teachable Moments I received in this redemptive experience of grace was that it is a mistake to abdicate our spirituality to our religion. Whether you attend religious services regularly, use your prayer beads faithfully, or follow pre-scribed prayers daily, something more awaits you with infinite patience and longing. It is all too easy to slip comfortably into form without spirit. Our spiri-tual lives can become like a dry but dutiful marriage in which two people live parallel lives, are pleasant to each other but never really touch.

I have some grief about the fact that for a period of years the stress of over-work took over my life, and I allowed it to rob me of this amazing, accessible grace. It was my choice to remain in the FOG of Fatigue, Overwhelm, and Guilt, but who knew? One morning during my prayer time, I felt the presence of my fa-ther's spirit softly brush against my cheek. He said, "Don't get caught up, sweetie. You're just a whisper away from eternity."

Some of us have allowed our Fatigue, Overwhelm, and Guilt to become a lifestyle. It literally takes us out of our minds. We are so externally focused and pressured to keep up with the demands of an excessive life that we forfeit the ca-pacity for being rather than doing. We are not truly present to our lives. Natu-rally, we feel bereft.

What is fundamentally missing is intimacy—first intimacy to ourselves, with love, respect, and gentle attention. In cultivating this practice of presence to ourselves, we are inevitably led to a deeper sense of reverence, and an experience of a greater presence. Our consciousness shifts from being a tourist in our own lives to being a pilgrim.

When at the advice of a friend in my mentors' circle I became the longed-for "good mother" to myself, as strange as it seemed at first, it was wonderful. I reg-ularly journaled during my reflection time, "What do you need today to keep your pace of grace?" If I felt anxious or irritable, I would ask myself, "What is it, sweetheart? What do you need?" I noticed when I was getting tired and would immediately stop and rest. I created a fun activity for myself each day, and in general applied the Ten Rules for Health with the same loving attitude toward myself as I would for one of my children. Most of us would never treat a beloved child the way we treat ourselves, driving ourselves without mercy.

I felt I could trust myself, for the first time, to protect my body from excess. This unfamiliar tenderness for myself had the effect of deepening my compassion for my husband and for everyone in my world. Judgments fell away. I experienced a growing sense of being loved by my Creator, cherished as a source of delight, even in my weaknesses and frailties. My heart opened to love as it never had before. I had heard all my life, "Love thy neighbor as thyself," but now that expression took on new meaning.

THERE ARE MANY WAYS TO PRAY

From my study of the world's religions and the privilege of working with communities of many varying sacred traditions, one of my particular interests over the years is the way prayer is understood and practiced. I have learned that prayer is an experience as varied as the people on earth. My own prayer practice as a Baha'i has been enriched by Native Americans and First Nations people of Canada, whose prayer life is a natural part of existence—not segmented off but infused into every activity with a sense of the deep connectedness of all living things. I have been blessed by an invitation to a vision quest on the land occupied for ten thousand years by the Tahltan First Nation. I have been with Aborigines in Australia who chant and dance their prayer, and Moslems in Kuala Lumpur who pray five times a day. I had a profound experience of sacred journaling in a Jesuit dream group. I have chanted in the presence of Guru Mayi (Swami Chidvilasananda) and received her blessing in a Darshan ceremony. My prayer life has been greatly enriched by Christian mystics and the study of Spiritual Direction, a special kind of counseling that focuses on one's prayer life. Formerly used exclusively for and by religious persons (nuns and priests), this practice is now commonly available to lay people, both as recipients and practitioners. For seven years I was in mutual Spiritual Direction with my friend Judi, who is a Sister of St. Ann. Through these years of rich multifaith experience, I have come to a profound appreciation of the common thread of devotion shared by all of humanity as well as a universal love for the virtues at the heart of every sacred tradition. In reality, we humans have far more in common than we do differences. As St. Paul said in 1 Corinthians 12:12, ". . . for we belong to one another as the parts of one body."

> God has infinite treasure to bestow, and we take up with a little sensible devotion, which passes in a moment. Blind as we are, we hinder God and stop the current of His graces. But when He finds a soul penetrated with a lively faith, He pours into it His grace and favors plentifully; there they flow like a torrent . . . which spreads itself with impetuosity and abundance.
>
> —Brother Lawrence

Do We Know How Wonderful We Are?

To truly know ourselves, we are told in the scriptures of the world's religions, is to know God. We were created in the image of God—a mirror of the Divine nature capable of reflecting God's peace, love, justice, gentleness, and all the Divine virtues. As described in the Second Epistle of Peter (1:2–4), we are "participants in the divine nature."

The virtues are our connection to the Divine nature. Godliness—being like God—is to live by patience, faith, peace, kindness, wisdom, and the other virtues.

Above all, prayer is a relationship with the Divine within us and beyond us. While deepening our relationship to ourselves in a reverent way, we are opening ourselves to the unknown, the ineffable. To know ourselves intimately is to connect deeply with our true reality and to move through the day in the presence of Grace. It is being mindful—knowing that we are in our bodies, alert to what is real, listening for the voice of spirit. It is being aware and willing. Brother Lawrence, who had to hide his ecstatic personal prayer life at a time when the church frowned on it as egotism and Satanic delusion, had a constant sense of God's loving presence. He wrote about the flow of grace those with a prayerful attitude invite.

We are so much more wondrous than we know. We have the capacity for a rich, spiritual life, whatever our circumstances may be. To partake of this inner wealth, however, we have to nurture it.

Create a Routine of Reverence

Many people wish for a spiritual connection but wonder how to create it. For years, when I have shared stories of my prayer life, people have come up to me after a presentation and asked me, "How do you meditate? I want to discern

God's will. I just don't know how." Many people these days seek a deeper personal connection, a way of discerning what they are meant to do with their lives.
One workshop participant told me, "I wish God would show me a sign, and tell
me what to do, but I don't see any." I remember wishing the same thing before
the spiritual turning point in my thirties, when I first experienced God's "embrace." I was clueless at the time about how to begin. Wanting a deeper connection with Spirit *is* the way to begin.

How do you begin any relationship? You take time to get to know the person. In this case, you are taking the time through a daily routine of reflection and
reverence to create an intimacy with your own spirit, and with the Divine.

What follows are some simple methods of prayer, meditation, and discernment, some that are my own practices, some from the experience of people of
varied beliefs and ways of connecting. I truly believe that anyone can cultivate a
relationship with the Divine at any time, whatever their past experience or beliefs. I recently read in Dean Koontz's wonderful novel *One Door Away from
Heaven,* these beautiful words about grace:

> . . . *your life can change for the better in one moment of grace, almost a
> sort of miracle. Something so powerful can happen, someone so special
> come along, some precious understanding descend on you so unexpectedly
> that it just pivots you in a new direction, changes you forever.*

Simple steps exist that you can take to cultivate a relationship with grace and
to enrich your spiritual practices. First, develop a regular routine of reverence.
Whether or not you consider yourself religious, the only way to keep a pace of
grace in your life is to have a time of deliberate silence in which to reflect each
and every day. By doing this, you are developing your inner life and your capacity to live reflectively and purposefully. Whatever your beliefs are, stillness and
reflection are as essential to your spirit and your character as food is to your
body. The discipline of regular reflection requires two things to begin with: sacred time and sacred space.

CREATE SACRED TIME

Any relationship you value takes time. Your relationship to the sacred, however you define it, requires first of all a commitment to take the time for deliberate solitude, a commitment to at least one definite time for prayer every day.

Find the best time of day that you can regularly create privacy for reflection and prayer. It must be a time that you are not too tired, so that you can have clear concentration. For us "larks" it is in the morning, before the doings of the day impinge. For "owls" it would be at night. I prefer to begin prayer before dawn, and it has become my natural pattern of awakening. I love to watch the sun rise as I begin my routine of reverence. For some young parents, their reflection time comes at the end of the day, when the dishes are done and the children are put to bed. Twice a day is ideal, with one being your concentrated reflection time and the other being a brief but gentle pause of gratitude with which to begin or end your day.

Eileen, a mother of two toddlers, had a very clear boundary that from one to two every afternoon was her private prayer time. The children were put down to rest and knew that even if they didn't sleep they were to play silently in their beds so that Mama could have her quiet time alone. She sat in a living room rocker beside a small table that held her books, her journal, and a pen. When her quiet hour was finished, she and the girls would do something fun together, beginning with a snack of cookies and milk.

Evelyn, a marketing director for a large suburban library, drives to her office a half hour early so that she can close the door and take time for silence. She sits with her eyes closed, recites prayers she has memorized, and gathers herself for the day, opening herself to peace.

Gary, a boat builder who specializes in caulking, told me that he once studied Tai Chi and uses breath as his way of centering. "I don't do the formal moves anymore but I do breathe. It's my way of connecting to the moonset and sunrise. I concentrate on my breathing, from my stomach area, and just slow down." Gary tends to do this throughout the day as well, even in the midst of "pounding away under the guts of a monster boat." He just stops and breathes. "It is a rejuvenation of my spirit at the time." Gary describes it as a sense of peace ending with a tingling in his fingertips.

Fred Rogers was an ordained minister whom millions of American children came to love as Mister Rogers, the kindly mentor in the daily television show *Mister Rogers' Neighborhood.* In a television interview, Charlie Rose expressed a

sense of wonder at the peacefulness that Rogers emanated, even during the interview. He asked him what he did to create this sense of peace. Mister Rogers responded that he got up no later than 5 A.M., and spent at least two hours in
prayer and reflection. "That's before I go swimming." He added, smiling, "Real
revelation comes in silence."

I normally spend between one and two hours for my routine of reverence,
sometimes less when I have an early-morning presentation or interview. I need
this amount of time because my practice includes a number of different things,
which I'll describe later in this chapter under "Start the Day with Your RPMS."
Yes, it's quite different from PMS, and yes, it does help.

Although my own routine of reverence may seem like a lengthy one, I want
to assure you that taking even ten minutes as a routine for reflection will make
an enormous difference in your life. There are many excellent daily books for
meditation you can use. I compiled *Sacred Moments: Daily Meditations on the
Virtues* for this purpose. The amount of time isn't important. The routine nature
of it, the regularity of your habit of tuning in on a daily basis is what really matters. It is the pattern of grounding yourself in the sacred, sourcing your day in inspiration and peace.

Just before you go to sleep, spend a few moments reflecting on something
you are thankful for that day, and if there is some problem on your mind, give it
over and ask for help and clarity upon awakening. Release your troubles as you
breathe peacefully, in an attitude of thankfulness and trust.

CREATE SACRED SPACE

Prepare a place for reflection so that the moment you enter that space your sense
of reverence is aroused. Keep it simple, using only things that are meaningful
and beautiful to you. You can turn even a small corner in your home into your
own blessed spot.

I recommend that you gather some materials:

- A candle to light and perhaps some fragrant essential oil
- A talisman: something that is special to you—a stone, a shell, a statuette
- A journal for recording your thoughts, prayers, meditations, and dreams
- A pen that has the right heft in your hand and flows on the paper
- Perhaps some colored pencils or watercolors for drawing
- One or more sacred texts

- An inspiring daily meditation book
- Virtues Cards (see description under Do a Virtues Pick on p. 235)
- A beautiful bag for your cards
- Prayer beads if that is part of your practice. (Prayer beads are used to count mantras, novenas, and names of God by Hindus, Catholics, Baha'is, Moslems, and others.)

I have two ways of creating sacred space, one when I'm home, the other when traveling.

At home I have a prayer corner in front of an East-facing floor-to-ceiling window in our living room. It is personal and private, and no one else sits there. Hanging from the ceiling are two exquisite stained-glass designs, one of which is my beloved fox, which happens to be my sacred animal symbol and a reminder of discernment, the other a symbol of my faith in pastels of green and pink. Both I found on our travels. Draped over my prayer chair (which I confess is a white plastic deck chair that I find comfortable) is a small quilt a friend made for me. She inscribed some words from a shoe ad on the quilt: "Improving your life is a matter of one step at a time. So think of your shoes as tools." In front of the chair is a small step-table (from a garage sale originally, I think), covered by a beautiful and now sun-faded Persian cloth. Standing in a neat row beneath the table are books that inspire me, including a number of holy books, a prayer book, and my journal. On the table are a pen, a string bag of beautiful tapestry for my prayer beads, and another bag of Fijian tapa cloth for my Virtues Cards. Several candles sit on the table, most of them gifts, including one that heats fragrant oil. The moment I sit in my prayer chair and light my candles, I enter a dimension of contemplative silence.

When I travel, I limit my sacred tools to the ones I need most. In an easily accessible outer pocket of my suitcase I pack my journal, pen, *Sacred Moments* (which contains inspirational quotations from many sources), my prayer beads, Virtues Cards, and a cloth on which to place my sacred things. For years my father's silk paisley scarf, which I received at his death, was my altar cloth. I felt moved to give it to my brother when his work with Disney took him off to Japan, so now I use a cloth from Fiji that is special to me. I sit in bed or in a hotel chair, spread my things on the cloth and begin each day with my routine of reverence. It grounds me in grace before a keynote talk or a seminar. It takes me home.

⤙ The Virtue of Prayerfulness ⤚

Call to me and I will answer you and show you great and hidden things that you do not know. —Jeremiah 33:3

Prayer is talking with God. We can practice prayerfulness in many ways. We can pray in silence or out loud—in any language. We can sing or dance our prayers. God always hears our thoughts and understands our hearts. Prayerfulness means living in a way that shows we are in the presence of our Creator. Prayerfulness is quiet reflection. We allow the Great Spirit to speak to us. We listen and receive God's guidance.

Signs of Success

I am practicing Prayerfulness when I . . .

- Take time every day to pray and reflect
- Talk to God as I would to a really good friend
- Share my innermost thoughts, hopes, needs, and fears in prayer
- Trust, listen, and watch for God's answer
- Take action with trust
- Have an attitude of gratitude

Affirmation

Thank you, God, for the gift of prayer. Help me to live in Your presence. I find Your answers in quiet moments. I dedicate my actions to You today.

A friend of mine who is a filmmaker in Dallas says, "Nature is my church." His sacred space is his morning walk into the desert. He sings, chants, and sometimes lights a sage stick, but mostly he walks in silence in the presence of beauty. He says it is often the place where his most creative ideas come to him—out of the silence.

Arlene, a gifted massage therapist and very wise woman, does not go to a single place for her routine of reverence. She dons a prayer shawl and instantly enters the silence, whether outside on her deck in the sun or in a favorite chair inside on colder days. Pulling her prayer beads from a silk bag, she readies herself for several rounds of her mantra.

THE RPMS OF SPIRITUAL FITNESS

So, when you have created sacred time and sacred space, then what? What do you do?

A simple formula that I find helpful is what I call my RPMS. We associate this with revolutions per minute, which I vaguely understand has something to do with the get-up-and-go of a vehicle's engine. Well, this formula is a means of getting going with spiritual practice. It stands for:

- Reading
- Prayer
- Meditation
- Service

You can complete this formula in ten minutes or two hours, depending on what is right for you and the time you have available. You may find it helpful, as I do, to journal throughout this process. The RPMS of reverence includes four basic steps:

1. Read something inspiring, and reflect on what it means in your life.
2. Pray in a way that is genuine and meaningful to you. There are many ways to pray, from petition—asking for what you need—to opening yourself to guidance or dialogue, offering praise and gratitude, or experiencing communion—being in the presence of Spirit.
3. Meditate in a way that suits your learning style, whether walking, breathing, reflecting on the meaning of scripture, seeking guidance, or simply entering stillness.

4. Serve. Focus on your day as an opportunity to be of service in some way. You may feel moved to take immediate action on what came to you in prayer. Picking a virtue as your spiritual practice for the day can give you the theme for how to be of service.

Let's look at each of these elements separately.

Read

Read what inspires you

In my own practice, I lay out my thoughts first by journaling, basically checking in and writing how I am and what's on my mind or anything special about the day before. Then I seek wisdom in reading something inspiring. I need to empty before I fill. Others prefer to read first, then journal or reflect in silence.

I believe that the sacred texts of the world's religions have great power. The "creative word" is generative. It is an ancient thread of revelation going back before the days of Krishna, Abraham, and Moses. It holds the collected wisdom about the Divine, and some believe it is the direct word of God. I always include the sacred texts in my daily readings: the Baghavad Gita of Hinduism, the Upanishads and Dhammapada of Buddhism, the Torah and the Pentateuch of Judaism, the Bible of Christianity, the Qur'an of Islam, the Book of Certitude of the Baha'i Faith, and other holy books. They have such pure, undiluted power.

Read moderately

You may choose to read from the holy book of your faith or obtain a book of inspiration from the library or a bookstore. Whatever you read, I advise moderation. Read a few lines, and take time to reflect on their meaning. Reading a single verse of scripture with understanding is worth more than a long, tedious reading of many pages. As in any relationship, quality is worth more than quantity.

Read reflectively

As you read a passage, reflect on what this passage means to you and what virtues you need to embody the message you find there. For example, read the following verse from the Book of Mormon reflectively:

> *Hope cometh of faith, making an anchor for the souls of men, which would make them sure and steadfast . . . if there be no faith among the children of men, God can do no miracle among them. —Ether 12*

This passage, as most scriptural passages do, mentions four virtues: hope, faith, certitude, and steadfastness.

Spend some time reflecting in silence about the meaning of what you have read. Create one or more journaling questions to apply the meaning to your life. For example:

> *Should a person recite but a single verse from the Holy Writings in a spirit of joy and radiance, this would be better for him than reciting wearily all the scriptures of God. . . .*
> —Bahá'u'lláh, *Kitab-i-Aqdas* (Baha'i book of laws)

How hopeful am I right now?

What is my deepest hope?

What would help me to anchor my hope in faith?

What would make me sure and steadfast?

How open am I to God's miracles?

Create an affirmation of what you have read

The rest of the day, use an affirmation such as "I am open to miracles" and stay calmly and deeply alert to what happens. This is an active way to participate in prayer, and literally attracts Divine assistance. Expect miracles and you will have them.

One morning when I was at home with my sleeping six-week-old son, I felt a stirring of boredom, a restlessness to do something meaningful. That morning I had read a line about the importance of service and it resonated with me strongly. I decided to wash and wax the kitchen floor, but sat there afterward praying my boredom. "God, that just doesn't cut it. I'm bored! Please, can't I do something to be of service today?" I felt a sudden urge to go for a drive, so I wrapped the baby up, got into our old station wagon and headed off. I let the car take me in new directions and found myself on the rural outskirts of town, where I had never been before. Suddenly, I pulled off into the parking lot of a converted bowling alley, with the sign Manpower Development Program crudely painted above the entrance.

I took the baby out of the car seat, still sound asleep, and went inside to find utter bedlam. People were running around wringing their hands and crying. I went up to a woman and asked her, "What's going on?" "One of the boys has locked himself in the bathroom and says he's going to kill himself!" I handed the baby to her and pushed my way toward the door, saying, "Let me through. I know what to do." Before my maternity leave, I had worked as a therapist at an inner-city mental health clinic, specializing in suicide prevention and intervention. "What's going on?" I yelled. I could hear him crying and ranting inside. I began to companion him through the locked door. Finally, the door burst open and a tall seventeen-year-old boy fell into my arms. Billy became the first member of a teen sharing circle I facilitated in my home, and later became a leader in his community.

Pray

Among the many paths to prayer, find your own

There are many paths to prayer, and many ways to pray. Many of us avoid praying because we have not yet found a method that resonates with our soul and our style. Some resist prayer because they aren't sure what they think about the existence, much less the nature, of a Deity. Some have been hurt by religious institutions, which have turned them away from a relationship that I believe is meant to be as natural as breathing.

The sacred teachings of the world describe the nature of the Divine in different ways, yet they all speak of faith as a sacred relationship. Buddhism is a nontheistic religion, yet His Holiness the Dalai Lama says in *The Good Heart:*

> *[It] is just as important in Buddhism as it is in the Christian context that one's spiritual practice be grounded in a single-pointed confidence and faith, that there is a full entrusting of one's spiritual well-being in the object of refuge.*

He speaks of "entrusting your spiritual well-being to the guidance of the Buddha. . . ." Single-pointed confidence and faith—what a way to spend the day. What a sense of focused mindfulness.

My friend Nancy Reeves has written a deeply insightful and intimate book about the diverse ways we pray and seek spiritual discernment, *I'd Say "Yes," God, If I Knew What You Wanted* (Northstone Publishing, 2001, www.joinhands.com). The examples she includes come from a broad spectrum of individuals—from Mother Teresa to Teresa of Avila—as well as contemporary stories from individuals of many faiths and backgrounds whom she interviewed, including myself. I love Nancy's book because it so clearly describes how people uniquely connect with the Divine; particularly, their desire is to say "Yes!" to the spiritual adventures possible to them.

Pray the real

Whether you think of the Divine as the Source of Life, the Holy Spirit, a distant Creator, or as One you can talk with in prayer, in the context of *A Pace of Grace,* I ask that you think of prayer as a gentle and honest look at what is real in your life and at the same time an encounter with a loving God. Pray the real.

> *Trust in him at all times. . . .*
> *Pour out your heart to him;*
> *hold nothing back.*
> —Psalm 62:8

The first time I ever took a directed retreat, Judi, my spiritual director, told me: "Linda, pray whatever happens. If you feel antsy, pray your antsyness. If you feel worried, pray your worry." I remember being full of earnest intention, holding tightly to my specially bought retreat journal. I went outside, perched on the edge of my deck looking out over the Pacific, and took a deep breath. I held my pen aloft awaiting revelation. The first words I heard were: "Linda, put down the book and pen, and go deep within." I was unprepared for the stream of memories, some quite painful, that flowed before my mind's eye. I sat and wept. Then I went to sleep. Judi had explained to me that often on retreat we need to sleep a good deal. When I awakened, I journaled, and then shared what had come to me with Judi. It was truly revealing and an unexpected start to a lifelong practice of spiritual retreat. I once read the words of a Jesuit whose name I cannot recall. He described prayer as "a long, loving look at the real."

Some people have been taught to pray as an insurance against damnation, to assuage a stern, authoritarian, and exacting patriarchal Godhead. Some of us, and I admit I was guilty of this at one time, believe that we are only entitled to pray when we are on our best behavior. I call this the "good girl syndrome." If in truth God is a being of infinite love, patience, wisdom, tenderness—and yes, justice— one who loves us like a mother, I can only imagine that such studied, painstaking, and upright prayers must be tedious to listen to, producing a big cosmic yawn. Have you ever had anyone "suck up" to you? The insincerity alone is enough to make you pull back and escape from their company as quickly as possible. Artificiality doesn't bode well for inviting intimacy.

In my work with the dying as spiritual care director at the hospice, I was often called in to help when someone was severely agitated or making so much noise moaning and groaning that they were disturbing other patients. One afternoon, I was asked by the nurses to companion a very agitated man, who was groaning loudly. "Go do that thing you do, Linda. He's really upsetting the other patients." Matching his tone, I loudly asked him, "What's on your mind?" He seemed to "come to" and calmed down immediately, and began to talk. He was able to tell me how bitter he was to be dying at sixty just as he was about to re-tire, after dreaming and saving for years to travel the world with his wife. I felt moved to ask him whether God was part of his beliefs, and he said, "Oh, yes. A very important part." I then asked, "Have you prayed your bitterness?" "Can you do that?" he asked, with a huge smile on his face. I said, "I'm sure God knows what you are going through, but I think God wants to hear it from you." He drifted into a peaceful sleep, still smiling.

Start where you are, with what you feel—pray your bitterness, your anxiety, your gratitude, your boredom, your anger, your shame, or your hopelessness. Whatever state you are in, this is where Spirit longs to reach you. Speak it, jour-nal it as if you are writing a letter to the Divine friend, or think it, but be real. Let Creator meet you right where you are. This is one of the most intimate forms of prayer.

Ask for what you need

We are invited to ask for what we need or want. Matthew 7.7 says, "Ask and it shall be given you; search and you will find; knock and the door will be opened for you." Petition is a legitimate form of prayer. There are times when a simple request is the purest prayer of all.

After speaking at a conference in Salt Lake City, I was interviewed on an African-American radio station. The producer and I hit it off and went to lunch together. She invited me to attend the Sunday service of her church. After the thrilling experience of listening to the Mormon Tabernacle Choir with hundreds of conference participants, I slipped out to join my new friend, who drove me to a small AME Zion church in the suburbs. As we drove up, it fairly rocked on its foundation. She escorted me right to the front pew, where I was warmly wel-comed by the congregation. After several hours of glorious singing, accompa-nied by a rousing four-piece band, passionate preaching, Bible readings and prayer, a soft-voiced, elegant elder offered to drive me back to my hotel. "This is a beautiful car," I said, sitting back on the plush seat of her powder-blue sedan. "Yes," she said, "this is my miracle car." She explained that her minister had said to her one day, "Nelda, it's time for you to get a new car. You don't need to be driving that rickety automobile." "Well, I don't have much money," she replied. The reverend told her, "If it's God's will for you, it will happen." "What happened?" I asked. She described how she had gone to a car dealer after praying to be led by the will of God. She walked in, told them she needed a new car, and the salesman pointed her to this luxurious-looking sedan, and said, "What can you afford?" It was all over in ten minutes. "I just stepped out on the word of God," she said.

> *Dance, when you're broken open.*
> *Dance, if you've torn the bandage off.*
> *Dance in the middle of the fighting.*
> *Dance in your blood.*
> *Dance, when you're perfectly free.*
> —Jalal 'u' Din Rumi,
> thirteenth-century Sufi mystic

Pray with trust in God's will for you

We are told in all the scriptures to ask whatever we wish or need of God. However, when that's our *only* way of praying, prayer remains at a shallow level, devoid of trust. One of the barriers to prayer as relationship is what I call "supermarket prayer." "Okay, God, I'll take one of those, and that over there, that better job, and could you please let me have a half pound of luck. . . ." Petition is only one form of prayer. Just as in a marriage, if all we ever talk about is what errands need to be done and never look into one another's eyes, or pause to say words of love and appreciation, intimacy erodes. When we habitually badger God for the things we want, our prayer life becomes a superficial, unilateral sort of warding off of difficulties. In terms of cultivating a deeper relationship, this hardly invites openness or discernment. I believe this kind of prayer is based on fear—fear of facing life's Teachable Moments rather than delving into them to discover the pearls of learning that occur in every circumstance.

I heartily agree with Christian theologian Harry Emerson Fosdick, who cautions us against using prayer to order the Divine around: "God is not a cosmic bell-boy for whom we can press a button to get things." How often I have told God what I think should happen, sniveling and whining if I don't get it, and just praying harder, like an insistent child who feels that eventually her begging will wear down the Great Parent. "Oh, please, God. Please! Please! Please!" Whenever God has granted me my wish in such a moment, probably with a proverbial shake of the head and a sigh, I get to learn the hard way that this was not the easiest or the best path at all. Rather, if we have sufficient trust to open ourselves to the

> *Is prayer your steering wheel*
> *or your spare tyre?*
> —Corrie Ten Boom

Creator's wisdom, our prayer will more often be an expression of willingness to discern the path that is ideal in the moment.

When we demand that the Almighty fix things that aren't going according to our will, we are asking for far too little. Prayer is not meant to be demanding, but discerning. This is the only way to receive the soul gifts that are contained in everything that happens and everything that is.

Asking for God's will rather than seeking to impose our will on God means that we understand there may be reasons beyond our ken for what is happening. To ask for a miracle in order to be healed of an illness that has many gifts to give us may not be in our best interest. The prayer "I will to will Thy will" is more courageous. It provides an opening to grace, a willingness to proceed on the spiritual adventure offered by our unique destiny.

In a conversation with an elderly Jehovah's Witness whom I have admired for years for his steadfast and wholehearted faith, he revealed that he never prays for God to fix anything. He prays for God to fix *him*—to replace his weaknesses with wisdom, love, and forgiveness. He prays for virtues. Above all, he has utter faith that to pray for God's will to manifest in his life is to ask for the very best Jehovah has to offer him.

Pray with passion

The Greek writer Nikos Kazantzakis describes a robust, passionate, and utterly trusting relationship with the Divine in prayer:

> *There are three kinds of souls, three kinds of prayers. One, I am a bow in your hands, Lord. Draw me lest I rot. Two, Don't overdraw me, Lord, or I shall break. Three, Overdraw me, and who cares if I break. Choose!* (Cited in *International Journal of Spiritual Directors*)

My husband, Dan, and I have had an amazingly adventurous life. We met at a conference on spirituality and psychology in Grand Junction, Colorado, where both of us were speakers. We were married six weeks later. We felt an immediate powerful attraction, but not in the ordinary way. That came later. It was more of a sense of some shared destiny. During a plenary conference session, I was seated behind him, and my chair kept sliding forward as if drawn like a magnet. I kept planting my feet and looking around to see what was moving the chair. At the time, each of us was in what I call a "Whatever" state. Each of us had prayed for God to use our lives in whatever way God chose. We were married within six weeks not because either of us was in a hurry but because

> *Those who wait on the Lord shall renew their strength. They shall mount up with wings as eagles, they shall run and not be weary, they shall walk and not faint.*
> —Isaiah 40

synchronicity after synchronicity—miracle after miracle—showed us that this was the Creator's will. For example, even though Dan lived in Colorado at the time and I lived in South Carolina, during the third week after we met, we were both appointed to a national task force on marriage and had the opportunity to work together. All our decisions—where to live, what to do with our time and energy, The Virtues Project itself—have all been "out of the blue" productions based on guidance. I look for answers in prayer. Dan observes the patterns of events around us. In more than twenty years of marriage, we have never once been bored.

Trust the desert times

If you find that you are sincerely praying for guidance, asking for God's will to be revealed or for your path to be made clear, and you get nothing, trust that response. I have found that dry times, desert times, are fertile periods requiring great patience. Ask, "Is there something I need to learn at this time before clarity will come?" I have always found that that prayer is answered soon after. Also, it may be that other circumstances need to fall into place for the right way to be revealed to you with perfect timing. Trust that this is a fertile period of waiting and know that movement and stillness are both directed by God. Trust the timing.

Meditate

Do you realize that you are already meditating? Whatever is on your mind most of the time, whatever you think about frequently, the thoughts, concerns, and intentions that are central in your thoughts, are the focus of your meditation.

Worry is a form of meditation that deepens anxiety and fear. It can be paralyzing at times. The meditative faculty is like a mirror. When you turn it toward material cravings, fears, worries, or preoccupations, it reflects and amplifies them. When you turn it toward a desire for discernment, love, patience, or peace, your meditative capacity reflects and attracts these virtues. As a great teacher used to say, "You are already doing it willy-nilly. Why not do it willy?"

The methods described here can help you to focus your meditation in a deliberate way that will serve you rather than trouble you. Instead of being at the mercy of haphazard or troubling thinking, you can employ conscious, positive, daily discipline—meditation can literally transform your life.

After my moving experience of "the embrace" in the midst of my dark night during my divorce, I cloistered myself for months, spending peaceful time connecting deeply with my children. I quieted down into reading, prayer, and reflection. One morning, while doing my RPMS, I came across a short sentence in Moslem scripture that was like an explosion of light: "One hour's reflection is preferable to seventy years of pious worship." One hour of true meditation is worth more than a lifetime of righteous living? My first thought was, "But I don't even know how to meditate!"

So I began to learn. I read a couple of books about meditation, talked to people, and prayed for help to learn. I discovered that there are many ways people define and think about meditation. For some, it is an emptying of the self and a journey into stillness. For others, it is the use of a mantra to enter total silence and peace. For others, it is an active process of discernment, a conversation with God.

Call on your A-team

Before we explore some simple ways to meditate, I want to reiterate a point I made in chapter 1. Experts say that most of us use only 10 percent of our intelligence. I believe we use only 1 percent of our spiritual powers. The sacred traditions of the world teach that there is a spiritual dimension that is more real and more abiding than the material world.

In my study of sacred traditions, and in my own experience, a vast array of helpers are available to us at every moment. They are the greatest untapped source of power, help, and inspiration in the world—because we fail to use them! There is an entire "team" of beings whose fervent wish is to be of service to you, to guide you and help you to get the very most out of your short span on earth: angels, ancestors, and advisors.

Angels of many kinds exist, as well as your own family and friends who have passed on, and other souls who are available to help you, though you may never have met them. Their job, and their joy, is to assist you. When you fail to call on their help, you're promoting unemployment after death!

So, although I might say casually to my husband, "God told me this . . ." or "Spirit said to me that . . .," I don't really believe it is the Creator of all life, the Maker of the universe speaking to me. I believe it is whoever is serving as my messenger from God in that moment. The meaning of "angel" is messenger. I do believe it is part of God's design that spiritual beings are part of our lives and that from a spiritual perspective we are always capable of living in both worlds.

Prayer is a way of communing with our own spirit so that we can then connect to the power of the spiritual realm. As I began to learn how to meditate, I discovered several methods that opened me to amazingly clear guidance. Life-changing ideas began to come "out of the blue."

One morning, I was in a peaceful state of meditation, envisioning myself walking through a meadow where each morning I would meet a holy figure who would give me guidance. Suddenly, my reverie was interrupted by a commanding voice saying, "It's time for The Virtues Project to go to a wider audience." I was a bit shocked by the "interruption" and by the statement, since the Project was going quite far and wide by then. About an hour later, the phone rang. It was Theresa Park, a literary agent from New York, who said, "Linda, I've heard of your work with The Virtues Project and I think it's time for it to go to a wider audience. Have you written any books?" I almost dropped the phone. I told her of my first two books, which we were self-publishing. She asked me to send them to her. The books went to auction because of the number of publishers who were interested. I spent an entire day in my nightie answering the phone as editor after editor wanted to know, "How did you sell sixty thousand copies of *The Virtues Guide*? What was your marketing approach?" We had never done any marketing, and all I could say was "word of mouth," or "I guess it's just an idea whose time has come." When I flew to New York to meet the marketing director and her team in the offices of Penguin, they asked the same question. I said, "Now that we are working together, I'll tell you our secret." Everyone leaned forward. I just pointed up. They looked puzzled. I said, "To be honest, we never had a chance to market it. We've had lots of media coverage, but they called us. It had to be 'Out of the Blue Productions.' It was God. We never did a thing."

A source of great spiritual power to us humans, according to all the sacred texts, are the angels, one of whose tasks is to assist us in this world. According to Origen, an early angelologist of the Catholic Church, the guardian angels assigned to us are our instructors in virtue. The Fathers of the Church teach that "they protect the soul against troubles both within and without; they reprimand and punish the soul that turns aside from the right way; they assist it at prayer and transmit its petitions to God" (Jean Danielou, *The Angels and Their Mission*). There are also the Angels of Virtue themselves, who are considered higher in rank than the archangels. Think of the power of calling on a specific Virtue. Rather than saying, "I should be more patient," we can invite the presence of the Angel of Patience and lean against her for support. In the Qur'an, Mohammed tells us that when we are born, two angels are assigned to guard us, one at our foot and one at our head. These guardian angels remain with us all our lives.

The First Nations people speak of "the grandmothers and grandfathers"—the ancestors who come to our assistance. There are also advisors and saints, whose task is to assist us on earth. My personal favorite is St. Anthony, the patron saint of lost things and lost causes. He is amazingly helpful and has become very dear to me. One time I had lost my Daytimer, which contained the only record of my schedule—my entire life for the coming year. I frantically turned the office and the house upside down looking for it. Suddenly I stopped, hit my forehead and said, "St. Anthony! I don't know why I didn't ask you before. Will you please find it?" There was a deafening silence, rather than the usual swift, efficient location given in a thought or image. "Hellooo," I called rather impudently. I sensed a sternness in his presence. "St. Anthony, is there something I need to learn or understand before you locate it for me?" "Yes," he answered immediately. "Plan nothing without asking us first." I made an instant and sincere promise to pray about all future plans, and the phone rang immediately. "We have your schedule book," a school secretary said. "You left it here after the workshop." "Why are you so good to me, St. Tony?" I asked him. "Because you're one of my best customers," he said, laughing.

Simple ways to start

I'd now like to describe the simple steps with which I started as a beginner in meditation. I'll also provide concrete descriptions of daily practices others use to make the connection with Spirit, to tap into this vast source of Divine assistance available to every one of us.

Meditate in stillness

Psalm 46:10 says, "Be still and know that I am God." I have a very active mind. It is not easy for me to empty my mind of thoughts. They babble and burble continually unless I'm utterly physically engaged—gardening, dancing, making soup, making love—and, I confess, even then my mind sometimes has to be corralled back to the moment. Even when I'm looking at an exquisite sunrise, my mind is *thinking*, "Isn't that gorgeous?" I have heard this same complaint of "busy mind" from many others in my workshops. When I was first learning to meditate, what helped me to quiet my mind was focusing on my breath in a number of ways.

Meditate through breath

Sit upright, either kneeling on a meditation stool or in a relaxed but erect sitting position, with your feet grounded on the floor. Picture a thread being pulled from above from the crown of your head.

Curl your tongue gently up against the roof of your mouth. In Yoga, it is said that this keeps energy circulating. Relax your abdomen and breathe from there, rather than filling your chest. First, exhale, counting slowly, numbering each breath; then, expanding your abdomen, inhale, counting your breaths. Then hold your breath for several counts. Work toward doing each to the count of ten. This will help to free you from thought.

Focus your mind on a part of your body involved in the breathing process, such as your nostrils, noticing your breath passing in and out. This helps you to center your attention and calm your mind.

Meditate with energy

Stand erect, as if a thread is pulling up from the crown of your head. As you inhale, imagine the powerful energy of the earth moving up from the soles of your feet, through your veins and arteries, filling your body with energy and moving out through the crown of your head up to the heavens. Some believe that it is best to do this outside in bare feet.

As you exhale, imagine the power of the heavens flowing down through the crown of your head, filling your body with energy, then flowing out through the soles of your feet and deep into the earth. As you repeat this, let the energy become a constant, steady flow, circling through you.

Do a walking meditation

Still yourself by regulating your breath, counting as you inhale, as you hold, as you exhale. Do this several times, then let your breathing return to normal. Place each foot down gently and reverently as if you are stepping on a path strewn with fresh flowers. Count your steps as you breathe in, then as you breathe out. Three slow steps as you inhale, three or four slow steps as you exhale. Allow your movements to flow. Concentrate only on the earth you are stepping on and your breath. Walk for several minutes. Thich Nhat Hanh, who has found mental clarity even in life-threatening stituations of religious persecution, describes walking meditation as something that clears his mind and places him in the moment in a joyful way. "Every step makes a flower bloom under our feet," he says.

Use a mantra

A Zoroastrian priest once shared with me the "golden triangle" of chanting prayer aloud: the mind conceives the words, sends them to the mouth, which sends them to the ear, and back again to the mind.

"I'm not into chatty prayer," my friend and neighbor Rita, a retired nurse, told me. "For me meditation is contemplative. I enter the stillness." Rita is a Roman Catholic who learned to meditate from a Buddhist meditation group. "An encounter with Buddhism really helped me to understand who Jesus is." When I asked her to describe specifically what she does, she explained that she spends twenty-five minutes both morning and night in her meditation chair in silence. "I simply go into the stillness and just *be* in the presence of God. I try not to have feeling or thought, just pure still silence so God can infuse me with courage, humility, gentleness, or compassion." I asked Rita how she remains focused and how she keeps her mind from wandering. She explained that she uses a mantra to stay focused. If an extraneous thought or feeling or anxiety arises, she gently gives it over to God and resumes her peaceful presence. "The center of your being is the indwelling God. The stillness helps us to live from that center. When we meet our true selves we will meet God face-to-face." Rita is one of the most giving, generous people in our community. Her personal ministry is to be of service wherever she is needed, whether offering soup and a listening ear when someone needs to talk or milking cows for a young farming couple needing a holiday. She is one of the happiest people I know.

Find your own meditation style

In my work in spiritual care at the hospice as well as in the virtues development workshops I have given around the world, I have actively explored the varied ways people pray and meditate. As I reflected one day on the seemingly endless ways that people engage in prayer, a fascinating discovery dawned on me. Just as we all have a particular learning style that allows us to process information, whether auditory, visual, or kinesthetic, the same principle applies to our capacity to pray and meditate. We have different ways to access meditation that work best for us. One person needs to be moving—walking, running, dancing, or swimming—in order to connect deeply. Another needs to be sitting in silence and listening. Others meditate best while writing. It will be very helpful to you to discover your own meditation style in order to access the rich source of grace and guidance that is available to you. Perhaps, like me, once you get into the practice as a regular discipline, you will find that you move between styles.

Auditory: If you learn best by listening, your best method of meditation is to listen for a still, quiet voice within your mind. You may find it most conducive to meditate while sitting still in your prayer corner, or you may find it better to walk and listen. My first experience of responsive, conversational prayer was a quiet voice. At first, it was like listening to a whisper in a windstorm—very faint. Now that I have come to trust it, it often comes without my asking and is quite clear. One day, I was turning a corner at home, and several voices said, "Prepare yourself. Something will happen tomorrow." The tone was somber, and I spent the day gathering strength for what was to come. The next day I got the call that my father had collapsed in a coma, and that his death was imminent. My husband and I immediately flew to Tennessee, where my father was hospitalized.

For auditory prayers, music can connect you deeply to Spirit. I have witnessed amazing changes in people at the hospice when their families brought in music that they loved. They would often emerge from coma with a smile, and if agitated, the music would calm them.

Meditate as dialogue: Another form of meditation that is auditory in a sense is dialogue or conversation with Spirit. Enter the conversation expecting to be answered. You may want to journal the dialogue in order to remember it. This is very powerful, even for people trying it for the first time. I learned the method below of "A Letter to God" from Reverend Janet Garvey Stangvik, an inspiring minister who is also a Virtues Project facilitator.

Correspond with God: Write a letter to God, then write God's response. Write a few lines addressing Spirit, then write back as if Spirit is speaking to you. Does it resonate as real? Are you surprised by the wisdom flowing to you? In Bermuda, a workshop participant told me he was utterly amazed at his experience with "A letter to God." He was in tears feeling he had just received for the first time a clear answer to an issue he had been praying about for a long time. "I guess I never took the time to listen to God's answer," he said.

Visual: If you are primarily a visual learner and have to see things to understand them, your best means of meditation is likely to be visual.

Structured visual meditations will provide a means for you to freely open yourself to guidance and use your imagination vividly to see what you need to see or what Spirit desires for you to see. Here is an example of a guided visualization I often use in workshops:

↦ A Visual Meditation ↤

Take several deep cleansing breaths, relaxing and breathing from your abdomen. As you breathe in, breathe in peace. As you breathe out, allow any tension you are holding to be released. Allow your breathing to return to normal.

In the center of your mind, picture a hallway—the hallway of awareness—at the end of which is a doorway on which is the name of a virtue (e.g., peacefulness). Gently move down the hall toward the door, noticing the shape and color of the door, and how the virtue is inscribed on it. Then enter the space of peacefulness.

Allow yourself to visualize a place of beauty, either a room or a scene in nature, a beach or a forest. It may be a place of beauty where you have been before. Notice the temperature of the air around you. What do you see? What sounds do you hear? What scents do you smell? Allow your body to be still or to move as it needs to in this space of peacefulness.

In the distance see a holy figure moving toward you to speak to you and show you what you need. Allow yourself to picture this being now close before you, knowing you can bring anything to them for assistance.

Allow yourself to receive whatever this being has to give you, whether a thought, words, or touch.

Open the palm of your hand and receive a small symbol or gift. Look into your hand and see what it is. Thank this being of peace, and bringing your gift with you, gently move back to the hallway of awareness, bringing yourself back down the hallway. Notice your breathing. Come back to your surroundings.

Journal what you saw, felt and heard. What is the gift for you in this meditation?

Kinesthetic: If you are a person who tends to move around a lot and loves to be physically active, you may need to be moving to go into a meditative state. While you are running or walking or swimming, open yourself in prayer and be in the presence of Spirit. Joseph is a man who meditates while running. He will often sense a companioning presence with him and sometimes hears brief, meaningful phrases of guidance or expressions of love.

Take a spirit walk

This is an activity I developed for Virtues workshops inspired by the reverence of First Nations people. People of many backgrounds, from corporate executives to teens, have found this meaningful.

1. Spend ten minutes walking outside slowly and contemplatively, with a spirit of openness. (It is best to do this in a place of natural beauty but I have also done this in cities.)

2. Allow your attention to be drawn by something. It could be a leaf, the sky, a bridge, a gate, a flower. Contemplate it with gentle concentration. Ask the question: "What is your message for me? What is your gift to me?"

3. Journal the dialogue with your object of contemplation for ten minutes, giving it voice and answering the question. If there is a particular issue on your mind, let the message be about that.

4. If you are doing this in a group or have a friend to companion with, share the message with them.

5. Discern what action you can take in response to this message and the virtues you need to do so.

I experienced a very special spirit walk during a retreat in Sedona, Arizona. Each member of the group spent the afternoon doing their own spirit walk, then returned at a certain hour to companion another member. I went out into the desert and climbed up to a ledge, where I sat looking down on the saguaro cactus and rock formations below.

My attention was drawn to a tall stone spire with a round plateau at the top. It stood solitary and quite far from the mountainside, like a huge sculpture. After contemplating it for several minutes, the question formed, "Lord, what are you carving out of me?" I received only silence, and gradually made my way back to the retreat center still holding the question. A woman walked up to me and asked if I would like to companion with her. "First," she said, "may I give you something? I thought you might like it." It was a sheet of paper on which was written these words of Michelangelo, the great sculptor: "I saw the angel in the stone and carved to set it free." This meant to me that the pain and difficulties of my life were sent not to hurt me but to set me free, to release the virtues in my nature. A sense of relief and gratitude swept over me. It's all good, I realized. It's all grace.

Trust your imagination

One of the sources of resistance to meditation that I often hear from people is: "How do you know it's not your imagination?" as if the answers received in meditation are fabricated from self-deception. This is a legitimate concern about being misled by one's own ego or at the very least wishful thinking. Our materialistic culture teaches us not to trust in our intuition, and to scorn imagination. My answer after companioning them about their concerns is, "Of course it's your imagination. How else is Spirit to reach you?"

While facilitating a Virtues workshop with a faith community at a lakeside retreat center outside Alberta, Canada, I invited the group of about fifty people to go on a spirit walk. I asked them to commence silence at that moment, and most people filed slowly out onto the grounds. A couple remained in their seats and appeared to be arguing, so I walked over to them. Angela was trying to convince her husband, Jim, to go on the spirit walk, pleading with him, "Jim, maybe it will help you." Jim covered his face with his hands and kept shaking his head. I had observed and felt the man's bleak, distraught presence in the group since the retreat began. I asked Angela to go and have her walk while I talked with him. Reluctantly she went. Jim and I then had an experience that I can only describe as mystical.

As I sat beside him, he leaned forward, resting his head on his arms on the chair in front of him. I placed my hand on his back and began to companion him:

"Jim, what's happening?"

"I can't take it anymore. I'm so depressed." I remained silent, just making a soft sound of acknowledgment, "Mm."

After some silence, sensing that he felt enclosed in some way, I asked "What's it like in there?"

"It's like a dark cave."

"What position are you in?"

"I'm curled up in a fetal position."

"What's the temperature like?"

"Very warm. Hot." I noticed the heat and perspiration coming through his shirt.

We were silent for a while and he was weeping quietly. I stayed focused with total concentration, compassion, and detachment, vigilant to his experience. Suddenly, I felt the ethereal presence of a holy figure moving toward us from across the room. When he reached us, he turned and faced Jim. At that moment, Jim gasped and then began to sob. I witnessed this encounter in awed silence.

Finally, I sensed this spirit gently withdrawing. Jim then sat up and smiled, tears streaming down his face.

"He came. He was standing right here. He told me I was his beloved son."

When Angela returned, Jim took her in his arms and said, "I'm going to be okay. He came," and shared his experience with her. Angela's face lit up as she admitted, "I wasn't doing the spirit walk. I was praying to him to help you!"

"Oh, Angela," I said, "you did your spirit walk."

This was more than a visual experience that I shared with Jim and Angela. I *felt* the presence of this holy person. For the rest of the workshop, Jim was joyful and active, contributing illuminating insights. I learned some months later that from that point his depression had lifted completely. This is an example of the intimacy and outpouring of grace that can come to us when we allow our imaginations to serve as a bridge to the spiritual realm.

Be a participant in your meditation

One way to use your imagination in meditation that is both visual and in a sense kinesthetic is an Ignation method related to the exercises of St. Ignatius of Loyola. This approach allows us to personalize scripture in our own lives by placing ourselves as observers or participants in the scriptural passage. This method opens many people up to a deeper sense of God's grace in their lives.

For example, in Luke 10: 38–42, the story of Mary and Martha's meeting with Jesus is recounted:

> . . . *a woman named Martha welcomed him into her home. She had a sister named Mary, who sat at the Lord's feet and listened to what he was saying. But Martha was distracted by her many tasks; so she came to him and asked, "Lord, do you not care that my sister has left me to do all the work by myself? Tell her then to help me." But the Lord answered her, "Martha, Martha, you are worried and distracted by many things; there is need of only one thing. Mary has chosen the better part, which will not be taken away from her."*

Place yourself in the role of Martha, then of Mary. This exercise is appropriate for men as well as women. You don't need to be a woman to understand envy, resentment, or adoration. Envision yourself being distracted by your many tasks, and your sense of injustice that all your hard work is not acknowledged. How do you feel as you hear Jesus' response to your plea for recognition and help? Then place yourself meditatively in the same story as Mary. Record in your journal your thoughts and feelings and what insights you have received from this reflection.

My friend Rita says, "If I come upon scripture that really talks to me or really disturbs me, I meditate on it. I stay with it. I become an actor in it, discerning its meaning to me."

Meditate on your dreams and visions

Some individuals receive their purest guidance and their deepest spiritual connection in dreams. As a therapist, I always asked about my clients' dreams and found powerful symbols within them, symbols that had particular meaning for each person. One of my clients was a four-year-old boy who was grieving and withdrawing after his father moved overseas following his parents' divorce. He had a recurring dream of being in a small boat and crossing a turbulent sea, then drowning. By working with him on the story, telling it, drawing it, and retelling it, it gradually changed, and he was able to cross the sea unharmed. His father took him into his arms and that was the ending of the story and the boy's grieving process.

Our dreams often hold symbols, the meaning of which can help us to grow in understanding. I find that journaling both our dreams and visual meditations is very revealing and helpful. I have found that asking the sea, the boat, and the persons in a dream "What are you to (in) me?" "What is your message for me?" extremely illuminating.

Journaling Questions
For Images and Symbols in Dreams and Meditations

- Who/What are you?
- What do you represent?
- What is your meaning for me at this time?
- What part of me do you represent?
- What is your message for me?
- Why are you here?
- What do you need?
- What virtues do I need?
- What actions can I take?
- How can I serve you?
- What is your gift for me?

The following is an example from the journaling practice of my friend Kate:

For many years off and on I have been having dreams of flying. Typically, I find myself flying, fairly low at first and then I continue to climb until I am soaring above the earth and I feel an extraordinary trust in Spirit, totally free.

I discovered through a yearlong circle I attended that the Divine often speaks to us in symbols and archetypes, especially through our dreams. In a meditative state I asked the Creator three questions about these flying dreams.

Why have you come to me in this form?
I represent the authentic you that soars and plays and finds life exhilarating. I call you to your destiny and your capacity to rise above it all, to see the bigger picture, to detach from what's right there in front of you and attach to the process of life that carries you, like the wind, and your spiritual wings (strengths) through this world and all the worlds to come. I come to you in this form so you can see and feel the contrast between living a life

*of true freedom to be yourself and living a life with your wings weighted
down, focusing on things you can't control and wouldn't really find fulfilling even if you could.*

What message are you bringing me?
*Trust in the winds of change, the winds of time, trust in your spiritual
wings, that as you fly and fall, you will become stronger and able to fly
higher and longer. Trust in your instincts. You'll know the flight path. The
winds of destiny carry you to your own true self. They carry you home.*

Meditate to discern guidance

I think of praying as the speaking, asking, opening of the conversation with
Spirit. Meditation is the listening, receiving, discerning part. Prayer is my voice.
Through meditation, I hear Spirit's voice. In my first book, *The Family Virtues
Guide,* in the description of the virtue of prayerfulness, I wrote about the importance of the receptive part of prayer: "Without the listening part of prayer, it
is like dialing someone's number on the telephone and then hanging up before
they can answer you. Becoming very still and listening for an answer is a way to
connect your spirit to the Great Spirit."

During an interview on the television show *Biography,* singer and actor
Della Reese shared that her second career began in her sixties when she was offered a role in the pilot of *Touched by an Angel.* She wasn't very enthused about
it and prayed that she would only do the pilot and nothing further. There was
some doubt about whether the show was too blatantly religious for the public, so
she felt it might go no further. But when she prayed, God said to her, "Della, you
will do this for ten years." Clearly God's will was different from Della's. Not only
was the show a huge hit, but also Della was able to use the power of her presence
in the character of the angel Tess to serve her personal ministry of teaching
people about God.

Cultivating the virtue of discernment to strengthen your capacity to receive
guidance in meditation is just like building the muscles of your body. It takes
time, attention, and energy. As you develop your prayer relationship, you will
most often be able to "separate the wheat from the chaff," to know intuitively
what is coming from Spirit and what is coming from ego or mere wishful thinking. You will learn by the results of acting on your guidance. In this way you will
strengthen your intuitive muscles.

What's the worst thing that can happen? You'll see or hear something in meditation, you'll act on it, it won't work, and you might feel foolish for a few seconds. Obviously, you wouldn't follow anything that involves causing pain to others or violates the integrity of your moral code. In my experience, there are three tests of the reliability of what comes to you in meditation:

1. To the best of your awareness, your intent is pure.
2. The actions you take based on it are for everyone's highest good.
3. The actions you take based on prayer bear positive fruit.

I wouldn't dream of making any decision without discerning my true direction through prayer and meditation. In the early days of The Virtues Project, shortly before we finished self-publishing *The Virtues Guide,* we prayed for guidance about what to do with it. We had no particular marketing plan in mind. "First Nations First" was the message we received in meditation. That day, a call came from a First Nations community asking us to "bring the virtues to our people."

Release your illusions of control

There is a destructive trend in New Age thought to take a time-honored teaching of the great sacred traditions about the power of thought and to overrender it. The idea that we create everything that happens to us by our own thoughts is a distortion by overemphasis. It is an oversimplification. It omits mystery—ignores the reality of God's surprises. I believe that we need to be spiritually nimble—supple, ready, and open to the promptings of the spirit—in order to live as richly as we are intended to live. That is very different from being in control of what happens.

A colleague with whom I worked at a management consulting firm in Denver had a car accident in which he cracked one of his lower vertebrae. After taking a very expensive course that was meant to transform his life, he came to me very depressed one day saying he had "created" the accident and was feeling terribly guilty. From my perspective, this usually cheerful, confident marketing specialist was guilting himself needlessly for playing God. I told him, "Sid, what arrogance. Stuff happens. Who died and made you God? What matters is how you respond to it. How do you know it isn't a test to help you grow spiritually or learn some lesson?" He was stunned by this response and walked quickly away. The next day he thanked me. "Linda, the worst pain wasn't my back. It was thinking I had caused it." Even illness or accident can be a spiritual adventure when we are present to its gifts.

> *Silence leads to Prayer*
> *Prayer leads to Faith*
> *Faith leads to Service*
> *Service leads to Peace.*
> —Mother Teresa

Pray with faith and confidence

If you desire spiritual guidance, you must issue a full invitation to Spirit to answer you and show you things that of your own power you have no way of knowing. Shoghi Effendi Rabbani, Guardian of the Baha'i Faith, spoke about the magnetic power of meditation, "Have faith and confidence that the power will flow through you, the right way will appear, the door will open, the right thought, the right message, the right principle, or the right book will be given to you."

The investment you make through the daily discipline of prayer, meditation, and discernment will bear surprising dividends. Not only will you find that you are more peaceful, but you will have greater access to your intuitive powers, and to the guidance available to you from the spiritual realm. You may well find yourself embarking in surprising new directions in your life. However, you must meet two conditions if you intend to reap the full benefits of prayer. First, you must put doubt aside, and have faith that your prayers have been answered. Second, you must act on your prayer, and as you act you will become a magnet attracting divine assistance. Several times I have had a faint sense that something or someone was calling to me, then moved in that direction—gotten into the car not knowing where I was meant to go—only to meet someone's need in a crucial moment. The more you act on prayer, the stronger the connection of guidance will become. Your reflection time is just the beginning. When you open yourself spiritually, be ready for adventures.

Serve

One of the ways to live with a pace of grace is to use our time well, as it was intended. Time is a gift, and we are meant to use it not only for ourselves but in the service of others. Service gives us a sense of meaning and a joy that can come in no other way.

After you have read a few inspirational lines, prayed and meditated, the final part of the RPMS is Service. As you close your routine of reverence, be open to guidance about how you are meant to practice the presence of God today. There are simple ways to weave service into our day so that we can experience the opportunity to *be* God's grace to others. It may be spending ten minutes on the phone with a friend, or playing with one of our children, or stopping to ask a stranger who looks confused, "Can I help you?" No matter how busy we are, we always have time for kindness, moments in which we can choose to be of service.

Being an instrument of Divine peace, kindness, love, forgiveness, or justice is an essential part of the prayer process. Putting inspiration into action completes the circle of prayer.

Work is prayer

Work done in the spirit of service is one of the highest forms of prayer, and it begins with the attitude with which we rise from prayer and begin to move through the day. Whatever we are doing, we can allow it to be infused with the spirit of service, whether we are cleaning a sink, changing a diaper, presenting a paper, pumping gas, or conducting a meeting.

Restaurants in our island community don't have a great record of survival. However, one restaurant has remained open for years, and it is busy at all hours. Although the food is quite ordinary and there is nothing special about the coffee, it's a favorite gathering place for the locals. I believe it's because of Wendy, a waitress who has been there for years. She greets everyone with a warm welcome, calls people by name, and trades affectionate insults with some of the regulars who like to tease her. She is nothing short of radiant. She calls everyone "Love" and "Darling," and when she says it to you, you feel that at that moment you are her dearest friend. I watched her once with a group of mentally challenged adults from a group home as they wrestled out of their coats and came over to their regular table. Every face lit up when Wendy went over. She spoke to each of them, gave a little touch and a word of encouragement or love. "Joe, you did your buttons yourself. Good on ya." "Got a bit of a cold, Clara? A nice cup o' tea will fix you right up." Wendy is one of my role models, as a woman whose service is always a joyful prayer.

Do a Virtues Pick

I find that one of the most efficient ways to spend a day of grace is simply to ask during my routine of reverence, "How can I serve today, Beloved?" With willingness and focus, ask how you are meant to serve or how you are meant to be. I often find the answer in my Virtues Pick, which I do at the end of my routine. I ask, "What virtue do I need to practice today?" and then reach into my bag of Virtues Cards to select one.

Sometimes practicing the presence of Spirit has nothing to do with doing, but rather with being. It may be a gentle virtue that calls to us, such as moderation or acceptance. To me, it always seems as if one particular virtue is calling each day. The Virtues Pick is also used in places like schools, offices, and treatment centers as a way to focus a meeting or focus the actions of staff for the day or the week. It can be done in a sharing circle as well.

One card is randomly picked from a pack of fifty-two, on each of which is a description of a virtue with signs of success and an affirmation. (The virtues in each chapter of this book are examples from the pack. The entire list of virtues is on page 13.) After reading and reflecting on the virtue, you then hold the virtue in awareness throughout the day.

Classrooms of middle school students in Texas hear their principal or a "student of the week" read a passage about the virtue from one of our books or from the Virtues Card over the public-address system, and the students reflect on it for a few minutes, then look for ways to practice it throughout the day. Some teachers take time for a brief sharing circle in which students share how they have used the virtue in the past and how it can help them in their lives at the moment. Each individual receives virtues acknowledgments from the others in the circle when they finish speaking.

I received a report about a violent offender in a Fijian prison who received the virtue of obedience in his pick at the end of the first day of a workshop given for inmates and corrections officers. "He was very upset and angry as it challenged everything that was happening and had happened in his life. He found himself with obedience on his mind after being locked up for the night. He could not get rid of it and struggled with it all night, not even getting much sleep. When he arrived at the workshop the next day, he went straight to Gilbert, the facilitator, and asked, 'Could I have the card you gave me yesterday?' Gilbert replied that he would be given the whole set at the end of the workshop, but the inmate insisted he wanted just that card and he needed it now! Gilbert went through his 'spare' cards and found it. The man kissed the card—he was so happy with it." For Virtues Cards, see virtuesproject.com.

Do a Family Virtues Pick

Some families create a sacred time each morning to pick a virtue or read from *The Family Virtues Guide* about a virtue they have picked for the week. Six-year-old Adam invented a virtues game to go with the pick so that he could extend the time his family spent together. He would pick a virtue, then act it out in pantomime, and the other members of the family guessed which virtue it was. Then, the family would choose a last virtue and make a commitment to practice it throughout the day, and acknowledge it in one another as well.

Focusing on a virtue a week, or a virtue a day, allows us to deepen into mindfulness, to meet circumstances with some spiritual help in our pocket.

Be alert to opportunities

In the course of your day, be alert to opportunities to practice your virtue or to be of service to others. You don't have to add to the amount you are doing, you just need to be open to moments of grace when they come. Smiling at someone who makes a request of you, asking a colleague to lunch, calling your mother and giving her the best ten minutes you have, asking a friend how his day is going. It could be anything. Practicing the presence of grace is a state of mind.

Pray without ceasing

At first, I didn't get how Rule 6: Pray Every Hour, would be feasible. I wasn't aware at the time of what it meant. I admit it took many months for me to truly understand that it was about cultivating the spiritual practice of God's presence, whatever I was doing, or however I was feeling.

Thessalonians 1:5 describes this state of practicing the presence through ongoing prayer: "Rejoice always, pray without ceasing, give thanks in all circumstances." I now understand this as a sustainable state of grace, an ideal possibility.

In this passage, sustained joy—"Rejoice always"—is linked to unbroken prayer ("pray without ceasing") and continual gratitude in all that happens ("give thanks in all circumstances"). What would it be like to be always joyful, thankful no matter what, and to pray without ceasing? How does one integrate such an attitude of reverence into a full life of laundry, work, family chores, and financial concerns? I cannot do it every day—there are days I become totally task-focused, reverting to my habitual workaholic attitude. However, when I'm in a pace of grace, I find it possible to sustain the joy of presence. Those are my very best days, and they are deeply pleasurable.

I discovered a clue about sustainable, ceaseless prayer in the letters of Brother Lawrence, who described this state of hourly prayer as "a little lifting up of the heart." The Baha'i writings of the nineteenth century describe it as being open to spiritual guidance: "To thank God for His bounties consisteth in possessing a radiant heart, and a soul open to the promptings of the spirit. This is the essence of thanksgiving."

On the third day of a Virtues Project workshop in Seattle, Washington, a group of about forty people shared their ways of honoring the spirit—the fourth Virtues strategy. I remember the deep quiet that settled on the room as each one of us spoke of a sacred moment. We were a diverse group, made up of clergy, day-care workers, therapists, Asians, African Americans, and Caucasians, and including individuals who were Jewish, Siddha Yoga, Catholic, Anglican, Quaker, Baha'i, and agnostic. One person described a moment of pristine oneness while he ran at dawn; another of a sense of being mysteriously comforted in her grief; others related hearing God's voice. The last to speak was a minister, a gentle man in his sixties. He stood up slowly and faced the hushed circle. There was a tremor in his voice. "I have never been able to pray like some of you. I have tried many times. The connection just doesn't happen." He paused to regain his composure. "All I get are hunches." He went on to describe a time he was in a hospital intending to visit a parishioner only to find that she had already checked out. "I started to leave, but some nudge told me to enter the next room. The person in that room needed comforting. That's all I get—hunches." His humility filled the room. (Story excerpted from *Sacred Moments*.)

Remain thankful

"Give thanks without ceasing" is another way to have a contented mind throughout the day, and to bring oneself to awareness of the presence. Stop regularly to breathe deeply, and at the same time be aware of something in that moment you are thankful for—a warm house on a cold day, a tasty cup of tea, the opportunity you have today to do meaningful work, your health, the beauty outside your window, appreciation for a friend or loved one in your life, an act of kindness you are able to give. I have found that residing in an attitude of gratitude pushes the edges of my joy. It generates enthusiasm for life. I recall a story out of the Hindu tradition that a miserable wretch came to the Master and said, "I am so sad and unhappy, Master. Can you cure me?" The Master replied, "Have you done something kind for someone today?"

Trust synchronicity

I first learned of the existence of the Angels of Virtue in the early days of The Virtues Project. Dan is the researcher in the family, and he originally discovered the virtues as the common thread in all sacred traditions. One night, I said to him, "Dan, there is some power in these virtues that I don't understand. What *are* they? They are more than just concepts or qualities." The next night he asked me to sit with him after dinner. With tears in his eyes, he said, "Linda, they are angels. In all the sacred texts they are described as angels. The angel of peace, the angel of joy. They are direct emanations of God." I was stunned. Then he said, "I imagine humility as a great presence that casts no shadow." We just sat together silently crying in recognition.

A few weeks later, I was driving down the steep dirt road from our home, having doubts, wondering, "Is this a hokey New Age thing, or is this really true about the angels?" I reached down and switched on the radio. The announcer said, "This song has just been released." I almost had to pull the car off the road as k. d. lang began to sing "Calling All Angels." I parked in front of the post office and went inside with some packages to mail. As I stood in line, I looked down and a single white feather was on the floor. "How did that get in here?" the postmistress asked.

After that wherever I went, feathers appeared. I was having tea with some friends looking out at a beautiful old spruce tree outside their window. A single white feather came floating down, yes, just like in the film *Forrest Gump*. My friend David said, "Linda, that's for you."

My first visual impression of one of the Angels of Virtue outside my prayer window was remarkable. I saw a huge feathered being and somehow knew it was the angel of trustworthiness. I took its message to heart with a major business issue confronting me at the time. That night, our elderly neighbor called me and said, "Linda, I feel inspired to paint you something. What would you like me to paint?" "George, would you paint me an angel?" George got very agitated, and started sputtering, "Why did you say that?" and then said something about if I knew what had happened to him that day I would put him away. "Did you see an angel today, George?" "Yes, it was huge. It was flying toward your house this morning." "I saw it too, George, I saw it too." Now let me say that both George and I "saw" it with our mind's eye—not as we would see a bird flying, but as an image superimposed from within the mind on outside reality. The synchronicity of our seeing it at the same time was a sign that this was something not to be ignored. Seeking guidance in the many ways open to us is not merely recreational. Signs are meant to direct us in some way to take action based on one or more of the virtues. If we have the courage and trust to say, "You choose, Lord," wonder upon wonder occurs. Prayer is an excellent career move.

Pay attention to signs

One of the ways to pray without ceasing and to live in the presence of spiritual reality is to pay attention to urges, nudges, and signs. Many people ignore signs or are simply too busy to pay attention. This is really an impractical way to live, doing it the hard way, without all the help available to us. Unless we slow down into awareness, the signs right in front of us elude us. When we fill our attention with busyness, we cannot be present in the moment. We cannot enter the Divine presence that is always there. We don't know what we may be missing. The Qur'an, chapter 12, says, "How many a sign there is in the heavens and the earth which most men pass by and ignore."

In chapter 8, I shared a story about my experience on the *Oprah* television show when I was having my makeup applied. Now I'd like to share how I became a guest on the show, as an example of the active part of prayer—paying attention to those little nudges and signs. One morning I awoke at 5 A.M. as usual, washed my face and brushed my teeth, put on my robe and went into the dark living room toward my prayer corner. Normally I would go into the kitchen, prepare a cup of fresh ginger tea and then go to my prayer corner, and light my candles. Before I even turned on the kitchen light, an invisible hand seemed to stop me. I heard, "Go to work." "Don't you want me to pray first?" I sensed that I had better just be obedient and went into my home office and sat. "Yes, what shall I do?" "This is the day to write to Oprah." My publisher had already tried several times to get me on the show, sending fancy packets of information on my books with cover letters on Penguin stationery, but with no response. "Okay," I said, clicking my computer on. I very quickly turned out a one-and-a-quarter-page proposal focusing on the Five Strategies of The Virtues Project as a way to live and raise children with integrity.

I sat in silence for a few minutes. I was then told by the same guiding voice the name of the producer to send it to. I had noticed the long list of producers at the end of the show, and in this moment, one name stood out strongly: Katy Murphy. Before mailing off the package of books and materials with my proposal letter, I felt I should call my editor and the marketing director as a courtesy to ask for their blessing. I was told by the marketing person, "If you want to have any chance at all, you'll have to send it to at least four producers, but be my guest." I thanked her for sharing and went ahead and sent it out to Ms. Murphy. I found a picture of Oprah in *Life* magazine and put it up on my bulletin board. I envisioned myself with her, and even dreamt that she reached over and took my hand and said something special to me. Several weeks after sending the package, I felt guided to call the producer, using a special number provided by my publisher. A receptionist answered and said, "Oh, the producers don't actually speak to people on the phone." "Would you be willing to just give her my name and see?" Reluctantly she agreed. The next voice on the phone was Katy Murphy's. "Linda, I've been walking around with *The Family Virtues Guide* under my arm all day. I'll definitely pitch it to Oprah." Several weeks later, I was sitting beside Oprah on stage. At the end of the show, off camera, she reached over, took my hand as in my dream, and said, "Bless you, Linda, for the work you're doing."

Marcia Yudkin, creator of the excellent e-zine *Marketing Minute,* shares the story of one of her subscribers, networking specialist Diane Darling. It illustrates the power of synchronicity and the value of following signs that are placed in your path. Every couple of months Diane would send out an e-mail newsletter containing tips on better networking to a growing list of more than a thousand subscribers. In May 2001, she announced an upcoming seminar on networking in the newsletter. Fifty participants attended, among them a woman who was later asked by a *Wall Street Journal* reporter about the role of networking in a job search and mentioned Darling. *Journal* reporter Joann Lubin attended Darling's next seminar and described it in vivid detail in an article. *NBC Nightly News* called after seeing Lubin's article and filmed a networking session led by Darling that night. A month later, that segment aired. McGraw-Hill called: Would she be interested in writing a book? Diane Darling's book, *The Networking Survival Guide,* came out in April 2003.

Synchronicity is destiny seeking our cooperation. It is so much more helpful as a signpost along the right path than trying to push for things to happen. Whenever I have pushed, controlled, and schemed for something to happen, I lose time and usually money. When I trust "Out of the Blue Productions," everything flows as it is meant to. The mindset of a pace of grace allows us to transform our busy, distracted minds into finely tuned instruments of peace, love, kindness, and purposefulness. We are able to align ourselves with true power, which is not the insistent power of ego, but the trusting power of the soul.

When we are present to Spirit, we are present to ourselves. We have an intimate connection to our own intuitive powers and free the spiritual realm to be generous to us. Practicing the Presence gives spaciousness to the day, which helps us to think and act with more clarity and discernment. It allows us to notice the little things that happen around us and within us every day. It opens us to our destiny.

You are the deep innerness of all things,
the last word that can never be spoken.
To each of us you reveal yourself differently:
to the ship as coastline, to the shore as ship.
—Rainer Maria Rilke, German poet

⊷≏ EXERCISE GRACE ≎↞
Create Sacred Space and Sacred Time

Create a sacred area in your home, whether a spot on your living room table, a corner, or a separate room. Choose a time during each day that you feel you can have some silence and solitude.

Set boundaries around it with other family members, including children, or establish a time when you are already alone. Create your own routine of reverence and faithfully practice it every day. Spend some sacred moments each morning and night. Live each day with an awareness of a particular virtue. Notice the difference it makes within you and around you.

SUMMARY OF CHAPTER 12: PRAY
- Open yourself to grace. Be aware that your life can be a prayer.
- Cultivate a relationship of intimacy with God as you understand God.
- As you develop a loving relationship with yourself, as a person of virtues, you will come to know the Divine more intimately.

- Create a routine of reverence for yourself, with time for RPMS, reading, prayer, meditation, journaling, and reflection on how you can be of service.
- Remember that action is a form of prayer.
- Trust your dry, desert times, when you feel prayer doesn't get past the ceiling, or you are confounded by a situation in your life that seems unmoving. This is a fertile time for your spirit.
- Explore the best mode for you to meditate: auditory, visual, or kinesthetic. It may be writing, sitting, walking, moving, singing, using a mantra, or using visual meditation.
- Call on your A-team, angels, ancestors, and others waiting in the spiritual realm to help you.
- As you seek guidance, trust your imagination. How else do you expect to receive it? If your intent is pure and for the good of yourself and others, the guidance you receive will bear fruit.
- Use journaling questions and dialogue to get rich wisdom from your dreams and visions.
- Let go of the arrogance of believing you control everything. Have the humility to receive your Teachable Moments with grace.
- Focus on a virtue each day and let it infuse your awareness and your actions with grace.
- Pray without ceasing by living as if you are in the presence of Spirit every hour. This is keeping a true pace of grace.

Amazing grace comes to us when we practice the presence of Spirit through prayer, meditation, and service. It inspires us to walk through each day aware, awake, and able to be more present to the people in our lives.

❖ THIRTEEN ❖
Give the Gift of Presence

Let each one of God's loved ones center his attention on this: to be the Lord's mercy
to man, to be the Lord's grace.
—Abdu'l-Bahá

A lifestyle of grace finds its fullest expression when we are able to be the presence of grace to others, particularly those we love most. I recall one of my college roommates lying on her stomach on the bed as we talked into the night about our dreams of love and marriage. "I want a man who will cherish me," she said. To me, this simple dream was eloquent. To cherish is to hold dear, to cling to, to nurture.

In troubled times, particularly when catastrophe strikes, what we cherish most suddenly stands out in vivid relief. Our first response to a crisis is to call home. Love, family, friends, and a sense of the fragility and preciousness of life become utterly central in these moments. When life is threatened, it awakens our longing for something more in our relationships, a desire we can no longer ignore by immersing ourselves in the daily grind.

For some of us, any enforced pause in our busyness brings the harsh discovery that we are lonely. Either we have failed to invest sufficient time and attention to attract a close relationship or we may have allowed the relationships we have to become lifeless, distant, and wearying. Many people I spoke with after September 11, 2001, realized that their closest relationships were not as loving, as kind, as passionate, or as joyful as they could be. "I see all these people rushing home, and I feel so sad," Albert, a New York investment counselor said. "I haven't invested anything at home. There's a no-man's-land between my wife and me. Maybe it's time I did something about it."

BE A TRUE COMPANION

These times of personal or collective insecurity help us to realize that we want to give more to our relationships, but what shall we give? We are not used to sitting still long enough to make meaningful contact. In the midst of our habit-ual rushing through the overwhelming chores of the day, the idea of stopping to look deep into the eyes of someone we love may seem absurdly awkward. We don't have time to slow down into awareness and be truly present to some-one, so we whip off instant advice, check that off our list, and go on to the next task.

At any point in time, we have a way to bridge the distance. It is something that not only revives intimacy, but also sustains it. Although it is very simple, at times it eludes our awareness. Our capacity to be fully present to each other in the moment is the single most powerful way to sustain love and to show that we cherish one another. It is the greatest gift we have to give anyone. When we are present, we engage in each other's lives, take each other seriously, and meet one another with full, focused attention, with discernment and understanding.

Love is not just an emotion. It's a choice, an attitude, and a practice. It is a virtue in which one can become skillful through the practice of presence. Pres-ence is the conduit of love, the expression of grace.

THREE WAYS TO SUSTAIN GRACE IN OUR RELATIONSHIPS

I love the word "endow." An endowment is a fund that continues to give over the years. To be endowed is to be gifted. There are several ingredients with which we can create well-endowed, successful relationships, rich with a sustained sense of grace, abundance, and vitality. These practices apply to any relationship that is important to us in our personal lives and in our workplaces:

1. Concentration
2. Compassion
3. Curiosity

These are elements of Strategy Five of The Virtues Project: Offer the Art of Spiritual Companioning. Spiritual companioning is the art of soul-to-soul pres-ence. It allows us to enter another's world, seeing them as whole. It is being fully present to the reality of a two-year-old who has lost a toy or an eighty-two-year-old grieving for the loss of life. It allows us to catch people's joy, or confusion, or excitement. Companioning them illumines their experience, and above all pierces their loneliness. It allows us to *be* the presence of grace. And we can learn it at any point in time.

1. Concentrate: Give Your Full Attention

Paying close attention is the first step in communicating that we care. The quality of our attention is directly proportionate to our degree of concentration. We make immediate intimate connection when we give our full, undistracted attention, look into another's eyes, hear their words, and listen in a focused way to whatever is meaningful to them in that moment. I call it Spiritual Companioning because it is more than simply being physically present to someone. We are offering companionship of one soul to another, a willingness to enter their world, to witness their reality with accuracy, intelligence, and understanding.

Once the honeymoon stage of a relationship ends, the sense of being pursued and cherished wanes, and many women experience a sense of loss. We spend the rest of our married lives complaining about a lack of attention, trying to recapture that early intensity. Meanwhile many men move on to the next goal, as they have been trained to do, and wonder why we are so disappointed all the time. Men miss the sense of being treated as special and cherished as well. I believe at the heart of it is a need to feel loved and special, to sustain the intimacy begun in courtship. Intimacy can be renewed through spiritual companioning.

We can give spiritual companioning in less than a minute to the checkout clerk in the grocery store, a colleague or employee in a moment of frustration or celebration, or we can use it to discover a client's true needs. We can provide it to our intimates, those who need our presence most of all. Offering our peaceful, loving presence is one of the most meaningful ways to be a good provider.

Cultivate courtesy

How often have you been in a public place and noticed a parent completely ignoring a child who is chanting, "Mommy, Mommy" over and over while Mommy stares off with a glazed expression. How offended we feel when we have just opened our heart to a friend or partner only to have them flip off a bit of cheap advice as if we aren't worth the time to listen. The most elemental way to companion one another is to show the courtesy to listen, to simply be interested. It is looking at someone, reeling in our attention from what we are doing, and listening to them with our full attention, even if for a few moments. We need to give up multitasking when someone is speaking to us.

When my husband and I were out for dinner during a trip, we noticed a father and his son, who looked about eleven or twelve years old, enjoying each other's company. They had a peaceful, relaxed manner with each other yet seemed utterly rapt, unaware of anything or anyone else. When the boy spoke, his father put down his fork and looked at him with a smile of interest. He silently listened, then asked a question. His focused attention was palpable. The boy became animated, then sat back and resumed eating. I noticed my eyes were watering. I thought to myself, "What *was* that? Why should it seem so special?" It was a moment of true quality time, and it was clear this level of presence was natural between them.

It comes naturally to us to look lovingly at babies and small children, mirror their actions and facial expressions, and echo the sounds they make. It is our way of bonding with them and it is a pure form of companioning. This level of presence isn't necessarily verbal. It's about focus. During my travels, I have often encountered screaming, inconsolable babies being desperately bounced on a distraught parent's shoulder. I look deep into the baby's eyes and say, "What, baby?" with total focused compassion.

Sometimes I am just thinking the words. Typically, they stop crying and look as if "Finally, someone understands."

In the years I have been learning and teaching the Art of Spiritual Companioning, I have discovered that despite the challenge of describing that ineffable leap of connection that can occur between one soul and another, there is a method to it. We can show compassion by listening in receptive silence, which invites others to share their story, and we can also show compassion by asking questions.

Offer receptive silence

Receptive silence with total, focused concentration creates a safe space for others to speak freely. Silence can be a powerful compassionate response when our inner state is one of receptivity and nonjudgmental attention.

Having worked with many individuals who are in a state of grief, I have often heard from them the unhelpful things people do and say. One is to give little platitudes or Bible verses when they are in the midst of their pain, as if to say, "Get over it." Telling people "This too shall pass" when loss is fresh and wounds are raw is disrespectful. One young woman, recently widowed, was deeply offended when people said to her, "Well, you're young. You'll marry again." This utterly ignored the reality of her grief for her husband. She was in no position to project into the future at all. These kinds of expressions minimize the loss and trivialize the *meaning* of the loss. Simply being with each other, silent witness to our grief, is enough.

The mother of a twelve-year-old boy who was terminally ill with a brain tumor told me of the countless prayers, crosses, potions, and lotions the friends in her church bestowed on her. People came to lay hands on her son, prayed over him, and offered up endless magic remedies. Finally, realizing that this did nothing but upset him, she set a boundary and no longer allowed people to come into their home, "except for a few," she said. "What was it about those few?" I asked. "Oh, they would just sit with me, and let me talk and cry. And they brought food."

Grief is a natural and healthy part of life and it takes time. Giving someone our time, listening with gentle curiosity, and bearing witness to whatever they are experiencing—without pushing or pulling them along to a different state of being—is a rare gift that can bring them a measure of peace.

2. Offer Compassionate Curiosity

Love is involvement. Curiosity is care. Although in many families and cultures it is considered impolite to probe and ask personal questions, I have discovered that questions that get to the heart of the matter are an essential ingredient in the art of presence, whether I am companioning a villager in the bush or a corporate CEO. This is one of the most vital ways to give and receive grace in all of our relationships.

I have come to think of the practice of presence as a form of sacred curiosity. It is my impression of how the Creator looks on us, with eyes of love and compassion, fully aware of our foolishness and our frailties, and highly curious about what choices we will make, with eternal patience and all the time in the world.

Catch the ball

The courtesy of good listening is the bread that sustains our relationships. When we have had a bad day, have taken a great trip, or face a challenging issue, have seen something beautiful, or understood something new, most of us crave an opportunity to share it. Having someone's courteous attention through questions that allow us to tell the story more fully is a welcome gift.

When someone tosses out a comment that is obviously meaningful to him, don't drop the ball. Give the gift of your presence by offering receptive silence, or

⤳ The Virtue of Compassion ⟞

. . . Who is incapable of hatred toward any being, who is kind and compassionate, free from selfishness . . . such a devotee of Mine is My beloved.
—Bhagavad-Gita 12:13–14

Compassion is understanding and caring when someone is hurt or troubled, or has made a mistake. It is caring about others even if we don't know them. It is wanting to help, even if all we can do is listen and say kind words. We are a friend when someone needs a friend. It is important to show compassion to others and also to ourselves.

Signs of Success

I am practicing Compassion when I . . .

- Notice when someone is hurt or needs a friend
- Use empathy to imagine how they must be feeling
- Take time to show that I care
- Listen with an open heart
- Forgive others and myself for our mistakes
- Do some kindness for a person or animal in need

Affirmation

I have compassion for others and also for myself. I notice when someone is hurt or needs my help. I take the time to show that I care. I freely offer my attention.

a question that shows you care to listen. You want to know more. If someone says to you, "I had a fabulous holiday," you may ordinarily choose to say, "That's nice. I'm glad," or commit the all-too-common discourtesy of launching into a story about your own holiday. "Oh, good. Me too. When we went to Florida . . ." Instead, offer the gift of your presence in that moment by inviting them to share their story, with a question: "What made it fabulous?" or "What was fabulous about it?" Whether the interaction lasts for one minute or ten, that moment of shared intimacy will make their day.

What's the magic word

The best questions, I have found, are open-ended, nonjudgmental, and encouraging. They begin with the words "What" and "How." Asking "What's happening?" "What are those tears?" or "How is this for you?" gives people an opening to share their story. "Why are you crying?" or "Why are you upset?" puts us on the defensive. It implies that we had better explain ourselves or justify our tears. It is rarely a helpful word. "What" and "How" questions show simple, nonjudgmental curiosity, without an agenda to fix. They give others permission to empty their cups, which brings relief and the experience of being respectfully heard.

Asking the checkout clerk in a shop "What kind of a day are you having?" and giving her your full attention for that moment gives her consent to tell the truth about her day. "Oh, okay." "What's just okay about it?" you may want to continue. Then you are likely to hear her story, perhaps one or two sentences as she bags your produce. "I haven't had my day off this week." This gives you a chance to express compassion. "Bet you're really needing time off by now." That expression of interest, courtesy, and presence allows her to feel less alone. It will be a small bright moment of validation in her day.

I had a lovely companioning moment with a gentleman in a hotel elevator as I went to my room following a strategic planning meeting. I asked him, "How has your day been?" He said, "Oh, very peaceful, actually, very relaxing." "What made it peaceful?" I asked. He seemed delighted to tell me. "My wife and I are here for a wedding that happened this afternoon. We slept in, had a walk, then went to the wedding. It's been great. How about you?" "I had a very purposeful day. A great strategic planning meeting about a new plan for my project." "Fantastic!" he said. "I wish you all the best," he said as he got off on his floor. His face was bright with smiles. Companioning a stranger melts away barriers. It spreads a bit of friendliness and delight.

When you first see your partner at the end of a workday, be prepared that the same question may evoke a lot more cup emptying. So prepare yourself before you ask, and don't ask until you're ready to hear. If you need a break, a shower, a drink or snack first, do it. "Looks like you've had quite a day. Let me have a shower and then let's have a cuppa together." If your children fill all the space when you first get home, be ready to give them your full attention for a while and save some for your partner or a friend on the phone so that your need for adult conversation and theirs can be met.

Be a listener, not a fixer

In our relationships with our intimates, we have some rather ingrained habits that unintentionally create stress and block the flow of grace in our communications. They include:

- Belittling
- Advising
- Rescuing
- Fixing

Often we rationalize, "Oh, it isn't so bad" or "It won't last," as if that is meant to comfort. Instead, it invalidates.

It is rare to have someone to talk to who will truly listen, in a way that allows us to see and hear ourselves. Many women admit to not knowing how we feel until we hear ourselves tell a friend. It is all too common to be surrounded by family and friends, and yet still be very lonely, for lack of someone willing and able to be intelligently and compassionately present. Loneliness is our hunger to be met, not a need to be fixed.

In my twenties, I worked as a psychiatric social worker at Women's College Hospital in Harlem, New York. One of my roles was to offer services in the Cancer Clinic. Juanita, a dignified woman in her sixties with a lilting Jamaican accent, was a five-year cancer survivor. Her success story was a beacon of hope, and the clinic staff were all delighted to see her when she came in for checkups. Juanita gave me an unforgettable Teachable Moment about the simple value of presence. She taught me the importance of listening, not fixing.

Whenever Juanita came for a medical checkup, she would come to the Social Services office to see me. I remember her first visit, when she took off her black cloth coat, picked at a piece of lint on it and said in her lilting Jamaican accent, "Oh, my. I'm all lintified." Every time she came, she complained about the noise of "those nasty boys runnin' through the halls, with no thought about an ol' woman." She fussed about the little two-burner hot plate she cooked on, the fear of crime and so on. I became an aggressively helpful crusader to get her a new place to live. I began the long process of applying for a place in the long line of those awaiting apartments in a new housing project under construction. I filled out countless forms for her to sign. I commiserated each time she came with her stories of what was happening outside her tiny first-floor brownstone "hole in de wall," where she had lived for more than twenty years. A few days before her regular clinic visit, the notice came that she had been accepted as a tenant in the new building. I was thrilled to be able to surprise her with the news. When I told her, she looked absolutely panic-stricken and a tear slid down her cheek. "Do I have to go? I don't know that neighborhood. Everybody knows me where I live now. I wouldn't know what to do if I had to move."

I was shocked, but in that moment, it dawned on me that her complaining was a pastime for her, not a cry for help. She didn't really want fixing. She didn't need a savior. She just wanted someone to listen to her complaints—to understand how hard life is for an old woman alone. Her stories about her life in the brownstone were recreational. They were the color of her known life. She didn't really want to move. Some folks do need help to move, but it is really important to discover whether they just need to empty their cups or are really looking for a change.

Men are often accused of fixing rather than listening. Listening is not meant to be an engineering challenge. In the truest sense, it is lovemaking. In *Passive Men, Wild Women*, Dr. Pierre Mornell describes the frustration experienced by women working at home, waiting all day for an adult conversation, only to be driven wild by a man who comes home, takes in the facts and issues some cheap advice, then sits all night staring at the tube in his socks—an unresponsive, passive lump. Then he wonders why she rages.

At the end of a day of harried chauffeuring, diapering, scheduling, and meal preparation, when an at-home mom tells her beloved she's had a rough day, she doesn't need an engineer. She needs a companion. His blithe "Why don't you just . . ." will drive her wild. She needs her partner to empathize, to just be curious about what was tough about it. The simple act of asking—becoming curious—can make all the difference. Sometimes "How can I help?" works too, but only *after* she has emptied her cup.

Women, too, are inveterate rescuers, nurses, and caregivers. We think we are the emotions police and have the responsibility to keep everyone around us happy. We probe, question, advise, and wonder why we get snarled at. All we're doing is showing we care! I confess I too often lapse into this throwback habit with my husband. Sometimes all we are going to get from our partners is a snippet of a one-liner: "Tough day." Just ask a simple cup-emptying question, such as "What made it tough?" and if you get a shrug, let it be. "Sounds like you had quite a day. How does a nice cool drink sound?" This is not fixing. This is respecting the language your partner speaks—silence.

If you are the quiet one, know that your partner may not need a drink and a mild commiseration. He or she may need to talk. When you first see your partner after a long day, first get yourself refilled by some quiet time and then offer conversation to your partner sometime in the evening. Conversation to a talker *is* intimacy, and there is no substitute for it. Learn to ask cup-emptying questions. Engage with what they are saying by tapping into your curiosity. And remember, they don't need you to fix anything. Just relax and listen.

Seek to understand the story

Rachel Naomi Remen, author of *Kitchen Table Wisdom*, says, "Telling stories can be healing. We all have within us access to a greater wisdom, that we may not even know until we speak out loud." While working with people in the Solomon Islands, I heard an expression that enchanted me, "Story me." "Let's story together." I later shared these expressions with audiences in North America. It has come back to me as a gift. Malcolm Fast, one of our Virtues Project Facilitators, is a masterful chartered accountant who has integrated companioning into his practice. He has offered to me on a number of occasions the precious gift of his companioning presence regarding my own personal and corporate finances. He begins by saying, "Story me," and listens with rapt attention as my cup is emptied. Skillfully he leads me to my own wisdom about the most strategic way to move forward. At times he offers his own wisdom as the icing on the cake.

Nurture children's wisdom

Because we are hurried and harried, it is not always easy to listen to our children. Sometimes we feel we only have enough time and attention to put out fires or hand out instant advice. We often deprive them of their most Teachable Moments. We tend to rescue them, because it seems quicker and easier. "Mom, I don't like Janie anymore. I don't want to be best friends with her." There is a profound life lesson around the virtues of assertiveness and loyalty when our children have relationship challenges. Yet we are likely to offer superficial advice instead of helping them to find their own wisdom. We might say, "Oh, honey, you don't mean that. You and Janie have been best friends for a long time. You'll make up." For all you know, your daughter has just seen Janie shoplifting, and has a true moral dilemma on her hands, between loyalty to her friend and integrity about turning her in.

If you are living with a pace of grace, you recognize these moments as the mentoring opportunities they are. Rather than doling out advice, you would ask a cup-emptying question, "What's happening with Janie?" or "What don't you like about her?" Then listen. Get to the heart of the matter with questions such as "What bothers you the most about what happened?" Then you mentor her into her own clarity. "What do you think would be the right thing for a good friend to do?" Don't rush to dry those tears. Let them flow along with the virtues they reveal. Those Teachable Moments are gifts of grace in your children's lives.

When you are present to your children, you help them to respect their feelings and grow the virtues of their character. This is their soul work.

Get to the heart of the matter

The key to companioning is curiosity without judgment, and listening for the *meaning* of the situation in a context of virtues. You are a guide and a witness to the process of noetic integration—the discernment of meaning. The language of virtues is the frame of reference for the soul's clarity. There is always a virtue that can heal, redeem, or help someone move forward. I have never talked with anyone who was not expressing a virtue at the heart of their pain or confusion. It takes some discernment to see the virtue that is in the pearl of truth. Whenever someone feels angry, it is usually about justice. Whenever someone is guilty the virtues involved are usually integrity, righteousness (wanting to do the right thing), faithfulness, or loyalty. Listening others into their own clarity is a far greater gift than advising, rescuing, or fixing. You are treasuring them by honoring their Teachable Moments, which are the spiritual lessons of life.

Detach from your own agenda

In my hospice work I frequently observed that well-meaning relatives had an agenda to "comfort" people out of their feelings. A patient could be surrounded by loving relatives and yet feel utterly alone—trapped in their private feelings and thoughts, because they were basically being ignored. After the pillow fluffing smiling, patting, cooing, and praying was over, I would often slip in to see someone and find they had drifted away into coma, or that they were desperately agitated. I would sit with them, or rant with them, following their lead, whatever the dance. All I had to do was give them my full, concentrated attention. There was no agenda to fix them, and no pressure on them to be calm, yet they always found their own calm once they felt companioned in their experience.

I discovered that the key to giving full attention is to be present without an agenda. Even when the goal was to quiet down a patient who was making a disturbance, by being fully present in that moment with no need to change a thing, just open to whatever was going on, somehow this brought them to peace. When you have no agenda, you are free to give full attention without turning the volume up or down. You meet the other where he is.

Balance compassion with detachment

For years now, I have taught the skill of spiritual companioning to lay people, because I believe that if we are to live intimately, we need to meet each other's emotional needs more effectively. We shouldn't have to run to a professional listener to be heard. To be able to offer this gift to one another, which is part of the grace of true intimacy, we must learn to detach from our own agendas, and stop talking one another out of our feelings, no matter how loving the motive.

There is a great difference between sympathy, empathy, and companioning. With sympathy we feel sorry for someone and that merely amplifies their pain. With empathy we can feel their feelings and often feel impelled to rescue them. With companioning we can walk intimately with them without taking on their feelings.

The step of preparing yourself to companion someone is essential. Imagine placing a protective shield over your heart, one that is a strong weaving of two virtues: compassion and detachment. The shield allows your compassion to flow through to the other person, while at the same time detachment keeps you from taking on their pain. This balance is particularly challenging with those we care about most. However, without calling on your virtue of detachment, being truly present to your intimates will be impossible.

The spiritual definition of detachment as a virtue is quite different from our common connotations of the word. Detachment has very bad press. It is typically used to mean cold, uncaring withdrawal or lethargy—an "I don't care" attitude. In spiritual terms, however, it means the capacity to feel, and to step back from what we feel—to use thinking and feeling together in order to choose how we will respond. It is a gentle, loving, and often joyful quality. Detachment allows us to relinquish the responsibility for another's pain. It frees us to be present and frees them to be real.

One of the times we most need to call on this virtue is when our loved ones are hurting and they need us to be present to them. It can be incredibly challenging to listen with detachment to those we love. Our need to impose comfort is often greater than our willingness to be with them in their discomfort. And so, unintentionally, we isolate them in loneliness. Margaret Wheatley, author of *Turning to One Another,* says "The irony is that we want to help, but feel impotent, and so we withdraw the one thing that does help, our companionship."

The importance of detachment as an essential part of presence came home to me the first time I shared the Art of Spiritual Companioning with a family member at the hospice. A woman came charging up to me one day as I was walking down the hall. She practically pinned me against the wall with her anger.

"What are you doing to my husband?!"

"What do you mean?" I asked, startled by her assault.

"Why is he so happy to see you and so angry when I'm around? We've been happily married for over thirty years. What are you doing to him?"

"Do you really want to know?" I countered.

"Yes." I escorted her down the hall to a private room.

"What do you want to know?" I asked.

"Why is he so angry with me all the time? We're close. We've had a wonderful marriage, but now he seems to be so mad all the time."

I commenced an informative little lecturette about meeting him where he was. (Remember, companioning was new to me at the time.) I said, "Your husband is grieving for what he is losing—his life, you, everything. He's on a roller-coaster ride. Some days he's up and accepting it all, other days he's angry, other days sad. I've watched you. I can see you love him very much. You come every day. You're very loving to him. But you always try to cheer him up. He's lonely for you. When he has a down day, you're still up, smiling, patting, telling him that God loves him. You have to meet him where he is."

"No, no," she said, looking panicky, "I couldn't do that. I have to cheer him up."

The thought suddenly dawned on me, "Hellooo. Companion her, Linda. You can't put anything into a full cup."

"What is important to you about cheering him up?" I asked.

"Oh, I can't have him dying depressed. I was depressed once, and it was horrible. I can't let that happen to him." Her block to being present to her husband began to emerge as I put my agenda of teaching aside and continued to companion her.

"What happened to you?" I asked, following her lead.

She described her experience of abject loss when her mother died. "It was like being in this dark place and I couldn't get out of it. I needed someone to cheer me up."

"What was that dark place like?"

She described it in physical terms, which I then used as a bridge for her to understand her husband's experience.

"So, it was like a deep, dark, slippery place that no matter how hard you tried, you couldn't climb up out of it?"

"Yes, exactly. I really needed someone to cheer me up."

"Forgive me," I said, "but I believe what you needed was someone to enter that dark place with you, light a candle and help you look at what you were experiencing."

The look in her eyes altered in that moment. "Oh," she said, "I see what you mean. But I just want to keep my husband happy."

"Donna," I said, "you can't keep him happy, but you *can* keep him company. That's all I've been doing."

In that moment, Donna did a 180-degree turn. With some cup-emptying, she recognized her agenda to protect herself from the fear of her husband's depression. Donna became so adept at companioning her husband, Merv, that he no longer needed in-patient care and was able to go home for the last three weeks of his life. I visited only once. Merv's bed was in the family room where he could see and be seen. Their adult son escorted me in and I saw the two of them with their heads close together, talking quietly. I could see how easy they were with each other. Merv no longer needed a "specialist" to companion him. Donna ably called on her compassion and her detachment to offer him her presence. Whatever he was feeling, she gave him her full, relaxed attention. They enjoyed pure gentle intimacy for the last three weeks of his life. Merv asked his son to order Donna a new pipe organ and have it delivered on her birthday. A few days later, as she played and sang him out, he peacefully passed.

See others whole

The capacity to be present to others in their rage, their fear, their excitement, or their confusion takes a subterranean shift in one's own spirit, from the caregiver who feels responsible to make things better to the companion who trusts the wholeness of the other. Spiritually companioning others is grounded in confidence that the gift of your presence in that moment will help them to come back to themselves, that they are saying what they need to say, doing what they need to do, and always, always are expressing something that deserves to be heard.

In *How Can I Help?* by Ram Dass and Paul Gorman, a man who had been chronically ill with paralysis for twelve years following a stroke reveals important clues to what is helpful, and what is not. "I've gone to rehab program after rehab program," he says. "I may be one of the most rehabilitated people on the face of the earth. I should be President." He describes the well-meaning efforts of dedicated people who had worked with him steadfastly to restore his physical mobility. "But I must say this: *I have never, ever, met someone who sees me as whole. . . .* Can you understand this? Can you? No one sees me and helps me see myself as being complete, as is. No one really sees how that's true, at the deepest level. Everything else is Band-Aids, you know."

I have learned that one of the worst experiences of individuals with physical disabilities is the way people fend away their instant reaction of pity by looking away, averting their eyes. So, it is my habit to make eye contact, to offer that moment of "I see you." The first time I saw Jim was at an outdoor market; an attendant was wheeling him by. Our eyes met, and I smiled. He flashed back a crooked grin. Six months later, I was in the forward lounge of a large ferry and saw him again, sitting in his wheelchair. I stopped and looked into his eyes.

"Do I know you?" he asked, his speech slurred, his hands waving like limp flags.

"Yes, we met at the craft market," I replied.

"Oh, yeah."

"Are you coming or going?" I asked.

"Oh, I'm coming back from vegetable camp," he replied.

"What are you, a carrot?"

"No, a squash!" The sound of our laughter turned heads. His laugh was loud, a drawing in of breath that sounded like a donkey braying. His attendant came running, looking alarmed, but I told him we were just visiting and to please give us some privacy. He looked a bit stunned but went back to where he had been sitting some distance away.

I sat down next to Jim. Between jokes, he told me his story. He had a premonition in his teens that he was going to die. He even went out and bought a life insurance policy with his mother as beneficiary. Shortly afterward he was in a serious car accident that left him a quadraplegic. "But I never expected this," he said. "This is harder." He spoke of his love for Christ and what a difference it made in his life. At one point, I said, "Do you realize that you have a great gift? You have been able to share in Christ's suffering." His eyes misted with tears. "I never thought of it like that," he said. As the ferry pulled into dock, I asked him what was it that gave him such good humor. "I'm lucky," he said. "What else could happen to me?" "Well, your hair could fall out." This time he roared with laughter. The attendant came running, and started to wheel him away. "Wait!" said Jim. He took my hand somehow between his and brought it to his lips.

Don't get furious, get curious

It's one thing to offer compassionate curiosity when someone is sad. When they're mad, and particularly if you are the object of their wrath, it is much more challenging. On those occasions when a child or adult in your world is angry and upset, the worst thing you can do is get defensive, or try talking them out of their anger with a quick solution. Just by showing that you are curious enough to hear them, their anger will subside. This is one of those times you will want to take a deep breath and cover yourself with your virtues shield of compassion and detachment.

Instead of stonewalling them, ask a cup-emptying question. If, for example, your child says "I hate that friggin' school and I'm never going back," this is definitely not the time to correct his language or convince him that without a high school education he will never get anywhere in life. This is a time to take a breath of detachment, shield your heart, and let him tell you what's up in school. "What's happening?" or "What do you hate about it?" are respectful openers. If someone you love gets angry with you, put on that shield, and summon all your curiosity. Trust yourself to have an opportunity to answer them *after* you know what it's all about.

I learned about a wonderful companioning tool from Tod, a tall, handsome teacher in Western Australia. He stood up at a Virtues Project conference on character education, when we were focused on spiritual companioning in the school setting, and offered a pearl of great value. With males of any age, Tod said, they cannot access their feelings unless they are moving. He found he was able to companion young men far better when they were walking "shoulder to shoulder, not sitting knee to knee." I remember discovering this with my boys when they had some burden they were carrying. Coaxing them to talk rarely worked. But, get them in a moving vehicle and the words came tumbling out. I'm now convinced that keeping my eyes on the road was an important part of the safety they felt. I have also learned that if I really want to hear my husband's feelings, it is much more effective to invite him for a walk than to ask him to talk.

Always end with a virtues acknowledgment

After you have listened to someone's story, it is often helpful to ask, "What's been helpful about talking?" or "What's clearer after our talk?" This question helps them to integrate the meaning of what they have shared, to find the virtue in the situation. Once they have responded, give them an acknowledgment for a virtue you see right at the core of their story. "I see how much you love your husband," I told Donna after we had our talk about companioning. "Thank you for being so honest" we can say to a friend or relative who has shared some uncomfortable thoughts with us. "I admire your courage" we can say to a person who is enduring a difficult situation. It is a powerful way to restore their dignity after they have opened their heart to us.

BE PRESENT THROUGH PRAYER

I have come to understand that the power of thought is so great, the way we think and feel about someone can affect them, even across great distances. When I was having negative, hopeless thoughts about one of my children after a difficult phone conversation, Spirit spoke to me quite sternly, saying, "Don't you think his spirit can feel what is in your spirit about him?" I immediately began to use a form of prayer that Madeleine L'Engle termed "kything," which Louis M. Savary and Patricia H. Berne described in their book, *Kything: The Art of Spiritual Presence*: "You establish a spirit-to-spirit connection . . . so that the two of you become joined freely and lovingly to each other at the level of spirit. Although kything is a very elemental spiritual act, it is an affirmation and an experience of a profound union."

You center yourself and then send the energy of virtues such as love, peacefulness, or forgiveness to another. It literally changed my thinking, and hopelessness was replaced by hope. A week later, the phone rang and my son said in an unprecedented cheerful tone, "Hi, Mom. How are you doing?" "I've been thinking about you and praying for you," I blurted out. "Yes, I know," he said and laughed. "I can feel it." The power struggle in our relationship has never returned. This simple, gentle method of prayer was a turning point.

You can also help people who are expressing negativity by just surrounding them with positive thought. I was having lunch with my friend Robert, a First Nations man of great spiritual integrity. Some teens sat down at a nearby table and started cursing, just in the course of their normal conversational style. Without deflecting from our conversation, Robert noticed he was bothered by the words and then chose to detach and instead send love to the boys. He breathed it as a cloud surrounding them. All this occurred while he and I continued talking. The cursing stopped.

Send healing

Prayer is a form of companioning. When we are separated by distance from someone, our thoughts and prayers carry great power. I have experienced this form of companioning with a group. Aileen, a well-loved member of our faith community, was in the hospital the night before surgery for breast cancer. Several of us were at a meeting and decided to pray for her. I mentioned the kything method and we all decided to picture a holy figure going to stand beside her bed. We went into silence and just pictured her surrounded by love, healing light, and the presence of this beloved being. At that moment, Aileen later told us, a nurse walked into the room and found her laughing, radiant, utterly joyful. She said, "I just felt overcome with joy when I felt His presence."

The medical impact of prayer has been studied. I read a fascinating online interview with Larry Dossey, a physician in San Francisco. He said, "One patient I encountered during my first year in medical practice had terminal lung cancer for which no treatment was given; members of his church prayed nonstop for him and the cancer totally disappeared. I did not take these cases seriously, however, until the mid-1980s, when I discovered the existence of scientific studies dealing with humans and animals, showing the effects of prayer. After years spent researching this evidence, I became convinced that it is one of the best-kept secrets in medicine."

In 1998, Dr. Elisabeth Targ and her colleagues at California Pacific Medical Center in San Francisco conducted a controlled, double-blind study of the effects of "distant healing," or prayer, on patients with advanced AIDS. Those patients receiving prayer survived in greater numbers, got sick less often, and recovered faster than those not receiving prayer. Prayer, in this study, looked like a medical breakthrough.

In 1988, Dr. Randolph Byrd conducted a similar study at San Francisco General Hospital involving patients with heart attack or severe chest pain. He found that patients receiving prayer did much better clinically than those who did not.

Currently, Dr. Mitchell Krucoff at Duke University Medical Center in Durham, North Carolina, is studying the effects of prayer on patients undergoing cardiac procedures such as catheterization and angioplasty. Patients receiving prayer have up to 100 percent fewer side effects from these procedures than people not prayed for. Prayer is a way to practice presence to others and serve as a spiritual mentor to them.

The will and the skill to be a spiritual companion, offering the gift of our presence, allows us, as nothing else can, to serve as an instrument of grace. The gift is doubly blessed, because both the giver and the receiver experience a connection of reverence for what is real and true. Companioning gives us the opportunity for genuine intimacy and weaves bonds of grace in our relationships.

To "listen" another's soul into a condition of disclosure and discovery
may be almost the greatest service that any
human being ever performs for another.
—Douglas V. Steere, author of *Quaker Spirituality*

⋙ EXERCISE GRACE ⋘
Practice Being Present

Spend a day being truly present to anyone who speaks to you. In every phone call, every encounter, whether in the grocery store or the office, in the car pool or over dinner, be truly present. Ask at least one cup-emptying question of everyone. Ask "What?" questions rather than "Why?," such as "What bugged you about your teacher?" or "What made it the best day?" Follow their lead. Give them a virtues acknowledgment when they finish speaking. "You used a lot of patience today with your teacher." Or "I love your enthusiasm."

SUMMARY OF CHAPTER 13:
GIVE THE GIFT OF PRESENCE

- Show the people you love that you cherish them by listening with full, concentrated attention, free of judgments or an agenda to fix.
- Be truly engaged in the stories of their lives. Show compassionate curiosity.
- Avoid tossing out platitudes that demean, belittle, deflect, or invalidate suffering. All people need is your presence.
- Ask cup-emptying questions—what and how—to help others get to the heart of the matter.
- Shield yourself with detachment and compassion, to keep from becoming enmeshed with the feelings of others. It is a protection for them as well.
- Support people to discern the clarity of their own Teachable Moments. Meet them where they are.
- Don't get furious, get curious. Listening with openness is a gift of true grace.
- We can send grace to others through prayer and by changing negative thoughts to positive ones.

In living a pace of grace, it is not only blessed to give but also to receive. The next chapter explores simple ways to receive companioning and create community.

⊷ *FOURTEEN* ⊷
Create Community

I don't need a certain number of friends, just a number of friends I can be certain of.
—Alice Walker

As your life takes on a pace of grace, you will find that joy is becoming your natural state. As you develop the habit of being present in the moment and present to others, your capacity to love will naturally expand. Don't be surprised if people are magnetically drawn to you, providing you with new opportunities for genuine companionship.

A trend toward spiritual wellness is now transforming our society. More and more, we are recognizing the importance of community and healthy intimacy with partners and friends. Circles of people are coming together. Individuals looking for business partnerships are recognizing the assets that matter most— the personal integrity of a potential partner, and whether or not the partnership is grounded in joy and camaraderie. We are all searching for our familiars.

As You Are, So You Attract

Celeste, a woman in her thirties who worked as program coordinator for her church, said that ever since she had started spiritually companioning in her daily interactions with other staff, family members, and friends, ". . . all of a sudden, I'm the most popular person. People are beating a path to my door. Now I need new boundaries for how I spend time with people. Men are showing an interest in me. It's been amazing."

When you live in a state of joy, compassion, and love, you attract others who are also living at that level of awareness and virtue. Our own state of being determines the people and quality of relationships we attract at any given time in our lives. This is true whether we are seeking a new relationship or seeking to transform the one we are in.

To sustain a lifestyle of grace and to maintain joy as our natural state, we have some work to do. Just as we can habituate to a new level of order and grace in our environment, we can create an interior design that will remove our habitual barriers to intimacy. By clearing away the emotional clutter that prevents us from experiencing spacious love, we can become as adept at receiving presence as we are at giving it. Doing some housekeeping will help us clear out our unfinished business, making room for new levels of intimacy with others. First, we must make our own heart ready.

BE WILLING TO BE WORTHY

Many of us were raised with the belief that it is more blessed to give than to receive. I do believe it is more blessed to give than to take, but when others give to you, receiving their gifts freely and fully is an act of reciprocal generosity. The gift is twice blessed.

I remember a woman on a plane who rose from the seat in front of me and awkwardly tried to assemble all her carry-on packages and valises. "Let me help you carry some of those," I said. I took some off her shoulders. "You make me feel so bad," she said. I was struck that she was so constricted by her own guilt and embarrassment that neither she nor I could fully enjoy the grace of the moment. When someone offers to help you, does something considerate or kind, let them! Be a gracious receiver. It will increase their joy in the giving.

Too frequently, we are fiercely loyal to beliefs about the paucity of love picked up in childhood. What we must understand is that this is a choice we made long ago, one that protected us from constant despair or disappointment. It is a choice that no longer serves us. Consciously choosing now to experience the presence of love requires that we replace these habitual beliefs and attitudes with faith in our own deserving. The first step is to detach from the issues we have carried for our parents, who probably carried them for their parents, no telling how many generations back.

One of my clients, a handsome, competent executive, suffered from acute anxiety and "imposter syndrome." Joseph went from relationship to relationship fearing that if a woman really got to know him, she would leave him. Although he made good money and enjoyed his work, he was under constant fear of being "found out" as a fake. This was the repository of his legacy from his father, a man who suffered from feelings of inferiority and drank to medicate his anxiety. He constantly criticized and put Joseph down from the time he was a toddler. To compensate, his mother overprotected him and bolstered his ego by exaggerated

> *Each person is born with an unen-*
> *cumbered spot, free of expectations*
> *and regret, free of ambition and*
> *embarrassment, free of fear and*
> *worry, an umbilical spot of grace*
> *where we were each touched by God.*
> —Mark Nepo, poet and author of
> *The Book of Awakening*

praise. By the time he was ten, she was using him as a surrogate mate, driving the wedge between him and his father deeper. Joseph sensed, with the acute radar that children have in picking up the family dynamic, that his excelling at anything was a threat to his father. Yet he wanted to please his mother. Harboring thoughts of his own inadequacy was a gift to his father in his attempt to balance the tension in their home and relieve his own guilt for successfully competing with his father for his mother's love.

During one session, we used the gestalt method of dialogue with his father. "I give you back your pain. It isn't mine to carry anymore," Joseph sobbed. He then forgave his father and forgave himself for his lost years. He began to consciously claim his own worthiness—his sense of excellence, his joy in work well done, his loving nature. As he committed to and reclaimed his joy, he was able to attract a woman who could commit deeply to him.

In the years since The Virtues Project has been developed, I have discovered that it does not take years in psychotherapy to unearth these old patterns. Rather, one can challenge them—flush them out—little by little, day by day, replacing them with a new awareness of our worth. The light of our virtues dispels the outworn shibboleths about who we are. It's like spiritual stain remover.

TAKE CARE OF YOUR PRIMARY RELATIONSHIP

The first and most fundamental relationship you have is with yourself and your sense of the Divine. Your capacity to fully receive love is inextricably linked to certitude about your own worth. As you cultivate a more loving relationship to yourself through enriching your prayer life and learn to see yourself through the eyes of a tender God, you will find that your capacity to receive love from others grows.

This relationship is not merely based on comfort and reassurance, but takes us right to our limits, and is as demanding and fiercely affirming as the attitude of a world-class coach to a star athlete. This coach holds us as able, and expects us to give our absolute best. This isn't a mollycoddling brand of love, but a robust and always faithful presence cheering us on to live by the virtues within us. It gives no purchase to self-pity, yet offers a complete embrace of all that we feel, and all that we need.

By practicing the presence in this private way, you are reinventing your attitude toward yourself—releasing the old shame and nurturing that tender bud inside your being that turns toward the light.

HEAL THE DISEASE TO PLEASE

One of the ways we barricade ourselves against love is by believing that we only deserve it when we do something that pleases someone. This becomes a repetitive, self-fulfilling insult to the validity of our being. We seem able to receive or recognize love only when it is linked to something we have done to make someone else happy. Seeking to fill the vacuum of reassurance and validation, we turn our intimates into approval objects. Then, if they dare to want something different, we resent it. We receive it as a blow to our self-esteem.

I have known many people in therapy whose childhood experience of a parent's rejection or distancing left them with thick projection lenses that kept them from trusting intimacy. When rejection occurs early in life, we develop no natural trust in unconditional love. Any hint of criticism or even a courteous request for change from our partners sticks to our "Velcro spots" of inadequacy. It feeds our belief that we don't really deserve love, but it comes out as countercriticism of our partners for not loving us enough. We're used to rejection, so we make it up even when it isn't there. For better or for worse, it is our comfort zone.

Pamela, an attractive woman in her late thirties, revealed in a session, "It's really embarrassing to look back and remember the black hole of endless need for reassurance I was to my husband before we came for therapy." I remembered an early session when Keith, a gentle, caring man, shouted in utter exasperation to Pamela, "You're driving me crazy with your constant need for reassurance. I love you. Why can't you believe that?" Pamela remained parched even at the shore of the river. The answer to Keith's question was the primary focus of the individual work Pamela and I did together.

After several months, she was able to identify her place-keeper for rejection, a holdover from childhood with parents who believed that raising a child right meant constantly correcting her. Pamela began to admit to herself that her husband did indeed love her. To get there, she first worked on her own self-esteem, focusing on her shining virtues rather than her glaring faults. She was able to heal her hypersensitivity to being "slighted" or shaming herself when she didn't do something perfectly. She began to reinterpret her flaws as Teachable Moments and life lessons, and eagerly began working on her "growth virtues." For example, when she made a mistake, she called on humility to clear it up right away rather than nursing it as a wound. At her final session she said, "I've given up my pity party and now my whole life is a party. Keith and I are having a ball."

Let Love In

As you practice the art of presence to others, you learn to really hear their true issues rather than projecting your own story of unlovability. You will find that as you replace the habit of shaming yourself, and think in terms of the Language of Virtues instead, you develop the humility to face your Teachable Moments responsibly. As a natural consequence, habitual guilt falls away. It no longer serves. Your relationships no longer stagnate in power struggles or ceaselessly whirl on the wheel of circular arguments. You are relieved of supersensitivity in response to a problem someone has with you. You can face it as an opportunity for growth rather than an attack on your lovability. As your own self-respect and confidence grow, you naturally are able to honor your right to be treated as a good person, a being of value. You dare to set clear boundaries with people in your life, and their respect for you grows as a result. All these practices allow you to let love in.

Friendship Is an Investment in Your Health

Even if we are blessed to have a healthy and satisfying primary relationship, no one person can meet all our needs. Every one of us needs time for solitude, and time with friends. Friendship is a spiritual essential. The presence of a friend can soothe us, unleash our hilarity, amplify our joy, and diminish our sorrow. We need playmates, people we can hang out with, and we need soul mates who know us and accept us unconditionally. A friendship that includes both is pure gold.

I once asked Evelyn, my best friend from high school who has remained my closest friend for decades, "Why have you never judged me once in all these years?" She responded in an e-mail after our visit:

There is one basic ingredient for any loving relationship that is absolutely necessary and it is that there be no criticism of one person to another . . . that is what we have had all these years. You asked me why I don't judge you—I could ask the same of you. It just is that way and that is why our bond is so strong. It makes for a wonderful friendship and would be the same in a marriage. Also, we talked about being our own "loving" mother to ourselves and I think that is so important but very difficult to redo old tapes. As I think back on all the things you say to me, I believe you are that loving voice to me. I know you are gently allowing me to ask questions of myself, to determine what it is that moves me forward or holds me back. I always come away from our time together with renewed awareness and strength. Having time together is such a precious gift, and I treasure every moment.

> A friend is a person with whom I may be sincere. Before him I may think aloud.
> —Ralph Waldo Emerson, American philosopher

The gift of presence to one another as witnesses and companions is a critical ingredient for spiritual wellness. We must have someone in our life outside our family to bear witness, to never judge but always hear what is real in our lives. For some, this relationship surpasses the verbal. Especially in the lives of some men, the presence of a comrade, a buddy, who is just physically there is all they need.

A landmark study at UCLA by Laura Cousin Klein, Ph.D., and her colleagues, showed that women respond to stress by releasing oxytocin, which stimulated behaviors of caring for children and gathering with other women. According to Drs. Klein and Taylor, this "tend and befriend" response explains why women consistently outlive men. Study after study has found that social ties reduce our risk of disease by lowering blood pressure, heart rate, and cholesterol. "There's no doubt," says Dr. Klein, "that friends are helping us live longer." Other studies support this contention as well.

My husband has a very close friend named David. He once said to him, "Sir,

I admire you more than any man on earth, and I will be of service to you for the rest of my life." My husband is a graduate of West Point, and he has the soul of a soldier. He has traveled with David across North America to do service projects in many small towns. Both of them unite around their passion for service, and the bond is profound. In contrast to my experience with my women friends, they do not chat. They hardly ever talk. Yet, for them, this relationship is a haven and an essential part of life.

CREATE A SUSTAINING COMMUNITY

For many of us, the protective circle of the extended family and of the tribe has disappeared. I heard a researcher say in an interview that in Middle Eastern cultures, when a woman gives birth, the family cocoons her, cooks for her, takes care of her other children, shows her how to bathe and care for her baby, massages her, feeds her, and gives her time to just fall in love with her child. We were never meant to make our way through childbirth, death, and the other seasons of our lives alone.

A growing trend is afoot to create our own communities. Cooperatives are forming to purchase organic foods in bulk, share the home schooling of children, and set up shops where the works of artists are showcased. At the most basic level, we need community in order to have help with our children. I know of a large group of families that socialize together, trade off child care when they need a break, and plan marvelous child-friendly holidays, such as camping at a national park or beach, once a year. When one of the adults is hospitalized, this circle of friends are the ones who bring casseroles and look after the laundry. My closest friends and my siblings and I find ourselves thinking about aging now, concocting plans for moving closer together so that we can be there for one another as life becomes more fragile.

Thriving faith communities have learned the secret of sustainable community building. People don't need more meetings, they need to be touched. They need someone there when they are hurt or sick, feeling a loss or celebrating an anniversary. This loving embrace, when given in outreach from a center of authentic compassion, attracts others to join them.

Several members of my faith community attending the annual fall fair noticed how much garbage was being created by the use of paper plates and cups and the failure to recycle glass bottles and aluminum cans. They went through the garbage one year, picking out the recyclables, which inspired an idea. They proposed to the fall fair committee that we would rent plates for all the food concessions, and that we would wash the dishes throughout the day. The first year only a few of the booths participated. Now, a dozen years later, all you see are our plates. A lovely decorated booth has been built, and each year more people join us in the fun of fetching, sudsing, and rinsing. It has become one of our favorite activities of the year.

Schools have learned that one of the ways to heal violence, obliterate bullying, and inspire passionate school spirit is to build true community among the students through the virtue of unity and service. These schools create shared vision statements focusing on unity and tolerance. No one is left out. Every student is befriended. One of the ways they do this is through community service projects that connect students to the wider community and often with others around the world, building their self-esteem through helping others. The difference when you walk into one of these "character schools" is palpable.

CREATE A CIRCLE OF MENTORS

I am among those people who treasure having a circle of mentors to share our stories and honor our passages. Some circles meet weekly or monthly, some hold retreats once or twice annually without staying in touch the rest of the year. Some stay connected through e-mail or phone for regular companioning sessions. These circles are a powerful source of personal support and spiritual sustenance.

A group of men in California have kept up with one another through marriage, divorce, illness, new jobs, lost jobs, the births of children, and the deaths of spouses. Together, they continue to birth themselves. Carlos called me after I had given a retreat for his wife and the wives of the other men in this close circle of families. My husband, Dan, and I had facilitated marriage retreats for them over the years as well. "Linda, we want you to lead a retreat for the men too," he said. I resisted for years, believing they needed a male facilitator. Finally, I agreed, and it turned out to be one of the most moving experiences of my life. Until they shattered my illusions, I had no idea of the assumptions I had about men's emotional limitations. The first evening, we gathered for dinner in the large, beautifully furnished private home that was offered by one of the men for the retreat. As the men arrived, I felt like I was in a locker room and they were snapping

⤖ The Virtue of Unity ⤖

He who experiences the unity of life, sees his own Self in all beings, and all
beings in his own Self, and looks on everything with an impartial eye. . . .
—Bhagavad Gita vi, 29

Unity is a very powerful virtue, and it brings great strength. It is a way of
seeing the universe as one, designed by the One who created us all. Unity
brings harmony, like the sound of music made by the different instruments in an orchestra. Unity helps us to value what each part brings to the
whole. It helps us work and live together peacefully. Unity is the gift of
community. It brings a sense of belonging. With unity we can strive for
harmony with our family at home and our human family around the
world.

Signs of Success

I am practicing Unity when I . . .
- Treat all people as members of one human family
- See the gifts in differences
- Solve conflict through listening and finding solutions
- Do my part to build community
- Care for the earth and all living things
- Act like a peacemaker wherever I go

Affirmation

I create unity with others. The joy of one is the joy of all. The hurt of one is the
hurt of all. The honor of one is the honor of all.

towels at each other. I thought, "Uh-huh, I thought it might be like this." At the first session, when the circle came together, I set the boundaries for the weekend, one of which was to be fully present to one another from this point on without criticizing, interrupting, comparing, rescuing, or teasing. I wondered how capable they would be of abiding by these boundaries.

I thought they would keep things dry and heady. Instead, they revealed the longing they had for deeper love and acceptance by their wives and deep issues from childhood. I thought they wouldn't cry. They wept, sobbed, howled, and filled a huge basket with the tissues they used to wipe their tears. I thought they wouldn't touch. They enveloped one another in long embraces.

Two incidents stand out in my memory of this retreat. When Bill was sharing his story in the silence of the circle, he sang a song, "I go out in the rain, but I do not have a cup, I do not have a bowl." It was a song about thirst that could not be quenched. He wept as he sang. Suddenly it began to rain, a rarity in Southern California on a summer day. One of the men silently slipped out of the room and returned a few moments later. Each man in the circle then acknowledged Bill for the virtues they saw in him: "I honor you for your steadfastness, Bill. With all that has happened, you still hang in there." "You're the loyal guy I can always count on." Roger disappeared again and walked back into the room with something in his hands. He knelt in front of Bill, then with both hands presented him with a cup of rain. Then they held each other for a long time.

Gary, a married man with several children, revealed to this group, who had known him for many years, that he was gay and had been fighting it for years. They heard this in total silence, then spontaneously each one of them went over to him. They held him and rocked him. I could only sit there in wonder, tears coursing down my cheeks.

An Example of a Mentors' Circle

A group of nine women in their sixties to eighties has been gathering in one another's homes once a month for ten years since they retired. They refer to it as their "crones' group." They use simple practices to create a safe, sacred space in which to share the unfolding stories of their lives:

1. A regular meeting time

They meet on the first Monday of each month, deciding who will host it in her home the next time.

2. Use of simple rituals

They gather over coffee or tea, and soon a bell is rung. They use a talking stick or stone, which is passed around the circle.

3. Clear boundaries

There is no cross talk, no commenting when each person finishes, just silent compassionate presence.

4. Occasional play

From time to time, they take special outings to a place of natural beauty or overnight in a beachside lodge.

5. Food

A simple lunch of soup or salad and quiche awaits them after they have shared. Nothing elaborate.

Marilyn says of the circle, "It gives us a chance to reflect on 'where I'm at' as we go through different periods. I went through a depression last year, and it helped me to put it into words. Depression can spiral down until you share it in trust that it's okay to be there. It helped me to see the depression as a sacred place to be."

I belong to two circles, one for fifteen years and the other ten. They are lifelines. There had been five of us in the first circle until our beloved Liann died at age forty-three last year. The four of us who remain are writing a book about our sacred time together, weaving the stories of our lives as well as our recipes. We have shared survival from cancer, divorce, grief, joy, and emergence. When we are in one another's presence, time seems compressed and crystallized. Because we choose not to communicate much between times, we experience a striking mindfulness of where we have been and where we are now. We too begin with a simple ritual—the gonging of a Tibetan brass bowl, which Jo carries around the circle so that we each resonate to its tone. We hold the silence while each woman shares, and when she finishes, we sometimes ask questions, and always acknowledge her virtues. It gives us a sense of closure. And we feast—from the time we arrive to the time we leave. Whoever is hosting creates fabulous fare. New York boiled bagels, good cream cheese, and good coffee are an opening ritual. We luxuriate in food. We grow orgasmic over exotic, homey, voluptuous flavors. There is almost always chocolate. More often than not, we spend the night. We knit, listen to good music, nestle by candlelight.

My second circle of mentors is an ongoing support network of nine women in three countries. We are in our thirties to sixties. We retreat once a year, usually at a riverside lodge. Every year we seem to need more time. Last summer it was a full week. Our structure is flexible. Each woman has had intensive training and experience with spiritual companioning and the process is awesomely support-ive. We spend time in circle, and lots of time just being together. We paint each other's toenails in wild glittery colors, give each other temporary tattoos, swim, cavort, create fabulous crafts, and sign on for specific meals that are healthy and delicious. My annual contribution, which has been deemed a requisite ritual, is an old-fashioned roast chicken dinner, with gravy, mashed potatoes, corn on the cob, and piles of fresh vegetables, followed by something chocolate my husband bakes ahead of time as his gift to the group.

This group has become a life-support system for every one of us. We are in touch continually by e-mail. When Pat had surgery, two of us were there in a heartbeat. When Pam was burning out with job and children, Betsy invited her to her home for a week of respite care. We are the silken thread of awareness and love in each other's lives. We are the trapeze and the safety net.

The following is the end of an e-mail in which Pam shared the latest strug-gles on behalf of her special-needs teenaged daughter and how she had to deal with yet another crisis at school:

> *I'm making it up one day at a time. I hold the vision of that picture we shared at our last retreat. Placing my feet on the tight wire I am stretching out from my own hands. What helps?*
>
> * *Loving myself*
> * *Accepting my frailties*
> * *Not being it all*
> * *Taking it one step at a time*
> * *Calling on Courage*
> * *Calling on Detachment*
> * *Calling on Trust*
>
> *I see your eyes reflecting your love back to me when I look in the mirror. I call you close when I am lacking. I thank God for each of you every day. Thank you for your willingness to companion me through this. For walk-ing with me. Seeing me.*

CELEBRATE LIFE, CREATE CEREMONY

Christina Baldwin, author of *Calling the Circle*, says, "Ritual is the way you carry the presence of the sacred. Ritual is the spark that must not go out."

One joyful way to create a pace of grace in your life and to connect with community, is to have regular ways to honor and celebrate the passages of life. Honoring the Spirit is the Fourth Strategy of The Virtues Project. It consists of having a daily routine of reverence and also creating ceremony and ritual for significant life transitions. It is a way of being in community that celebrates and commemorates. It sanctifies our lives, reminds us of the meaning of our passages. It illuminates our virtues.

When a child makes a significant life change, as when they graduate from crib to bed or first go to school, pausing to celebrate it with a special cake, a new hat, an honoring dinner with simple virtues acknowledgments, marks it as soul progress. When a young man or woman comes of age, a ceremony, family celebration, or ritual such as the passing on of an heirloom piece of jewelry honors their life journey.

I know of several fathers who have taken their sons at the age of thirteen on a vision quest, in the First Nations tradition. They have gone out to a remote place of nature, set up camp and sent their sons out alone for a night or more of fasting and reflection. When their son returns to camp, they sat in silence and companioned him about the vision for his life that came to him, then gave him a special gift, such as a necklace or family treasure.

My friend Beth, in the midst of a very busy life, took some sacred time to honor her three daughters at a time when their life stories seemed to call for it. Her youngest daughter, at thirteen, had just had her first menstrual period; her foster daughter had just shown the courage to face her birth parents and visit them for the summer, while living within her own boundaries and for the first time returning to Beth's home free of depression; and her oldest daughter had just completed a year of service abroad for their faith community. Beth described to me what she had done to honor them:

> It felt like one of those uncanny "the stars are in alignment" sort of things and I needed to do something about it. I decided to have a wise-woman celebration. I alerted my daughters that I was holding a party in their honor on Wednesday night, that I was inviting some friends and that the men of the household were being asked to find something else to do that night. I contacted all my women friends and invited them to come to the celebration with some thought or wisdom that they would like to share with my daughters about being a woman.
>
> I asked my daughters to prepare themselves for the evening by bathing

and dressing themselves in their most beautiful clothes and adorning themselves with perfume. I set out the dining room table with scented candles, roses, fresh fruit, chocolates, and freshly baked bread and fresh jam.

My daughters were invited to come into the candlelit room and sit down. I welcomed them and then read to each in turn a letter that I had prepared telling them about this next stage of development that each was entering, identifying the challenges that were before them, acknowledging the strength virtues that each had developed that would help them on this journey and challenging them to use these strengths responsibly. I then presented each of them with a piece of jewelry as a symbol of this new stage of development. Then each of the older women present spoke, some sharing poetry or music as well as words of advice and wisdom. Each young woman was given the chance to speak. Then we ate and chatted together. My eldest daughter thanked me with tears in her eyes, "Now I know what I'm supposed to be doing, Mom. I was really lost after moving back home."

More and more schools are using the virtues to honor students as they graduate. Maxwell International School in British Columbia holds an honoring dinner, where each graduate honors the family members at their table for the virtues they appreciate. A woman named Charlene recounts that her daughter began by honoring her for "'the virtue of friendliness, Mom, because you're my best friend.' Fortunately I had brought a huge box of tissues for our table."

When I turned fifty, a friend asked me what she could give me for my birthday. "A dinner party," I said. I invited my twelve closest friends in town, and asked each to bring some words or a poem or a reading that signified what I mean to them or something I have given to them over the years. I took a weekend retreat to prepare for this passage, and a poem emerged, called "Trust," which I shared at the dinner and eventually included in my book *Sacred Moments.*

I felt a deep need to do a giveaway as a symbol of freedom from the things of this world, knowing I was closer to the next at this stage in my life. I spent days walking around the house or sitting quietly contemplating my most treasured belongings and choosing one to give to each of my friends. This was both painful and freeing. I wrote notes to each of them about the gift they are in my life, which they read aloud as they held the gift I had given them, then read the words they had for me. Ceremony is the portal with which we revere one another at the turning points of our lives.

The true spiritual wealth of our lives is found in friendship, kinship, mentorship, and worship. A pace of grace gives us the time to invest in these treasures.

*One of the most profound ways to share stories is in a council, or circle.
When we sit together in a circle we remember how we come from peoples who
gathered at the same well, who sat at the same campfires, who depended on
oral tradition to remind themselves of who they were.*
—Christina Baldwin, *The Seven Whispers*

⊶⇒ EXERCISE GRACE ⇐⊷
Create a Circle of Mentors

Select or attract your members

Make a list of several individuals you trust and with whom you would like to meet to have a sharing circle or a retreat. If this group is among people who know one another already, begin with the first person and make sure that he or she is comfortable with the others in the group. Truthfully, I have found that sometimes holding a retreat, getting the word out, and seeing who shows up attracts the people that are meant to be there.

Create simple rituals

Have a simple way to begin and end your time together, such as ringing a bell, lighting a candle, or saying a prayer. You may choose to end each turn with the picking of a card, such as a Virtues Card, reading it and saying how it speaks to you now. I suggest you always end each share with several virtues acknowledgments. "I honor you for your courage in the way you have dealt with this issue."

Set clear boundaries

Create a simple format that works for your group, with ground rules for your sharing circle. For example, there should be no advice-giving allowed and no cross talk during sharing. Advice can be very shaming and violates the need for a judgment-free environment. The key is to make this a safe place where your story is witnessed without judgment or the need to fix you in any way.

Decisions to make

1. How you want to deal with food
2. How often you want to meet and where
3. Your ground rules for sharing
4. An agreement about how someone leaves the group, for example, that they come one last time and say why.

Prepare the space

If you are hosting the gathering, prepare your home or the venue by making it clean and beautiful. Have a candle ready to light and food prepared ahead of time.

This is your mentoring group, so together you can make whatever guidelines or practices you need. You may find that over the years you want to add informal or physical activities to the practice of meeting. Continue to be open and trusting about your needs.

In some groups there is only talking; in others there is a need for physical touch, for being held. Have the courage to ask for what you want from one another. This level of safety usually occurs in a retreat setting, possibly a facilitated retreat to begin with. Focus on what it is you want and it will happen. Sustain it by making it a priority in your life.

SUMMARY OF CHAPTER 14: CREATE COMMUNITY

- As you keep a pace of grace in your life, cultivating the virtues of a more graceful life, you will attract your familiars.
- Your primary relationship is with yourself and your Creator. As that relationship grows more loving, you will be able to open yourself to receive more love from others.
- Heal the disease to please. Let go of the issues you carry for past generations.
- Don't try to control love. Let it in.
- Invest in friendship. It is essential to your spiritual and physical wellness.
- If you do not have a sustaining community, find one or create one.
- Form a circle of mentors.
- Create celebrations and rituals to grace the passages of life.

PART FOUR

PLAN A SUSTAINABLE LIFE

*It is only when we accept that we
do have choices and we exercise
those choices that we can
reclaim our lives.*
—Anne Wilson Schaef

⤙⋙ FIFTEEN ⋘⤚
Put Your First Passion First

Everyone should carefully observe which way his heart draws him, and then choose that way with all his strength.
—Jewish proverb

Living by a pace of grace helps us to focus our energies on our true values. We become more aware that whatever we invest our energy in will grow in our lives. I feel as though I have experienced a miracle, as practicing the Ten Rules for Health continues to regenerate my health and my energy. I have a new outlook on life. I am much more tuned in to my inner life, more adept at discerning the desires of my own heart, and willing to give myself permission to live a quality life. I now have a far better understanding of the ninth rule for health than when I first received it.

The ninth of the Ten Rules for Health was:

Rule #9: Prioritize

Put your first passion first. It is your most productive activity.

For me, putting my first passion at the forefront of my life meant a paradigm shift in my attitude. This rule held layers I had to peel before I could be free to pursue my first passion. It required deep discernment and profound behavioral changes, such as letting go of the habit of responding to the squeaky wheel, or letting high-urgency items monopolize my time, often leaving things of higher importance behind. It also meant making a radical shift from a responsibility-driven lifestyle to a joy-led life.

Start with what you love, the rule implied. First, do what makes your heart sing. It sounds so simple. However, this invitation in the ninth rule stirred up in me a major case of the "But-what-abouts." Pursuing our passion sounds nice, but what about my obligations? What about all those unanswered e-mails? An embarrassing memory surfaced of a time a few years before when I kept telling my friends I was going to slow down and do what I really wanted to do—be an author. At an employees' retreat where we presented amusing "awards" to one another, Adeline, my closest colleague at the hospice, gave me a strange package adorned with a huge red bow. The gift was a broken record.

It began to dawn on me that the virtue residing at the very core of a sustainable life is joy. What sustains us is what we find personally engaging and enjoyable. This is our true sustenance, not just physically, but spiritually. We don't need to fill our time with tasks that exhaust us, people that drain our energy, anxiety that taxes us emotionally, demands that overfill our time. We have choices. Everything works better when we are happy. Seeking joy in our work leads us to what we are meant to be doing. It helps us to find our true sphere of influence.

MAKE JOY YOUR PRIORITY

What a concept! Our first priority is meant to be our first love. Because I was so acutely conscious of the limitations on my energy, I realized as never before that I could no longer carry the administrative burdens of our global Virtues Project, and that in truth I could *only* do what would be life-giving to me, allowing my own gifts of writing and speaking to flower, instead of fitting them in around the daily grind of managing the details. It was time to stop contorting myself into the multitasking role of an administrator, a job others could do with great skill and enjoyment but which drained the very life out of me. I had made several unsuccessful attempts to turn over my "business" to others, but for various reasons it had not worked. This time, I was absolutely determined, one way or another, that I would shed the parts of my job that were limiting my joy.

I discovered that I no longer had to do hard work, just heart work. Putting my first passion first *was* my most productive activity—allowing me to be of greater service in bringing the message of The Virtues Project to a far wider audience, and at the same time producing far more income than when I was slogging through dozens of administrative tasks each day.

In the presence of my gentle observer, I took an honest look at how often I had wasted the time of my life in worry, or squandered it in great surges of effort, driven by an external goal instead of being led by inner wisdom. I entertained the possibility that work was meant to involve less duty and sacrifice, and more joy and freedom.

To live a life of grace, to live sustainably, we must stop letting the chaos of our lives dictate how we are living. We must see through the popular dogma that

⊸⇒ *The Virtue of Joyfulness* ⇐⊷

Joy gives us wings! In times of joy our strength is more vital, our intellect keener, and our understanding less clouded. We seem better able to cope with the world and to find our sphere of influence.
—Abdu'l-Bahá, *Paris Talks*

Joyfulness means being filled with happiness, peace, love, and well-being. Joy resides in each of us. It comes from a sense of being loved. It emanates from an appreciation for the gift of life. Joy flourishes when we are doing what we know is right. Joy is the inner sense that can carry us through the hard times, even when we are feeling sad.

Signs of Success
I am practicing Joyfulness when I . . .
• Look inside for happiness
• Believe that God created me and always loves me
• Enjoy whatever I am doing
• Appreciate some gift in my life
• Appreciate some gift in myself
• Feel an inner peace even when life is difficult

Affirmation
I am thankful for the joy I feel inside. I enjoy my work and my play. I appreciate the gifts this day holds for me.

"If I just work hard enough, I'll be okay." Now is the time to recognize that happiness is a natural outcome of living with a sense of grace. Our reclamation of joy does not come easy. It carries a price. We can no longer rush around, remaining disconnected from our feelings. We have to ask ourselves, perhaps for the first time, "What do I want and need?" and know that whatever it is, we are worthy of it.

We have a deeply ingrained habit of doing drudgery first, and only then what we enjoy. "Clean your room first," our mothers told us, "then you can go out and play." "Eat your broccoli first, then you can have dessert." The ninth rule for health radically reverses this notion. It called me to sacrifice my old way of doing things—gritting my teeth and doing the stuff I didn't like so I could get to what I enjoyed doing with the diminished energy I then had left. When all I had was four to six hours a day to work, I knew I had to prioritize.

What if we gave up what drives us, including the idea that we must have a certain income to be "successful"? What if we saw success as a simpler, more joyful life, pursuing work that moves us, and that fulfills our desire to make a difference? What if we could do what we love and love what we do?

Follow Your Heart

A huge step in planning a sustainable life is to make the decision to be happy—a commitment that what you do for a living will be life-giving to you. If you feel trapped in a job that doesn't use your gifts, ask yourself what livelihood would allow you to fully use yourself. Pay attention to your inner voice. What work would truly engage you? Spirituality is grounded in the meaning of life, and your spirit will be content only if you are doing what you find meaningful. It may be a world away from what someone else finds meaningful, but it will be an authentic expression of your unique gifts.

Simplicity guru Janet Luhrs made a leap of faith to follow her heart when she left her first job as a lawyer and pursued her passion as a journalist and writer. She had just finished law school and had hired a nanny to take care of her baby daughter so that she could work as a lawyer. She worked for two weeks before she asked herself, "What's wrong with this picture? I don't want a nanny raising my baby. *I* want to be with her." She also realized that working as a lawyer did not satisfy the call of her soul to be a writer and editor. At age eleven she had established a neighborhood newspaper, and she had never lost the bug. Janet is the author of *The Simple Living Guide.* She is also the editor of *The Simple Living Oasis,* a beautifully written quarterly journal full of rich ideas. Whenever it arrives, I devour it immediately, then savor it for weeks. The first time Janet interviewed me for *The Simple Living Journal,* we fell in love, and have remained fast friends. She became a great advocate and practitioner of virtues and includes chapters on virtues in her books. In *The Simple Living Guide,* Janet describes the simple living theory of work as something her father taught her:

1. Find something you love to do and get paid for it.
2. Live under your means. (Living under your means is when you spend less than you take home and sock away the rest.)

Janet was willing to live more simply and frugally to feed her soul. She also wanted a business that would allow her to be at home to parent her children. Her career as a writer has now burgeoned into a satisfying and sustainable career, and thousands of people each year read her books and enjoy her journal.

Follow your heart. Does this mean that everyone is meant to take a leap into a brand-new career? I don't think so. I think it is more a matter of cleaning house in the area of work, just as we can purify our bodies, our language, and our living spaces. Spend some time reflecting on what is cluttering your life. Whether you are working at a job outside the home or at home as a full-time parent, whether you feel you need to seek a new career or want to change your way of working in your current role, here is a way to redefine your priorities. If your children have too many extracurricular activities, they may secretly be feeling overwhelmed. Sit down as a family and ask these three questions together:

• What do you want to stop doing?
• What do you want to keep doing?
• What do you want to start doing?

If this exercise helps you to clarify that there are parts of your role you wish to eliminate, have a conversation with your boss, or your family, and creatively consider shifting these aspects of your role to someone else.

Take a good look at the level of materialism to which you have habituated. Are the things around you giving you joy, or have you drifted into the compulsive consumerism that pervades our culture? One of the things that has helped me to shed the objects around me is the thought that when I die, my sons will have to come and clean it all up. What do I want them to find in my home? Another goal is to have around me only those things that, as William Morris says, I "know to be useful or believe to be beautiful." I have truly found that less is more. I cannot describe the sense of lightness, freedom, and joy that I experience each time I clear up an area of "stuff" in my home or office.

You may not need to make the level of income you think you do. Likewise, you may find that when you allow your imagination to flower and find your true calling, your income will actually grow. If you are in a position in life when money is not an issue—and for that, be thankful!—it may be time to ask yourself what you want to say yes to. Take your time to discern what is calling to you now.

What Gives You Joy?

Helen Keller said, "Many persons have a wrong idea of what constitutes real happiness. It is not obtained through self-gratification but through fidelity to a worthy purpose."

Reflect on what activity fills you up. What gives you the greatest sense of true productivity and deep satisfaction? It may be using your hands instead of your degree. It may be an activity that allows you to be with people instead of in front of a computer. It may be taking time for acts of kindness—looking for ways to be of service in a job you already have. Perhaps it is something that taps into your creativity. It may be changing your role by envisioning a project rather than tackling the details themselves. It may be that you are a writer. Give yourself at least one hour to do a life-giving activity as the first task on your list after you have had your routine of reflection. Observe the flow of your productivity for the rest of the day when you choose to put your first passion first. Use this as a clue to build more of this into your work and your life.

Find Your True Calling

Buddhism teaches that right livelihood is a staple of the spiritual life. We are all born with some gift or virtue to be used in service to the world. We find our deepest self-fulfillment when we use our gifts in service to our community. Abraham Maslow, the father of humanistic psychology, coined the term "self-actualization." He said, "Self-actualizing people are, without one single exception, involved in a cause outside their own skins. . . . They are devoted, working at something, something which is very precious to them, which fate has called them to." Unless we take the time to discern our true calling, we may never know the joy of right livelihood, in which, as Maslow describes, "the work-joy dichotomy" disappears.

The purpose of our lives is to live a life of purpose. When we live only for the goals of ego—worldly success, recognition, prestige, or material gain—we will never feel satisfied. Only by tapping into our unique purpose can we be happy.

It isn't easy to do our soul work in the midst of an egocentric world. I remember well a wealthy man who flew in on his private plane to see me when

> *O Lord! Unto Thee I repair for refuge, and toward all Thy signs, I set my heart.*
>
> *O Lord! Whether traveling or at home, and in my occupation or in my work, I place my whole trust in Thee. Grant me, then, Thy sufficing help so as to make me independent of all things, O Thou Who art unsurpassed in Thy mercy!*
>
> *Bestow upon me my portion, O Lord, as Thou pleasest, and cause me to be satisfied with whatsoever Thou hast ordained for me.*
>
> *Thine is the absolute authority to command.*
>
> —The Bab, nineteenth-century Persian prophet

I was in private practice. Bill had set high material goals for himself and met all of them. In his mid-forties, he was a multimillionaire. He had bought and sold businesses, was CEO of a hugely successful company, and lived by the dictum that the difference between men and boys is the size of their toys. Yet Bill was plagued by a sense of emptiness. "Why am I so depressed? It's crazy," he told me in our first session. What came to light over the months I saw Bill in therapy was that there were two core virtues languishing within him: integrity and service. He was an incredibly purposeful man, but only in service to material wealth—to ego. Spiritually, he felt bankrupt. He was failing to serve a meaningful purpose. He was out of touch with his children, who had rarely seen him while they were growing up. He loved his wife but also had a mistress of several years he was very attached to. "Every time I try to leave her, I just can't do it." He was torn apart by guilt, having been raised with strong Christian values as a child. He also felt his life was useless. "I thought I had it all, but I don't feel I've really done anything with my life." Bill's soul task was to apply the same purposefulness and determination with which he had built his business empire to rebuild his life to be of service to others. He realized that he was holding his mistress back. She was (surprise, surprise) much younger and wanted a family, which he did not. He found the inner strength to let her go, and at the same time began spending quality time with his wife and two sons. He then spent time discerning and visioning what good he could do in the world with his money. He found his passion at last—giving young entrepreneurs a leg up—and began mentoring and financing their dreams. He didn't need to leave his profession. He just refocused his priorities.

The experience of single-pointed attention feeds the soul. I recently saw a *20/20* show on elderly workers. A factory manager deliberately hired people in their seventies and older. A woman of ninety-six with smiling, birdlike eyes said that she had tried retirement, "But it was boring me to death."

Finding our own unique purpose—saying yes to the grand adventure that is ours if we are willing to step out in faith, is not only a gift to ourselves but to our children. Seeing us working with joy leaves them a great legacy—the trust that if you pursue your true calling, by the grace of God, you will be given an opportunity to be the best and to give your best.

Pursue your service

If you use your sense of purpose only to pursue ego goals, as Bill learned, you'll never be fulfilled. Look at the goals you dream about. Are they merely material or do they meet your spiritual needs? One of the greatest sources of joy in life is the experience of making a difference. Within every person there is an inner craving to have an impact, to give something unique to the world. Only service can satisfy that call of the soul.

Malcolm is one of my most cherished advisors and has given countless hours of service to The Virtues Project over the years. As a chartered accountant, he has a successful practice that funds the work of his heart—to be of service to a cause he sees as changing the world for the better. He once explained to me that not taking money for what he does for the Project and for me gives him total freedom and joy.

At the age of thirteen, Canadian Craig Kielburger followed a calling that he could not refuse. He was watching a show on television about child labor in India and a passion ignited within him to do something about it. He pled with his parents to let him make a trip to India to see what he could do. By heeding that inner call and having the support of his courageous parents, Craig has built hundreds of schools around the world through his foundation Free the Children (www.freethechildren.org). He is often interviewed on talk shows such as *Oprah* and he speaks with great passion. His eyes shine with a strong sense of joyful purpose.

A rich world of opportunity in volunteering exists for retirees. You may want to serve as a mentor to children and youth, or participate in international projects such as Habitat for Humanity (www.habitat.org). Tim and Louise signed on for such a project and brought their grandson with them. Their lives were changed, and the bond among the three of them was deepened while giving true service.

Elders in various countries, such as the "character builders" in Bermuda, serve their communities as virtues mentors.

Alexina Keeling, a retired teacher in Texas, offered her services to the principal of a school in which many of the students had been in jail, some for violent crimes. When a student was suspended for carrying a weapon to school or an act of bullying, instead of just sending him out on the street, the principal would call "Miss Alexina," who would sit with the student each day companioning him about his life, doing Virtues Picks, exploring the strength virtues the student already had, and working out a plan to develop his growth virtues, the ones he needed to cultivate. Soon, the program was so successful that the school found funding for Alexina to start a "Virtues Camp." I received beautiful photos of the young people of her town beaming as they held up a virtues poster.

PLAY WITH POSSIBILITIES

Are you at a crossroad in your life? This is a signal that it is time for a change, one that will allow you to pursue your true calling. There is a relatively new industry of personal coaching offering mentorship to design your best life. This reflects the fact that so many of us are no longer content just to bring home a paycheck. We want our lives to count for something. A large part of finding our calling is identifying our unique gifts and pairing them with a job that allows us to give what we have to give. You may want to go to a personal coach or form a mastermind group, to help one another design a soul-satisfying vocation.

Give yourself permission to play with possibilities. In fact, think about how you play. What was your special gift as a child? What do you like to do? When your work is also your play, it is profoundly satisfying.

My two brothers are models of individuals who have had highly successful careers by paying attention to what gives them joy. As a child, John used to make innovative bulletin boards every week. For holidays, he created special place cards and centerpieces for the table, always with a theme for the occasion. Now he is the design director for one of Walt Disney's theme parks. He served as the first designer for Virtues Project books and materials and continues to serve on the international design team as well as being a director of the Project. Our brother, Tommy, used to pretend to be speaking different languages. I remember shrieking at him to stop when he would dramatically spout his "gibberish" in front of my friends, and I felt the excruciating embarrassment that only a pre-teen can feel. Tommy now speaks three languages fluently. He lived in Iran for a year and his accent in Farsi was so perfect that his friends successfully passed him off as a compatriot. He works as an interpreter for the federal court in Puerto Rico and as a bilingual television, stage, and film actor and singer. He's even made it into a Hollywood movie, thereby achieving both his dreams for drama and language.

DO WHAT YOU DO BEST AND DELEGATE THE REST

Have you considered that what you love most could be most productive for you, both for your health and your wealth? In a world that has become chronically stressful, with far too much on most people's plates, feeling productive is a strain. Our stamina is weakened, and our concentration is broken. We owe it to ourselves to give some thought to what we want to keep doing and what we want to delegate to others. I believe that organizations that are open to this way of re-organizing will find that people's productivity skyrockets.

Putting my first passion first led me to a change in my work habits I had never known was possible. Once I committed to doing what I do best, I was able to delegate the rest. Volunteers in several countries agreed to take on the various e-mail streams and a new international directory was placed on our Web site. I couldn't believe how the resources appeared once I had made the shift in my spirit to give myself permission to pursue my first passion.

A man who worked with my father during his many years in international development wrote me after his passing to share some advice my father had given him that he had found very helpful. Naturally it was the perfect time for me to receive it: "He gave some good advice that I have passed on to many others and strive to remember. During one of our meetings we were all consulting (I think maybe complaining) about our backlogs. Mr. Kavelin said that when we can't do everything, we don't do what we *must* do. We do what we *can* do. Then pray that it is enough and that it is acceptable in the sight of God. If he could follow that advice, with all the worries of the world on his shoulders, then I could certainly try it. This has meant a lot to me over the years."

I have heard it said that we can only focus on three things in our lives at once. This requires the detachment to sacrifice the important for the most important things in our lives. It takes a willingness to do what we love, to do what we do best, and delegate the rest—to employees, coworkers, and our family members, including our children.

Discovering our true purpose is so important. The attitude within your spirit is what leads you either toward or away from your passion. If guilt keeps sliding you backward, take some time and take a look at it. What purpose is it serving? Is it your way of feeling in control? Is it helping you to do your best work? Or are you just caught up in it, attached to it as the story you tell yourself about how downtrodden you are by all your responsibilities? Oprah Winfrey, on her television show on April 9, 2003, said, "Your real work is not your job. Your real work is to figure out what you're supposed to do with your life."

Irene, a mother of four, lived in a modest home not far from a beach. She complained bitterly that she spent all her time cleaning up after her four children and never had time to pursue her own passion for art. When I asked her to describe her typical day, the picture emerged of a compulsive cleaner who made her children's beds, did their laundry, prepared their lunches, all things that her children could easily do for themselves. When I asked her about this, she blushed a guilty red. "They're willing to do it, but I don't like the way they do it," she said. "What don't you like?" "Oh, they leave wrinkles in the blankets," she said. "Interesting choice," I replied, then put my hands out as if weighing things. "Blankets without wrinkles—painting by the beach. Towels folded just right—listening to the surf. Hmm." The story Irene was attached to was being the "good girl" in her family of origin, doing things perfectly for her demanding mother, who bitterly criticized her siblings for being lazy. Once she realized she was carrying on an old story, she marshalled the troops at home and began living her dream.

In their excellent book *The Power of Focus*, Jack Canfield, Mark Victor Hansen, and Les Hewitt emphasize the importance of finding your passion and then making it your first priority. Not surprisingly, they recommend that we focus on the high-leverage activity that we are best at, which is often what will earn us the most money as well. I have found that one of the barriers to this in myself and other leaders and business owners I know is that we get so caught up in the day-to-day survival activities and the fear that no one will do them as well as we do, that we procrastinate doing what we love and choose to earn far less money!

I asked Justine, a friend of mine who is also an author, what her current dream is for her life. She said she would love to write a column, and named other activities related to writing in addition to a quarterly journal she publishes. "What stops you?" I asked her. "Oh, I'm so busy running my business. I'm terrible at it, but I just can't seem to get out from under it." Seeing my friend in the same predicament that I had been in for years was another wake-up call. Find someone to do the things you are not best at so you can concentrate on your passion. I could see how much more financial freedom Justine would have if she took that one step. We both promised one another we would make delegation a priority.

The Power of Focus recommends the 4-D formula for prioritizing:

1. Dump it. Assertively say no to what you choose not to do.
2. Delegate it. Without guilt, turn these over to people who can do them.
3. Defer it. There are things that can be put off. File them in a follow-up file and look at it at a designated time. Give yourself a reminder.
4. Do it. These are the important things. Put them at the top of your To Do list and when they are completed, take a little time to celebrate.

THINK CREATIVELY

By tapping your creativity, you are sure to find a way to put joy at the center of your life and your work. Think "outside the box," as they say. What is the one thing that would make all the difference in the way you spend your time and energy? Is this what you feel called to do? If so, you will find your path or your path will find you. It may take a large step of courage and a leap of faith, but ask yourself this: What are you risking if you *don't* make a change?

There are at least three ways to live by your true calling:

1. The first is to find a job that allows you to fulfill your first passion.
2. The second is to create a job that you love.
3. The third is to have a vocation that supports your avocation.

Peter is a deeply fulfilled man. He worked by night at the central post office of a Canadian city for years to support his true calling. In his early fifties, he began studying spiritual direction, now open in some Catholic communities to the laity. Formerly, this was a role performed only by priests. He now counsels individuals to tap into the mysteries of their prayer life and leads guided retreats as a deeply respected spiritual director. I had the privilege of being partnered with Peter in a ten-day spiritual directors' retreat. As we practiced the skills we were learning each day with one another, I had a profound epiphany with Peter, who was able to companion me to my deepest place of doubt, abandonment, and grief in my relationship with God. At one point I was crying out to the God I felt had abandoned me as a child, "How could You let that happen?" I felt Peter's full, strong presence, with no agenda but to support me to go where I needed to go.

This deeply healing, transformative experience led me to a more authentic relationship with my God. The rare times Peter and I happen across one another's path, we enjoy a true soul reunion. Peter continued to support his true passions of spiritual direction, grandfathering, and softball through his work at the post office until he retired two years ago. Now he spends full time at his true career as a spiritual director. "The job provided a living wage, which supported my true career," he says. Peter added, "It wasn't something I actually chose, you know. Doors just kept opening. It chose me."

Do What You Love

A lyric by Duke Ellington and Irving Mills says, "It don't mean a thing if it ain't got that swing."

A Gallup poll found that 71 percent of North Americans do not find their work engaging. Being bored at work is actually quite stressful. We don't breathe deeply when we are bored and it takes only a slight shift for it to turn into depression.

We do not have to be stressed by work if we are willing to find a way of working that blesses and enriches us. Tod, the teacher in Western Australia, released himself from the "golden handcuffs" of the corporate world to follow his true calling of teaching. He was willing to take a deep pay cut in order to do his heart's work, yet his quality of life and his health improved greatly, especially when he included Yoga in his daily routine. We don't have to do what we don't love to do. When your work is not play, it takes a terrible toll on you. If your work is sheer drudgery, plodding, or boring and you have to force yourself to roll out of bed every morning, it may be time to look for or create a new job—something that will make your heart sing.

LOVE WHAT YOU DO

You may not feel that a radical change of job and lifestyle is your cup of tea. If your current choice of work feels right but is a bit joyless, there are ways to bring joy to any job. Reorganize your work so that you start with your first passion first—the activity that would give you the greatest pleasure and with the most meaningful result. Decide to bring some innovation to the job. Bring your mindful attention to the details and give them your very best today. Mother Teresa said, "To show great love for God and our neighbor, we need not do great things. It is how much love we put in the doing that makes our offering something beautiful for God."

Engage in your everyday tasks with a commitment to happiness. Rather than changing jobs, face the day with a shift in your spirit, a gentle transformation of attitude. It is said that work done in the spirit of service is the highest form of prayer. Often it is the spirit with which we work that sustains our joy.

When I worked as a social worker at St. Luke's Women's Hospital in Harlem, New York, I met Doreen, a young mother on welfare who was determined to break the poverty cycle in her family. She wanted to earn her own living but had little education and still had young children at home. I encouraged her to pursue her passion of independence, and together we created a plan. First she enrolled in night classes to get her high school equivalency degree. Fortunately, she had the support of family and friends to take care of her children in the evenings. We also found a day-care program for her children when she needed it. Then she got a job working at a McDonald's as a cleaner. She brought total enthusiasm and excellence to the work. The sinks and toilets shone, the windows sparkled, and Doreen's smile was bright. The manager noticed her excellence, and began to promote her. He saw her potential for leadership and enrolled her in a management program. Doreen was able to get off of welfare completely, fulfilling a dream she had had for years. She was just beaming when she came in to share her latest promotion with me.

NAME YOUR VISION

Putting words to the vision you have for your life is a helpful way to focus your purpose and attract confirmations. Create a simple vision or mission statement that captures your sense of purpose. It is most powerful when it is brief—just one sentence that includes one or two of your core virtues and gives you joy when you say it. Start with the vision or picture of your goal and add a "by" action statement. Here are a few examples of vision statements:

Keith, a gifted strategic planner with whom I have had the bounty of working, has his personal mission statement: "Foster human development while perpetuating that ability in others, leading to mutual self-fulfillment."

My own vision statement is: "I help people to make the sacred accessible in everyday life by an awareness of the transforming power of the virtues."

ASK YOUR ANGELS

As you discern what calls to you, ask yourself if what emerges is merely desired or is inspired. If you want all your possibilities revealed, think about tapping one of your greatest underutilized resources—the team of helpers in the spiritual realm who want you to be happy and to find your place of service in the world. If this is something that resonates for you, I strongly suggest it as a way to find your true calling.

First, prepare yourself for change. Are you willing to follow the leads that come to you after you begin praying? Ask for guidance. Then become acutely vigilant, alert, and mindful. Spend some quiet time each day listening to your inner voice. Pay attention to books people mention to you, things they say to you, your dreams, and your thoughts. Keep a journal about the patterns you notice, phone calls you receive, ideas that come to you "out of the blue." Fully trust that you will have an answer. Follow your intuitive nudges. As you act, you will become a magnet attracting Divine assistance. You are actively inviting grace.

I know a number of individuals who have prayed for more meaningful work—something that would allow them to pursue their true calling—and have had remarkable experiences leading them to put their first passion first.

Motherhood is my friend Kate's first vocation. She prayed for a way to homeschool her children and earn a living at the same time. An opportunity came to her attention when a friend spoke to her about becoming a distributor for Usana vitamins. Although at the time she wasn't too interested, her intuition gave her a nudge, so she opened herself to the idea. She is very proud of this quality product, and now has plenty of business each month. Her second greatest passion is helping other at-home moms earn a good living, and now she is able to do that and also has residual income flowing in. It gives her the time to pursue another interest, working as a researcher and editor for authors, another task with hours she easily regulates around caring for her children. I was her first author, and the way we connected was, of course, very synchronistic. Both of us were praying—I for the help I needed, Kate for a way to use her creativity and skill as a researcher. Those heavenly teams definitely talk amongst themselves.

Lead with Your Passion

My first passion is writing. Most days, it is like stepping into a warm, sunlit, softly flowing river and just moving with the current. Yet I was in the habit of attacking the difficult administrative things first, only getting to writing if I had time and energy left over.

I was amazed to discover that when I followed Rule 9 of putting my first passion first in my workday—before even checking e-mails—the rest of the day flowed effortlessly. I had already accomplished what was most important and could then relax with the pile of "little things" in my in-basket or on my goal list that didn't hold the same passion for me. It created a sense of quiet contentment and joy, a sense of "enough" early in the day. I find the same deep satisfaction when traveling to conferences around the world. I have done some of my best work in airports on my laptop computer, which accompanies me everywhere. When I spend a few hours writing on the plane, followed by a rest, I am quite refreshed when we arrive at our destination.

Putting our first passion first allows us to lead our lives, day by day, with the "edge of the wedge" in alignment with our true calling. It creates purposeful momentum for the rest of the day. Some days, this principle means beginning with what is most important—one of the "big picture" things, such as a proposal, an important call, or a major project of some kind, leaving the details for later. Sometimes the first priority is an act of kindness, writing a loving card to someone, or doing something special for someone we love. It isn't so much a productivity issue but a quality of life issue.

. . . Our calling is where our deepest gladness and the world's hunger meet.
—Frederick Buechner, quoted in *Soulcraft* by Bill Plotkin

⤞ EXERCISE GRACE ⟜
Discern Your True Calling

This exercise is a reprise of the assessment at the beginning of the book. This time it is focused not on the factors that are stressing you or blessing you, but on where you are in the stream of your life. It is focusing on the future in terms of what you are called to do at this time in your life.

Create a retreat experience for yourself, either in your own home, if it is conducive to silence, or at a place where you can walk, pray, reflect, and journal. Take along drawing paper or a roll of paper and colored pens. You may want to bring collage materials, such as magazines, scissors, gluestick, for the True Calling exercise. You may also want to go with a friend to companion one another about what emerges.

The river of life

Sketch a river on a long, single sheet of paper—symbolizing the river of your life—with simple words and pictures or symbols, such as a ring for marriage. As you draw the river of your life, notice the major events, the relationships, illnesses, and accomplishments that shaped your life. When was the current swift? When was it calm? When did you feel happiest? Come to the point where you are now and journal the words that come to you about what it feels like to be here at this point. Reflect on what will happen if you remain on this course. Write words and phrases that mirror your feelings about it. What do you want to keep about your current lifestyle? What do you want to release and replace? What do you want less of? More of? What will truly sustain you?

Mind Map your True Calling

On a large sheet of paper, create a Mind Map. In the center write "My True Calling" and the date. Reflect on one to three core virtues that are at the heart of your calling and write them above and below the central words. Around the page, write three goals that you feel are balanced, attainable, and sustainable and will help you to thrive. Beneath each goal put the first step you will take to realize your dream. What do you feel led to do with your time and energy? What would your perfect balance be? It may include activities or callings involving your spirituality, love life, family life, recreation, work, and/or service. It may be goals related to your chosen vocation. These goals will be measurable.

Create an "I have a dream" collage
I find that having a visual to go with the vision is powerful as a daily inspiration right in front of me. Create either an illustration of your true calling or a collage of words and pictures that represents your dream. Use colors and textures, pictures from magazines. Put it where you can see it. Envisioning your dreams helps you to make them come true.

SUMMARY OF CHAPTER 15:
PUT YOUR FIRST PASSION FIRST

- Place joy at the center of your life.
- Follow your heart. Pursue your passion.
- Assess your priorities by deciding what you want to stop doing, keep doing, and start doing.
- Find your true calling, which may also be your truest service.
- Do what you do best and delegate the rest, whenever you can.
- Think creatively. Play with possibilities.
- Do what you love and love what you do.
- Do everyday things in a spirit of happiness.
- Identify your vision and create your personal vision statement.
- Use prayer to find your most meaningful work.
- Lead with your passion. Be in tune with your purpose.

The final chapter of *A Pace of Grace* will give you tools for planning a sustainable life day by day in ways that reflect your personal vision.

·⇒ SIXTEEN ⇐·
Plan for Grace

In the beginning, love.
In the end, love.
In the middle,
We have to cultivate virtues.
—Swami Chidvilasananda

The morning I received the Ten Rules for Health and had my first glimpse of living with a pace of grace, I was struck by the brevity—and mystery—of the tenth rule:

Rule 10: Plan a sustainable life.

No further details were revealed as there had been with all the other rules. It seemed to be a summary of all the others, and at the same time a call to action demanding radical change. Yet I had little or no understanding of the meaning of these words that first morning.

I started with the first rule and took it step by step, day by day. As I constructed a new lifestyle around the practices of immersing myself in water, inside and out, breathing more deeply, eating more nutritious foods, and pacing myself with work, rest, and play, something new within me began to unfold. As I created a gracious, orderly space, set clearer boundaries about how I spent my time and with whom, focused my thoughts and language on the virtues, and replaced my internal critic with a gentle observer, a new sense of fullness and delight emerged. I was practicing the presence in a more fluid and constant way, and for the first time in my life I began to *experience* the meaning of sustainability. I realized that it was not just about surviving an illness or making it through the demands of a pressured life, but thriving.

Now I have learned to refill my energy level every day. I feel healthier and happier than I have ever been in my life. My mind has come back more lucid than ever before, and creativity flows. Every day I am aware of the precious gift of time. Every day I ask myself, What would a day of grace look like today?

CREATE A PLAN

The daily practices of a pace of grace lifestyle can help us restore our energy, provide a sense of peace, and enable a gentler flow in our lives. They can provide relief from the chaos and exhaustion that constantly threaten our quality of life. Preserving this new level of well-being calls for something more. There must be a way to sustain positive change in light of the inordinate level of stress under which we are living. What is required is a trustworthy plan to safeguard our intent to live gracefully.

I gradually discovered that hidden within the final rule was the key to sustaining a lifestyle of grace. The key word was "plan." The plan is the chalice that holds the elixir. It structures our resolve. It is the container for grace.

Years ago, I spent a week at a conference center in Michigan in a course on creativity. I was assigned a roommate from Tennessee, who was a woman of great size. As Cora and I got to know each other and shared our stories, I shared a challenge I had been puzzling over for some time. I was deeply impressed by Cora's brilliant ideas for how the situation could be resolved efficiently. My brother John once tactfully described me as "physics-ly challenged" because the technical and pragmatic details of life often confound me. I am easily awed by the mastery of the practical. Cora was a blues singer and a highly creative artist. Even the way she dressed was an art form. Yet she was so pragmatic. When I expressed my surprise about this dual gift, Cora said, "Honey, if you ever need to get something done right, ask a fat woman. She has to plan every move."

When post-polio took over my life, I received my own empowering lessons in planning firsthand. It became an engaging form of soul work for me to become more aware of my body, enabling me to cultivate more subtle, mindful discipline. When one's energy is severely limited, every hour has to be planned. If I had too much rest, I found it made me sluggish. If I didn't get enough, I would slide into fatigue. If I failed to exercise sufficiently, I lost muscle strength. If I overexercised, my muscles and joints would stiffen with pain. The process of discovering the balance point took unaccustomed delicacy, introducing me to a new level of mindfulness.

I had to continually discern what was "just right." I learned to plan the shape of each day with wisdom, in order to get as close to perfect moderation as possible. My recovery offered an invaluable Teachable Moment about the power of moderation, order, and balance in managing time and energy. Once I saw it as a

⋯⇒ The Virtue of Purposefulness ⇐⋯

I have awakened to the truth and I am resolved to accomplish my purpose.
—The Gospel of Buddha, The Bodhisattva's Renunciation, para. 12

Being purposeful means having a clear focus. We begin with a vision for what we want to accomplish, and concentrate on our goals. We discern what we feel called to do. Do one task at a time, without scattering energies. Some people just let things happen. When we are purposeful, we make things happen.

Signs of Success

I am practicing Purposefulness when I . . .
- Have a clear vision of what I want to accomplish
- Know why I am doing it
- Focus on a goal
- Do things one at a time and finish what I start
- Keep myself from getting scattered or distracted
- Persevere until I get results

Affirmation

I am purposeful. I am clear about what I am doing and why. I stay focused on my goals. I concentrate on what is most important. With God's help, I can accomplish great things.

virtues challenge, I took to it gladly. Gradually, I realized that a life of grace required this same "just right balance," not only for physical wellness but also for the health of my spirit.

These lessons are a core part of the practices that continue to safeguard and sustain my excellent health. In this final chapter of *A Pace of Grace*, I want to share with you the best practices I know for planning a sustainable life. They include creating a balanced design for your life and simple ways to organize your year, your week, and your day, not as something more to burden or restrict you, but to free you to live your easy, grace-filled life.

1. Find Your Balance

Moderation is the fulcrum of a graceful life. The first step in planning a sustainable life is admitting that you can't do it all, and that if you are to have quality of life you must choose how you will spend your energy and your time, and then plan for it. Find your own way of balancing the elements of your life that works for you and gives you a sense of spaciousness, grace, and accomplishment. This requires scrupulous honesty and detachment from the expectations of others, including those heavy ones you have carried around since childhood.

After a conference keynote address in which I talked about the necessity for leaders to practice a pace of grace, a saleswoman came up to me in tears and said, "I feel really moved by what you said, but I have four boys at home, and I love them to death." "Whose death are we talking about here?" I wondered silently. I told her that it wasn't serving her boys to see her sacrificing her own well-being for them. "Think of their wives," I said. "They need to learn when they're still young that a woman's role is not one of total sacrifice. You must model for them that women take care of themselves and must be respected." She really cried then, and I knew my statement had hit a nerve. I recommended a visioning retreat for her to plan a new balance for her life.

It's time to undress and take off your hair shirt, no matter how comfortable it has become. If, on the other hand, you have been a dilettante in your own life, never committing to any path, full of confidence about your own talents but waiting for a magic opening to appear, it may be time to take a deep breath of courage and plunge into deeper water, to set your direction, and make a plan.

If you are like most people, you are overloaded by a sense of too much to do, and the idea of planning your life sounds like an impossible luxury. Give yourself the gift of sitting down now and looking at the pieces of your life, just as if you were cleaning out a cluttered shelf. Lay them out in front of you. What do you want less of, what do you need to release, and what do you want more of? Review your answers to the exercise from chapter 1, "What Blesses You and What Stresses You?" Think in terms of the basic elements of your life in light of what you value:

- Relationships
- Community
- Work
- Spiritual practices
- Service
- Creativity
- Personal health and exercise
- Fun
- Rest and relaxation

What would the perfect balance look like at this time in your life, given your most valued priorities? What do you feel you are neglecting? If you lived just as you wanted to, and could magically change it all in an instant, what would be different? What would you eliminate? What are your greatest time wasters? Are you watching too much TV because you're exhausted and feel you have no choice? What activities restore your energy and build your joy? What are the best times you have as a couple or as a family? Do you need to plan more of them?

Place all the ways you use your time out in front of you and look at them. You are the designer, the architect of your life. You can rearrange, eliminate, or add what will give you a sense of grace. Finding your balance and reinventing yourself in light of your vision, your needs, and your joy takes a leap of faith and a step of confidence that you are worthy of a good life. And that means a moderate life.

By putting your first passion first, many of the things that drain your energy will naturally fall away. It may be time on the phone, or it may be time wasted in some activity that is joyless for you. Give yourself permission to make changes in the way you use your time so that it reflects how you truly choose to spend your life.

The problem is that we have been conditioned to live with a constant external focus and to value ourselves only in terms of what we produce or do for others. It takes so much less energy to just bob along on the swift current of momentum. Habit is seductive—and so much easier than change. Yet if we decide to continue living unconsciously and reactively, we are making the choice to experience depression, anxiety, and resentment—which will continue to drain our energy. Irritability is proportionate to the degree that we are failing to live authentically, by our own design.

At a women's retreat, I invited a participant to create a psychodrama of the roles she played. She chose various women from the group to play the parts of her life: her children, her job, her husband, her faith, and her creativity. She directed them to move into positions that showed how it felt to be in her life. Her children pulled on her arms, her husband was at a distance, half turned away. Her faith was beckoning to her from afar. Her job was pushing down on her shoulders. Her creativity was curled in a ball at her feet. She had each "part" speak to one another about what it needed from the others and rearrange themselves into a pattern of how they wanted to be. Then she gave them final "adjustments." Her children held her hands gently. Her husband came and stood in front of her looking lovingly into her eyes, with one hand on her face. Her faith held her in its arms and supported her. Her job took its rightful place on the outside of the family circle. Her creativity danced around and through all the other parts. She then went and journaled a plan to transform and structure her life as she had seen it revealed in the exercise. She named the virtues that she would cultivate in each part to allow it to take its rightful place.

2. Schedule Self-Care First

In his groundbreaking classic *The 7 Habits of Highly Effective People*, Stephen Covey speaks of time for self-care as "sharpening the saw." Rather than just working harder and harder, thereby dulling our effectiveness, we need to work smarter. This requires us to take the time for self-care. Covey shares a story about taking time out of his busy life to go to Hawaii to write, because this was what was calling to him. Think of the millions of people who have benefited from this soulful decision.

One of the ways to make self-care more central and reliable is to plan for it, to specifically schedule restoration time on an annual, monthly, weekly, and daily basis.

Annually

Plan for some adventure at least once a year with a group of friends, your partner, or your family. Make sure to plan for some solitude as well. Once a year, my husband and I meet our children and grandchildren, who live across the world, for a family holiday. Plan something that will truly restore you—a kayaking trip with a friend, a retreat or a trip away. Deborah, an editor for a New York publisher I worked with, would plan a rafting trip or a hike to some place of beauty across the United States at least once a year. She returned radiant from the Grand Canyon or Yosemite. Wisely, she knew that these trips needed to be booked far in advance, and she includes it in her planning process each year.

You can find inexpensive ways to restore yourself wherever you live. My friend Betsy goes to a retreat center near her home several times a year to restore, reflect on her life, and just be. I have found that exploring the tourist attractions within a few miles of where we live is a wonderful way to have a "holiday at home." The key is to plan your year with restoration in mind, so that you have something wonderful to look forward to.

I remember the courage it took the first time I planned a retreat with a friend instead of a holiday with my husband. I stood in front of our wall calendar, tears running down my face, and told him, "I need time away, love, and I need to go alone. I want to spend some time at Boo's wilderness cabin this summer." He was silent for long moments and then said, "Do what you have to do." That sacred time every summer for more than ten years kept me sane during the stressful times and nurtured my soul for the rest of the year. My husband happily created a sustaining ritual of his own, going off to help his friend David build something. I have two women's circles that meet for retreat at least once a year, and those dates are inviolate. If you don't plan them first, your time can easily be eaten up entirely by the shoulds and obligations of your life. First things first. Sharpen the saw.

Monthly

Using a calendar, whether on your computer or one that hangs on the wall, plan for monthly "Me" days. It may be for a massage, an outing, time with a friend, or special time with your partner. Be sure to include time for reflection and creativity. There are many wonderful workshops you can attend in spiritual growth or art or community building. Angeline, a supervisor for a telecommunications firm, uses a red pen on her paper calendar and reminders on her computer calendar for "Angeline Days." "I'm already booked for that day," she says if anyone asks anything of her on the day in question. Schedule these free times even if you don't yet know what you will be doing. Leave space for spontaneity.

Weekly

Take time off! By that, I mean take time to be, to do nothing, to play. Make sure that you plan your weekends or whenever you can take time from your regular daily work so that you have time just for being. Engage in peaceful activity. Build or sew or craft something that requires your full, contemplative concentration. This is one of the best ways to relax your mind and take it off of work mode. Often our minds keep working away even if we are trying to be in relaxation mode. The key is to be engaged in something that soothes your mind and restores your body. Physical activities such as skiing, kayaking, canoeing, and gardening are ideal. They help us to glide into a zone of peace and remain there, refilling our spirits and refreshing our bodies.

Plan something fun for yourself with a friend or with your partner every week. Plan for family fun as well. Put it into your schedule and keep it sacrosanct. Our children need noncompulsory time too, alone, with their friends, and with us. Hanging out with a child or a teen doing something fun and peaceful like fishing or hiking or crafting something together builds trust and intimacy.

My husband and I have our inviolable Tuesday date whether we are traveling or at home. In the summer months, when I am at home, I meet a friend for brunch and then we go to Saturday market to browse the local crafts and buy fresh local vegetables.

Susan and Greg live in New York with their five children. When their children were still young, they were drawn to move from a quiet town in British Columbia to this high-energy city. Greg is a physician and Susan has an active life as a mother and volunteer in her children's schools. They often go on adventures with their kids without ever leaving home. Susan described with delight a school holiday when they went to museums, played sports in the park, and took the subway to an out-of-the-way ethnic bar and restaurant where they were the only people in the place not speaking Spanish. They basked in the color, the food, the noise, and the music. This lifestyle choice has given them a sense of rich abundance and they make constant use of the wealth of opportunities around them.

When you refill your cup in ways that nurture you, you will find that you have more energy for the rest of the week. You will naturally have more patience, acceptance, love, and generosity to give. When your own cup is full, you have plenty to give others. It doesn't serve anyone for you to go empty.

Daily

Structure your day to include regular pauses for self-care. Begin with your routine of reverence, sourcing your day in prayer and reflection. Ask yourself what a day of grace would include today. Take time for at least ten minutes of reading, prayer, meditation, and journaling, along with choosing a virtue to focus on for the day.

Have a nurturing breakfast. Relax and enjoy your food. If this means getting up ten minutes earlier, do it. Then, your first priority for a joyful, sustainable workday is to lead with what gives you passion. Make sure to spend about five to ten minutes at the end of each day clearing your work area and putting it in order. This short investment will help you begin each day with a sense of a clean slate.

Include self-care in your daily routine. Always have fresh water at hand to sip on. Stop about every two hours to literally take a breather, take a short walk, have a stretch, or a face, head, and foot massage.

Shoulder rolls: Lift your shoulders straight up beside your ears, then roll them back. Rotate your hands and wrists.

Mini-massage: Rub your palms together to heat them up, then smooth your forehead and cheeks with both palms. Press your scalp gently and firmly with your fingertips, then the base of your neck and your shoulders. While sitting in your chair, massage your feet in the same way, firmly pressing with fingertips and massaging with your thumbs. You can stimulate any part of your body through the pressure points on your feet. The thinner part of your big toe relates to your neck, your arch is connected to your back, and the adrenal gland can be stimulated by finding the sensitive point just inside your arch and pressing on it for a few seconds.

Take a breather: Do some abdominal breathing, breathing in for several counts while letting your stomach out, holding your breath for a few counts, and then as you exhale, pulling in your abdominal muscles tightly. This is an excellent muscle toner as well as a good way to restore oxygen.

Pause for prayer: Offer a prayer of gratitude for something going well in your day, or whatever comes to mind about life that you appreciate.

Remember to rest proactively: About four to six hours after you awaken, plan a ten-to-twenty-minute rest or Yoga pose. Take more time if you suffer from fatigue. Make sure you rest *before* you get tired.

End your day with inspiration: End your day by reading something from your bedside table, whether a prayer or a brief passage of inspiration. Think of three things about the day for which you are thankful. If you have a problem to solve, ask for clarity and wisdom, then sleep on it. When you awaken you will see the world differently.

I know from experience as someone who easily gets lost in my work—something I actually enjoy about myself, by the way—that if I don't plan for self-care, it doesn't happen. These simple practices based on making self-care a priority will sustain your enthusiasm, your mental acuity, and your creativity, three of the most important qualities enabling you to effectively meet your goals.

3. Transition Gently

Gentle transitions help us to sustain a sense of grace in our busy lives. We must resist the habits of procrastinating, overstuffing our time, and rushing from one thing to another, which rob us of peace. We need gentle bridges from one state to another each day.

It has become fashionable to "hit the deck running." We need to stop barreling into activity as if we are in a race to keep up with our day. When you rise from sleep, don't hit the deck running. Step into the day prayerfully. Move into the day gracefully. Give yourself the gift of time. Make preparations the night before that will allow you to have a peaceful morning. One habit that makes a big difference in my life is that before a trip of several weeks or months, to make sure I will have a pace of grace the day of departure, I pack two or three days ahead rather than scrambling at the last minute. I have a tendency to pack more than I need, so it is helpful to have the time to then put back things I won't absolutely need. A checklist of essentials such as camera, reading light, flashlight, and sacred materials remains in a pocket of my suitcase.

So, take your time getting up in the morning, using orderliness to help the day begin as peacefully as possible. One of my happiest memories of my mother was her coming into my room each weekday morning to wake me for school, singing her silly morning song, "Tra la tra la, the birdies sing. Awake, awake, tis morrow." Even as a teen, as much as I grumbled about her invading my privacy with her cheerfulness, she was wise enough to know that this small ritual still helped me to start the day right.

Create simple rituals

Simple rituals help us to move into the varying activities of our day. When you begin your reflection time, lighting a candle is helpful in drawing yourself into the presence of spirit. A gentle transition ritual as you move into your workplace for the day is very helpful in keeping your pace of grace as well. Take a breath, and say a prayer or an affirmation such as "This is an excellent day. I now begin my peaceful, productive work."

As I walk into my home office or prepare a work space in a hotel room, I put my hands out to either side, picturing two writers who lived some time ago and whose presence I feel assists me with my writing, taking each hand, and thank them for their help.

Begin with order

Putting your work area in order if you have not done so the day before will immediately reduce potential stress. Having lived for years without this practice, I can now assure you it will make a huge difference.

Plan your day

Before you enter your work area, stop and invite excellence, courtesy, or grace into your day. Be alert to opportunities to be kind, to be the presence of grace to others. One of the ways to get a sense of perspective on your day, rather than just plunging in, is to sit down, turn on your computer or put a pad of paper in front of you, and make a plan for the day. I have a "Today" file on my computer, which is the first thing I pull up. It contains a plan for the week, and each day I refresh the daily goals.

Whether you work inside or outside the home, design a daily transition from your work to home that helps you to restore yourself and refocus on your relationships. Perhaps it is a ten-minute rest, a shower, walking the dog, a quiet drink, or a story with your children. Design a pleasant way to help you cross the bridge between away and home or between day and evening.

I once asked James, a business consultant and friend, how his holiday had been. "It was fabulous!" he said. "I had a great time with my wife and daughters, but I'm having a devil of a time getting back to work. I've been in the office for a week, and I just can't seem to get into the swim of things." James seemed to have left his spirit behind on holiday, and his inner resistance to reentry was keeping him from getting anything done. I asked him what would serve as a gentle bridge or transition to work, one that would allow him to keep the joy of his holiday. He designed a simple ritual of sitting at his desk each day, and before beginning work, taking a few peaceful breaths, permitting himself to recall happy memories of playing on the beach, or swimming in a warm sea, then bringing that same joy to his work. What gave him pleasure, James realized, was to avoid wading into the accumulated pile, and instead organizing from highest priority to lowest priority, and filing it in that order as well. He placed his first passion—the project that excited him most—in the closest file, and spent the first two hours of each day on it. This gave him a deep sense of satisfaction. Instead of fighting his joy, he used it as his transition bridge.

4. Pause for Applause

Because we always have more to do, we rarely take the time to pause for applause, to celebrate as a way to give ourselves closure when a project is finished. Yet we crave closure. We need to reestablish kinder rhythms. Every culture of the world celebrates the fruits of the harvest. After the hard work of planting, cultivating, and harvesting, people enjoy dancing, celebration, and feasting, and rest from labor. Because most of us work in an information environment, or a family environment where people's needs never stop, we need to create our own passages, our own ceremonies of completion and closure.

In the workplace, rewarding staff for the successful completion of a job is important. Small perks such as a gift, a spa day, or a trip to see a movie are remembered and show our people that they are important to us. We need to do this for ourselves too.

I have learned from years of experience with overseas travel that after a long trip I experience a sense of letdown or loss, despite my excitement and delight about being home. My pattern is that the first day I feel elated, and riding the last waves of adrenaline I zip around the place. The second day after travel my adrenaline slumps, and if I didn't know better I would interpret it as depression. My energy levels shift dramatically, and I feel a sense of loss about what is now over. Perhaps it has to do with the less-than-glamorous piles of mail and other things calling for my attention.

When Maria, one of our conference coordinators and facilitators in Malaysia, was driving us to the airport, she confessed she felt depressed after each conference was over, including workshops at which she was the facilitator. Dan and I companioned her, and she emptied her cup about the feeling of letdown afterward. It's not easy to get back to a humdrum daily routine after a demanding and exhilarating activity has stopped. After Dan told her about the "adrenaline slump," I asked Maria what would help her to transition gently, and realized that I too needed something for this same syndrome. We both realized we needed to "pause for applause." And at the same time, we needed a creative way of structuring the shift to a lower level of energy required by our waiting tasks.

Doug, a retired advertising executive, and his wife, my dear friend Evelyn, who retired from her job as marketing director for a large library, recently completed a project of two years constructing and decorating a large home in the suburbs of Chicago. They have taken some time to travel the world. When I asked Evelyn how she transitioned from the huge building project as well as their travels, she said: "We took lots of pictures during the building of our new home. We could see not only the before and after, but all the 'baby steps' along the way. We started a photo album and noted dates when advances were made. After our home was completed and we were exhausted, we kept it available to look at daily. It gave us great pleasure to relive all the challenges we faced and the problems we solved. I even took pictures of the house completed without furniture and continued to photograph the rooms as we added furniture, drapes and accessories. Having the album has been a fun way to share the experience with family and friends as well as to enjoy looking over it all by myself.

"I take time to think about what gives me the most pleasure about the house. After a trip, I do the same thing. I like to keep my calendar clear for at least a week after a trip so that I can slowly unpack; look over the photographs, postcards and memorabilia I collected while traveling; think about the people I met and places I visited so they get implanted in my memory; reflect on how I handled a long trip and what I would do again or do differently." Evelyn's transition gives her the pace of grace to savor her experiences.

Our friend David, who has built schools around the world, says that "You have to take time to sit back and look at it. You think about how you would do it better next time. Most of all, be glad you did it." He also piloted internationally known speakers across the country in his private plane as a service to his faith community. "When you get back from a trip, suddenly it's all over. You're all alone, and it can be very depressing. You have to sit back and think about all you accomplished."

Donna, who is in sales and training, says, "One way I transition is to take my time cleaning up and putting everything back in order—from a trip, a workshop or a home project. It seems to appeal to my sense of having control. I find it grounding and meditative. It puts me back into my body. Also, I can go into quite a slothful state and just laze about for a while, which brings me to a state of peacefulness by just being, and gratitude for the things in my life. Then I can get up and running again."

Dan and I always end a long speaking trip by going to a beautiful spot for a week or so of beauty, silence, and pampering. This is why we so often end a trip in the Fiji Islands. That week of rest is utterly restorative before flying home. Then, the transition at home involves making our environment beautiful, cleaning the house, arranging fresh flowers in a vase, and calling friends to share highlights of the trip. One of our homecoming rituals is that the first night, I make Dan his favorite meal—meatballs and spaghetti. The next night I make my favorite—a full roast chicken dinner. We reminisce about the beautiful people and favorite spots we have enjoyed. Dan always asks me, "What was best about it?" And then I ask him the same question.

Being a task-oriented gal, I also get great pleasure in reviewing my current ninety-day plan and seeing what I have accomplished. I check off the goals that have been accomplished, and spend some time in prayer reflecting on the next ninety days. This method of focusing is extremely helpful. Let me tell you more about it. Not only is it a bridge between past and future plans, but it is also a brilliantly simple way to organize our lives.

5. Make Manageable Plans

Time is our most precious nonrenewable resource. Life is too short to spend it heedlessly, in ways that fail to fulfill us and bring us joy. Once you have explored how you want to balance your life, and have a vision in mind of what you feel called to do at this stage of your life, it is time to create a plan for your life and to set some goals.

Creating a life plan may sound daunting—as if it requires the gift of prophecy, or at least the ability to fore-see your life for the next ten years. The planning I am referring to is a simple, renewable process, which is meant to be refreshed every ninety days. It is a plan that is manageable, moderate, and doable. It will guard you from excess and protect you from chaos.

> *The difference between a dream and the vision is the work plan.*
> —Stuart Schroeder,
> prison chaplain

Make ninety-day plans

I received an invaluable gift during a walk on a beach in Western Australia with Rob, a management consultant who is also a passionate advocate of The Virtues Project. He told me about one of the best time-management tools he knew—making a ninety-day plan. There is something resonant and right about the number three—three months, the Holy Trinity, and the idea some management gurus propose that we can effectively focus on only three priorities at a time. I have found that my ninety-day plans, which are written out on my bulletin board in my home office and in the journal that I carry with me on trips, are an invaluable sustainability tool. They help me to focus on what is most important and give me a constant visual perspective on what is important.

I have found that a project orientation to my work keeps me from feeling overcome by the multitude of miscellaneous tasks. A project has a clear purpose, a beginning, an end, and a definite result. Cleaning the house can be a project, or finalizing proposals with clients for the coming year, or writing a book. Keep this in mind as you create your ninety-day goals. What do you really want to accomplish in this period of time?

On a large sheet of paper or a white board, I draw a heart or circle in the center with the dates, such as September 1 to December 1. Just above the dates, I write the core virtue I feel is guiding me at the time, such as purposefulness or commitment or trust or grace. I place a short, meaningful phrase or a line from scripture, such as "All things work together for good" or "Joy gives us wings." Other phrases I have used are: "Clear Sailing," "My true calling," "Free and Clear" and "I love my easy, grace-filled life." You may choose to use your personal vision statement in the center.

Around the perimeter, I name three to five achievable, measurable goals that capture the main tasks I want to accomplish in this three-month period. I put them in the present tense as if they are already accomplished. Mine at the time of this writing are:

1. *A Pace of Grace* is completed
2. French products are finalized
3. All client proposals are sent
4. Family holidays are planned for next year
5. An international design team is formed

Keep your goals in your line of sight. Then, as you plan each day, your three-month perspective on what is most important will support you to be purposeful. Is what you are doing today responding to the squeaky wheel, or is it serving your goals? You have to balance both, but you need never leave your own goals behind.

This simple planning tool helps us to maintain our natural rhythm and provides the structure for a pace of grace and an abiding sense of balance. We will recognize our plan when we find it, because as we put it into practice, most of the time we will be smiling.

6. Make Moderate Lists

Are you a list maker? Do you find that your daily list is so long that you have unwittingly doomed yourself to failure? How do you feel when you look at your list at the end of the day? If more often than not you heave a sigh of defeat rather than a smile of contentment, then your list is too long.

If your goal is to remember all the small and large commitments you make, keep them in a spiral notebook along with notes from phone calls so that you have one place to look for details like this. This one practice has made a huge difference to me. Instead of having bits of paper floating and piling all around, and easily getting lost, I have one source for ideas, notes, and commitments. A small sturdy notebook for the times we are away from home or the office can be kept in purse, pocket, or briefcase. A trusty spiral pad for keeping track of calls and promises ought to be a fixture in your office or kitchen countertop. Always put it in the same place.

As for your daily list, that is not the place to put everything that needs doing. That is a place to put moderate, reasonable goals for the day. Mine is computerized and I change it easily and print it out first thing after I enter my office and have my transition prayer. It contains my weekly goals, the virtue I picked that day, an inspirational quote, today's date, and my top three priorities for the day. (To download a Virtue of the Week, go to www.virtuesproject.com.)

⊶⟹ This Week ⟸⊷

Purposefulness
With a clear purpose, I work from the fullness of my heart.

GOALS: WEEK OF (Date)

Complete Chapter 12

Arrange European trip

Finalize 3 proposals for fall

Update Web site

Desktop is clear and completely filed or actioned

TASKS: TODAY

Book: Spend 2 hours

Update Web site

Get new mattress

Finish thank-you letters to clients

Send family e-mail

On a second page, I have permanent categories that I fill in when I need to recall specific details. The categories include:

Writing

Personal

Family & Friends

Faith Community

Corporate

Clients

The virtue of orderliness is imperative to sustain peace of mind—and memory. Putting it all down on paper is not meant to be one more task to do. It is meant to be the structure that protects you from distraction.

7. Make Discerning Decisions

Change is a constant in today's world. Unless we have a structure for responding to the world—a strong ship with which to ride the waves of change—we can easily become overwhelmed. We need to be decisive directors of our course, yet our decisions need to be sustainable so that we won't be helplessly blown off course. I remember being with Doug, an adventure guide in his open handcrafted boat in a large lake in northern Canada, when we were caught in a sudden storm. The waves swelled higher and higher all around us, and the boat bobbed and twisted with an unusual flexibility. I was alarmed to see that the front of the boat and the back were moving in different directions. I looked at Doug, and he smiled and nodded with an expression of "See? Isn't this boat cool?" He had designed it for just such a crisis. He had foreseen the need for flexibility. We rode out the storm and arrived safely on shore.

Being decisive doesn't mean rushing into decisions. In the midst of today's horrifically pressured work environment, successful business leaders and entrepreneurs apply an abiding virtue. They take the time and cultivate the patience to think through their decisions. They know that determination alone is nothing without discernment.

I have found that a pace of grace is essential in making good decisions. Decisions we rush will not be sustainable or abiding. Sometimes things simply have to take their natural course. Unless we allow the timing to be perfect, it will be imperfect. Have you noticed that when you rush decisions the outcomes tend to fall apart? I have learned the hard way that any time I push, rush, or overexert myself to move a decision forward, it will end up costing me time, money, energy, and often tears of regret. It is equally true that at times an opportunity will present itself and we must move boldly, decisively. The key is whether our intent and inner experience is fear or wisdom. We cannot act on both.

I remember a time when I was quite worried about money. I had a "brilliant idea" and feverishly began putting it in place to make it happen. I had always had great success facilitating small, private, unpublicized women's retreats. The word would get out and the retreat would immediately fill, with a waiting list. So, when I needed money for my sons' university fees, I figured I could hold a large women's conference at the brand-new Victoria Conference Center. I planned to bring in well known speakers, a First Nations drummer, and so on and so on, and hundreds of women would flock to attend. While I am very experienced at facilitating retreats and speaking at conferences, I had never organized one. I soon learned that is a whole different skill set. Instead of the 250 women I planned for, eighty turned out. It also happened to be on Earth Day, an event in our area that attracts everyone, and I had totally forgotten it was a holy day in my faith on which work was not allowed. So indeed, I didn't earn money that day. In fact, it cost me the last five thousand dollars remaining in my inheritance. I stopped speaking to God for quite a few weeks, since in my feverish excitement over this conference I had naturally dragged along expectations of Divine assistance. When I cooled off, I had a whine session and asked, "Why didn't You help me?" Immediately I had an answer. First, a gentle reminder that I was the one who chose a date on which money was not supposed to be earned, and secondly some words I will never forget. "Sometimes you are a Mack truck, and sometimes you are as gentle as a deer. Your power is in your gentleness." I felt quite insulted at first, and to release my frustration I went for a walk on our forest path. Of course I came face-to-face with a deer—for me a symbol of gentleness—who didn't move but stared into my eyes. I started to laugh and took in the Teachable Moment. I learned never to presume on the generosity of God. Determination without discernment is a risky business.

Pacing ourselves in making decisions is to hold them lightly, with trust that the right thing will come about without having to control it or make it happen. We can make no decision before its time. Things have to take their natural course. A well-paced decision is a lasting decision.

I find that sustainable decisions have the following steps and virtues in common:

- Discern the true question
- Trust in the timing
- Carefully consider all the facts
- Full and honest consultation by everyone concerned
- Identify the core virtues needed to make it work
- Balance determination with discernment
- Build in an opportunity to revisit the decision once it is implemented to evaluate and fine-tune.

> *Pay attention to your intuition. That gut feeling will guide you. Don't let your heart rule your head. When we are too emotionally involved, we often make bad decisions.*
> —Jack Canfield, Mark Victor Hansen, and Les Hewitt, *The Power of Focus*

This method is useful in business, and it is also one that can keep us from being too impulsive in buying something we will regret, or making a family move, or choosing a school for our child. Time is too precious to waste on poor decisions.

Peter Drucker, a leading management thinker for decades, says, "Management by objectives works if you first think through your objectives. Ninety percent of the time, you haven't." Applying some of the lessons of successful business leaders can help us to lead our lives with sustainable success, a sense that we are thinking and living in the flow of grace.

To create plans that will actually work, it isn't sufficient to merely push up our sleeves and forge on with grim determination. Planning by logic alone will not work. Many entrepreneurs learn the hard way that a business plan is only as good as the truth of its basic assumptions. You cannot expect a business to grow just because you construct a logical plan. Plans created by determination without discernment are like a house of cards. They fail to be realized because they are not based on the truth. This principle also applies to making a plan for our lives.

Discernment is a fundamentally different process from mere deciding. A sustainable life plan is sourced in what I call "contemplative vigilance" about the opportunities that are before us. After my expensive "Mack truck" experience, I went to the other extreme and became overly timid in prayer. I became too compliant, excessively submissive, and in all honesty, fearful in seeking guidance. I was sniveling a lot, "Oh, Lord, just tell me what to do." One morning I was startled awake by a thunderous inner voice pronouncing: "Dare to discern!" I sat up, my heart pounding, wondering what could cause this usually gentle inner guide to take this tone. I realized that I was in a bog of indecision about the direction of my life. What I needed was the courage to reclaim my wisdom to discern my direction. I interpreted these words as a call to relinquish my helplessness and sacrifice my fear of making the wrong choice. It was time to discern what I truly wanted and then act on it with total commitment. A few months later I learned about the gift of contemplative vigilance from a fox.

Robert is a gifted medicine person, friend, and spiritual advisor. He took me to the sacred land of the Tahltan First Nation in northern Canada and left me for a day in the solitude. As we were winding through the deep forest toward the cliffs of this primeval area in his battered blue truck, a fox darted out of the bush. It seemed to me as if time had stopped for several moments as it gazed into my eyes, and then suddenly with a flick of its silvery tail, it vanished. "Robert, did you see that? The fox looked right at me." "No, Linda, that was for you." The next morning after he prepared a "bush breakfast" of skillet bread, eggs, bacon, and coffee, it was time to pray. He led me out to a meadow beside a rushing river held between high canyon walls. After he had prayed for some time, he opened his eyes and said, "Creator has a sense of humor with you, Linda. Creator says, 'Catch the rabbit.' I have no idea what it means." "I do," I said laughing. Robert then left me there for the day, the only sign of life the occasional bald eagle that soared overhead. As I moved deeper into prayer and meditation, I saw the fox very clearly in my inner vision. She had two lessons for me. The first was seeing her curled around her kits in her den. "Always take care of family first." Then she gazed at me again very intensely, as if to say, "Watch this." She showed me how to catch a rabbit. She didn't run around madly looking for rabbits. She crouched down in the thicket, peacefully waiting yet deeply alert, with very clear intention. The moment she spotted the rabbit, she ran like the wind to capture it. "Contemplative vigilance" was the phrase that came to me. Remain peaceful, alert, and discerning. Seize the opportunities that come. Don't waste energy wandering around searching. A few months later, on the patio of an urban hotel, as I stood to shake the hand of a new colleague at the conclusion of a business agreement, a rabbit hopped by. My colleague looked mystified by my laughter. "Just a private joke," I said.

Discernment involves trusting our own intuition, and our wisdom to *reveal* the truth, rather than manufacturing the truth based on logic alone or what we or others think we *should* do. Revelation is a gentle process. It is letting the truth unfold based on true needs, genuine feelings, and accurate perceptions. It is having the courage to dive deep, to tell the truth, in order to discover what is calling to us.

One of the women in my international mentors' circle had been working in a personnel and recruiting position with an international agency for more than five years. When a position in another department opened up, she was thrilled at the possibility of working in this new role, but hesitated out of guilt at leaving her former department in the lurch. She considered not even applying until a friend gave her the wisdom she needed. "Five and a half years as recruiter has been good, but I also realized that I needed a change. When Frances told me she was leaving, I was immediately drawn to her position, but did not consider to apply for it as three out of the current six staff in the recruitment section will be leaving by July. Thanks to my sister Deloria in Canada I did it after all! She said to me on the phone 'How will the wind know where to blow you if you don't put yourself out in the wind?' That set the process in motion. I did get the position, and I'm very grateful for this new opportunity of service." It is always good to leave some space for God to work the bigger plan for our lives.

We can glean some wise and practical trends for planning a life of grace from successes in the world of business. Eighty percent of new businesses fail within the first year. Women own eighty percent of the businesses that succeed. What do they do differently? Studies of the Federal Business Development Bank of Canada show that, interestingly, one of the virtues that leads to success is humility. Their study showed that women business owners have the wisdom not to push ahead with a mere idea. They aren't arrogant enough to think that if they come up with a grand idea it should just darn well work. These are three practices that women use to build success in a contemplative and vigilant way:

1. They gather market intelligence by talking to people, and companioning their potential customers to learn what their true needs are.
2. As they gather information, they gather the resources. They are more financially conservative.
3. They build a culture of family in their teams.

When I am invited to give a keynote talk at a conference, I don't just rattle off a canned topic. I companion key people, spending time on e-mail and by phone to ask them what attracted them to me as a speaker. I profile the audience and ask for stories about acts of kindness or creativity or courage by individuals in the audience I can share during my talk. I ask about the best keynote addresses they have had before, and finally, I ask what would make this a truly excellent presentation.

These same business principles apply to planning a sustainable life. The challenge is that we ourselves are the client. When we have the courage to tap into our intuitive reservoir of wisdom to assemble the pieces of our life together with grace, we can then design a lifestyle that will sustain our joy, our health, and the health of our relationships.

LIVE AN IDEAL LIFE

When we dare to discern the changes that will keep us in balance and nurture us in all aspects of our lives, our quality of life and health improve dramatically. Even our appearance changes for the better. People often ask me, "How can you look younger now than you did five years ago?" I remember running into a friend who works at a government job. I did a double take when I saw him. "What are you doing with yourself?" I asked. "You look fabulous!" "I'm on sabbatical for a year," he said, grinning from ear to ear. His hair shone, his face was radiant, and his color seemed different. His whole aura radiated health. What a life-giving choice he had made.

As you develop new plans and practices that engage your soul and foster genuine happiness, you will find that the only thing that truly abides are your virtues. I saw this so clearly in companioning people at the end of their lives. All they truly valued at that stage were the virtues of love, loyalty, integrity, creativity, and joy. Through my illness, I received a sense that everything that comes to us is a gift, if we can only find the value—the virtue—within it.

As you cultivate your virtues, you will find that a life of grace comes more easily. Be kind to yourself. Live a kind life. Live with a pace of grace. What else really matters?

CULTIVATE CONTENTMENT

Contentment is both the seed of grace and its fruit. It grows when we accept whatever we are given this day, whether clouds or sun, whether our pace turns out to be exhilarating or slow and measured. Being happy and grateful for what we have is the sign that we have indeed adopted a pace of grace as our way of life.

These good qualities exist inside you. It's just a matter of time until they reveal themselves. When they do, you will recognize them immediately as your own. And then, as they begin to grow and grow and grow, you will experience contentment.
—Baba Muktananda

⤙≡➣ EXERCISE GRACE ☞⤙-
Create a Ninety-Day Plan

With your personal vision in mind, create a ninety-day plan, with four or five goals or action steps you want to accomplish in your personal life, health, and work life over the next three months.

1. In the center of a sheet place a virtue that characterizes the primary spirit of this period, such as joyfulness, purposefulness, or peacefulness.

2. Add the dates of the three-month period, for example October 15–January 15.

3. Find a brief quotation that fits your core virtues at this period of time, and place it at the top or center of the page.

4. Write the four or five concrete, measurable things that you wish to do. Examples might be: "Create a weekly exercise program," "Find a new preschool for Alex," "Start a mentoring circle," "Schedule a weekend family outing," "Write an article and get it published," "Reorganize my office in perfect order," or "Complete the ABC business proposal."

Post this sheet where you can see it every day. As you reach each goal, celebrate with something you enjoy—a special dinner out, a massage, a day trip with someone you love, a personal purchase just for you.

A life of grace is distinguished by joy, moderation, and mindfulness. It makes love our first priority—love for God, love for ourselves, love for others, and love for our rich, sustaining life. It is finding a balanced way to live a spacious life, and maintaining that balance. It is standing on holy ground as often as we can, with impeccable integrity and unfailing tenderness for ourselves and for others. It is living our very best life.

⊷ *Grace* ⊶
by Linda Kavelin Popov

Grace can be gentle like water
Its power hidden by the soft flowing
Yet wearing away rock imperturbably
No one watching can tell
How its cutting force is wielded

The trick is not to block the flow
With impediments silted by self-deprecation,
the accumulated muck
and rancid leaves of shame
to clog the way.

Grace flows only where there is an opening.
It pools at obstacles,
waits with infinite patience,
never trespasses where it is not free to go.
Yet, a single sorrow healed
and Grace floods through in an instant.

—(Excerpted with permission from
Sacred Moments: Daily Meditations on the Virtues)

SUMMARY OF CHAPTER 16: PLAN FOR GRACE

- Plan with a pace of grace in mind.
- Let moderation be your touchstone for a balanced life.
- Review the things you value in your life. What changes do you want to make to create true balance?
- Schedule self-care as your first priority, not your last!
- Create gentle transitions and rituals as you move from one activity to another.

- As you plan each day, ask, "What would a pace of grace look like today?"
- Pause for applause. Celebrate your victories.
- Make moderate lists.
- Make sustainable decisions. Be open to inspiration and discernment. Gather information. Determination alone will not get you where you need to be.
- Dare to live your ideal life.
- Cultivate contentment.

Afterword

Ten years have passed since I climbed my first mountain, amid the glaciers of northern Canada, propelling me toward a severe onset of post-polio syndrome. As *A Pace of Grace* goes to press, I have just climbed another mountain. This one required no rappelling ropes. It was a gentle ascent on a well-hewn track through tropical rain forest, leading steeply down to the sea on the west coast of New Zealand's south island. As I sat in the sun on a warm flat stone jutting out over the beach, I watched the surf pounding toward me, and smiled, pausing to give thanks. I recalled the days when I could barely manage a short flight of steps without leaning heavily on a cane and experiencing excruciating pain. I was deeply aware of the precious reprieve I have received from the pace of grace practices. I felt so free sitting there, knowing I could trust my body to climb back up, and then walk the two miles back to the beachfront cabin where my husband and our friends waited. I had a friend drive me to the head of the trail, preserving my strength for the hike and the walk back. Moderation is still my touchstone and always will be.

My heartfelt hope is that *A Pace of Grace* will be a lifeline for you as well, supporting you to refill your cup each day, sustaining your energy, your vitality, and your joy. You will need the virtue of self-discipline to keep faith with these practices. Genuine self-care is a lifelong commitment to purify our lives of negativity, listen to our bodies, rest proactively, create a space of grace around us, keep a routine of reverence, play every day, and plan a graceful life. Yet, these tender disciplines bring a sweet reward— the freedom to live as we choose—to be a willing recipient of grace and to be the presence of grace to everyone around us. May every day be a good day.

—Linda Kavelin Popov
January 2004

Bibliography

Purify Your Life

Baker Eddy, Mary. *Science and Health with Key to the Scriptures.* Boston, 1934, 1994.

Black Elk et al. *Black Elk Speaks: Being the Life Story of a Holy Man of the Oglala Sioux.* As told through John G. Niehardt (Flaming Rainbow). Lincoln: University of Nebraska Press, 1988.

Cameron, Anne. *Daughters of Copper Woman.* Madeira Park, BC: Harbour Publishing Company, 2002.

Carnegie, Dale. *How to Win Friends and Influence People.* New York: Simon & Schuster, 1981.

Church of Jesus Christ of Latter-Day Saints, The. *The Book of Mormon,* Salt Lake City, Utah: 1982.

Finnegan, John. *The Facts About Fats.* Berkeley, Calif: Celestial Arts, 1993.

Gottman, John Mordechai. *Why Marriages Succeed or Fail.* New York: Simon & Schuster, 1994.

Hendrix, Harville. *Getting the Love You Want.* New York: Henry Holt and Co., 1998.

Kavelin Popov, Linda. *The Family Virtues Guide.* New York: Plume, 1997.

Morganstern, Julie. *Organizing from the Inside Out.* New York: Henry Holt and Co., 1998. See also www.juliemorgenstern.com.

Orman, Suze. *The Laws of Money, the Lessons of Life.* New York: Free Press, 2003.

———. *The 9 Steps to Financial Freedom.* New York: Crown Publishers, Inc., 1997.

Peace Pilgrim. *Friends of Peace Pilgrim.* Somerset, Calif. See also www.peacepilgrim.com.

Schaef, Ann Wilson. *Meditations for Women Who Do Too Much.* San Francisco: Harper & Row, 1990.

Swami Chidvilasananda. *My Lord Loves a Pure Heart: The Yoga of Divine Virtues.* South Fallsburg, New York: Syda Foundation, 1994. See also www.siddhayoga.org.

———. *Inner Treasures.* New York: Syda Foundation, 1995.

Van Amerongen, Jerry, cartoonist.

Walston, Sandra Ford. *Courage: The Heart and Spirit of Every Woman.* New York: Broadway Books, 2001. See also www.walstoncourage.com.

Weil, Andrew. *Eight Weeks to Optimum Health.* New York: Knopf, 1997.

———. *Spontaneous Healing.* New York: Ballantine, 1995. See also www.drweil.com.

Web Sites

Bath and body products:	www.fruit-passions.com
	www.healinggarden.com
	www.gilchristsoames.com
Home and outdoor organizing:	www.grandoutdoors.com
	www.clutterbug.net/help/
My Feng Shui consultant:	wwwjanegibsondesign.ca
	Email: JaneGibson@shaw.ca
Vitamins and supplements:	www.usana.com
	www.unitoday.net/Justforthehealthofit

PACE YOURSELF

Bender, Sue. *Everyday Sacred.* San Francisco: HarperSanFrancisco, 1996.

Bruno, Richard L. *The Polio Paradox.* New York: Warner Books, 2002.

Cameron, Julia. *The Artist's Way.* New York: Tarcher, 1992.

Covey, Stephen. *The 7 Habits of Highly Effective People.* New York: Simon & Schuster, 1999.

DeMello, Anthony. *Wellsprings: A Book of Spiritual Exercises.* New York: Doubleday, 1984.

Dyckman, Katherine Marie and Patrick L. Carroll. *Inviting the Mystic, Supporting the Prophet: An Introduction to Spiritual Direction.* New York: Paulist Press, 1981.

Kornfield, Jack. *A Path with Heart.* New York: Bantam Books, 1993.

Plotkin, William B. *Soulcraft: Crossing into the Mysteries of Nature and Psyche.* Novato, Calif.: New World Library, 2003. www.animus.org.

Rolheiser, Ronald. *Against an Infinite Horizon.* London: Hodder & Stoughton, 1995.

SARK. *Change Your Life Without Getting Out of Bed.* New York: Simon & Schuster, 1999.

Satir, Virgina M. *The New Peoplemaking.* Palo Alto, Calif.: Science and Behavior Books, Inc., 1988.

Schaef, Anne Wilson. *Meditations for Women Who Do Too Much.* San Francisco: HarperSanFrancisco, 2000.

Thomson, Mark. *The Complete Blokes & Sheds.* HarperCollins Australia, 2002.

Winfrey, Oprah, editorial director. *O, the Oprah Magazine,* www.oprah.com.

Zerah, Aaron. *The Soul's Almanac.* New York: Tarcher, 1998.

Web Sites

Alternative Youth Adventures: www.mytroubledteen.com

www.wildernessprograms.org

National Youth Mentoring Network: www.nationalyouth.info

Practice the Presence

Baha'u'llah. *Gleanings from the Writings of Baha'u'llah.* Wilmette, Ill.: Baha'i Publishing Trust, 1952.

———. *The Hidden Words of Baha'u'llah.* Wilmette, Ill.: Baha'i Publishing Trust, 2002.

Baldwin, Christina. *The Seven Whispers: Listening to the Voice of Spirit.* Novato, Calif: New World Library, 2002.

———. *Calling the Circle: The First and Future Culture.* New York: Bantam, 1998.

Bhagavad Gita. Translated by Sir Edwin Arnold. New York: Dover Publications, 1993.

———. Translated by Swami Shri Purohit. Boston: Shambhala, 1994.

Dalai Lama et al. *The Good Heart: A Buddhist Perspective on the Teachings of Jesus.* Boston: Wisdom Publications, 1996.

Dalai Lama. *The Dalai Lama's Little Book of Wisdom.* New York: Barnes & Noble Books, 2002.

Danielou, Jean. *The Angels and Their Mission.* Dublin: Four Courts Press, 1991.

Dass, Ram and Paul Gorman. *How Can I Help?* New York: Knopf, 1990.

The Dhammapada: The Path of Perfection. Translated by Juan Mascaro. New York: Penguin Books, 1973.

Gospel of Zarathustra, The. Adyar, India: Theosophical Publishing House, 1978.

Holy Bible, The, King James Version. Thomas Nelson, Inc. 1990.

————, New Revised Standard Edition. Toronto: Bible Society, 1991.

Holy Qur'an, The. Translated by Usuf Ali. Oxford: Oxford University Press, 1985.

Jampolsky, Gerald G. *Love Is Letting Go of Fear.* Berkeley, Calif.: Celestial Arts, 1988.

Kavelin Popov, Linda. *Sacred Moments.* Chattanooga, Tenn.: Images International, Reprinted 2003.

Kidd, Sue Monk. *When the Heart Waits.* San Francisco: Harper San Francisco, 1992.

————. *The Secret Life of Bees.* New York: Penguin Books, 2002.

Koontz, Dean. *One Door Away from Heaven.* New York: Bantam Books, 2002.

McCarrol, Tolbert. *Notes from the Song of Life.* Berkeley, Calif: Celestial Arts, 1998.

Mornell, Pierre. *Passive Men, Wild Women.* New York: Simon & Schuster, 1979.

Remen, Rachel Naomi. *Kitchen Table Wisdom.* New York: Riverhead Books, 1996.

Reeves, Nancy. *I'd Say "Yes" God, If I Knew What You Wanted.* Kelowna, BC: Northstone Publishers, 2001.

Savary, Louis M. and Patricia H. Bernc. *Kything: The Art of Spiritual Presence.* Mahwah, New Jersey: Paulist Press, 1988.

Selections from the Writings of Abdu'l-Bahá. Haifa, Israel: Baha'i World Center, 1978.

Smiley, Jane. *Barn Blind.* New York: Fawcett Books, 1993.

Spiritual Directors International. *Presence: An International Journal of Spiritual Direction.* San Francisco.

Steere, Douglas V. From the introduction to *Quaker Spirituality.* Philadelphia: Religious Society of Friends, 1998.

Thich Nhat Han. *Peace Is Every Step.* New York: Bantam Books, 1991.

Wilkenson, Bruce. *The Prayer of Jabez.* Sisters, Oreg.: Multnomah Publishers, 2000.

Web Sites

World Prayers: www.worldprayers.org

An interfaith, intercultural site on world spirituality: www.thesacredsite.com

Music: www.ucamusic.com

Plan a Sustainable Life

Canfield, Jack et al. *The Power of Focus.* Deerfield Beach, Fla.: Health Communications Inc., 2000.

Drucker, Peter F. *Managing in the Next Society.* New York: St. Martin's Press, 2002.

Gibran, Khalil. *The Prophet.* New York: Knopf, 1964.

Hendricks, Gay and Kate Ludeman. *The Corporate Mystic.* New York: Bantam Books, 1997.

Luhrs, Janet. *The Simple Living Guide.* New York: Broadway Books, 1997.

————. *Simple Living Oasis* magazine. See also www.simpleliving.com.

Web Sites

Jill Campbell Galleries: www.jlcgallery.com and www.ilovethisart.com

Carol Evans art: www.carolevans.com

Retreats International: www.retreatsintl.org

Volunteering opportunities: www.volunteermatch.org and www.serviceleader.org

International volunteering: www.idealist.org and www.interaction.org

Information on The Virtues Project™: www.virtuesproject.com

Information on programs and how to book Linda Kavelin Popov as a speaker: www.paceofgrace.net

Resources

Programs and Materials

Visit www.paceofgrace.net

- To obtain a decorative poster of the Ten Rules for Health
- To learn about how to attend or sponsor a Pace of Grace workshop
- To obtain a schedule of presentations and workshops
- To book Linda Kavelin Popov as a speaker
- For information on how to obtain a set of Virtues Cards
- For definitions of the virtues listed in *A Pace of Grace*
- For links to other sites that will help you sustain your mind-body-spirit balance

Visit www.virtuesproject.com

- For information on Virtues Project programs
- To learn how The Virtues Project is promoting character throughout the world
- To view a catalog of virtues books and materials

To order materials in North America, call toll free 1-888-261-5611
To order materials internationally, visit **www.virtuesproject.com**

Index

ALSO BY
LINDA KAVELIN POPOV

THE
FAMILY
VIRTUES
GUIDE

Simple Ways to Bring Out the Best
in Our Children and Ourselves

LINDA KAVELIN POPOV
WITH DAN POPOV, Ph.D., and JOHN KAVELIN

www.virtuesproject.com

AVAILABLE WHEREVER PAPERBACKS ARE SOLD

Plume
A Member of Penguin Group (USA) Inc.   www.penguin.com